MW00440012

TIGER CREEK TALES

Memories of an
Oil Patch Kid

by

Billy Gene Carriker

Cover artwork and sketches on pages 1, 10, 15, 21, 31, 40, 42, 46, 50, 52, 74, 82, 98, 200, 235, 258 and 268 by Rachel Sager, graduate of Tyler School of Art, Temple University, and currently studying fine art animation in Edinburgh, Scotland.

Additional sketches by local artist, Amber Gresham, senior at Wichita Heights High School.

ISBN: 1-58597-253-3
Library of Congress Control Number: 2004102171

LEATHERS PUBLISHING

A division of Squire Publishers, Inc.
4500 College Blvd.
Leawood, KS 66211
1/888/888-7696
www.leatherspublishing.com

DEDICATION

This book is dedicated, first of all, to Elaine, my wife of 55 years. Although born an Iowa Hawkeye, she adapted well to an unregenerate, okra-eating Southerner and even learned to like both.

It's also dedicated to the memory of my sister, Frances, and brother, Willard, the two siblings nearest my age and the constant playmates of my early childhood. If you saw one of us the other two were close by. What fun we would have had with this project!

PREFACE

The story title for the book comes from a loose adaptation of a series of columns I have had featured in the *Drumright Gusher*, a weekly publication. In most instances the stories are a compilation of non-related, sometimes-disjointed memories of events and happenings in the Great Depression Era in and around my hometown of Drumright, Oklahoma.

I wanted to give the stories some direction rather than just publishing a series of a couple hundred tales, one following the other with no particular rhyme or reason. I experimented with various ways of doing it and finally decided on this manner of presenting them.

My first task was to compile a list of all the columns I felt would appeal as nostalgia to interested readers. I'll be the first to admit that there is a lot of overlapping in some stories and some would possibly fit in more than one category but decisions had to be made.

The list was refined several times and with much shifting and changing of topics and heading finally categorized into headings entitled; The Town; Personalities; Places and Landmarks; Oil Patch Living; Wing Schools; Lincoln School; Kid Activities' Holidays and Other Special Days; Memories Good and Bad; Food and Entertainment; Fun and Games; Adult Stuff; Autos and Travel and a concluding miscellaneous category called Just Stuff.

Now that I had the stories in some semblance of order I searched for a logical method to apply in carrying the stories along. One alternative would have been, once again, just a lengthy series of stories one following the other using the above headings. I decided to go to real life and use a technique I enjoy in my retirement, which is a weekly coffee session at a local restaurant with long time friends.

Accordingly, I created a dozen or so retired guys in the town of Drumright. They meet weekly for fellowship, conversation and coffee in the fictitious Boomtown Restaurant. It's a loose group of men who have known each other for many years so the mood and related talk is totally informal.

As the conversation spins languidly around the table various subjects are touched upon and discussed. Occasionally one of the old guys will bring up a subject that is the topic of a story column. At that point I have chosen to print that related story. Sometimes this will trigger a topic of another story. Using this method I have contrived to use the old boys as the vehicle to carry the stories along with some semblance of spontaneity.

A liberated daughter felt there was a need for a feminine touch so Ivey Jones was created to serve as the restaurant waitress and female foil along with a young waitress, Martha Belle Pines. Ivey will occasionally relate a story along with the men.

The sole purpose of the group of retirees is to serve as a vehicle and they are not meant to detract from the nostalgia of the written texts. They do have individual personalities but have no relationship to any person, living or dead.

ACKNOWLEDGMENTS

To Brent and Saundra Carriker, who planted the initial seed for a book and then provided encouragement along the way, especially the down times. It wouldn't have happened without you guys.

To Marla Carriker Denton, also an initiator and an enthusiastic cheerleader all the way, and John Denton, for his generous comments and words of support.

To Kimberly Carriker Ree, along with grandkids Logan and Ashley Ree, for technical assistance on the mysteries of the computer.

To Dave Carriker, my nephew, whose expertise and continued interest and technical help paved many of the rocky roads a lot smoother. He opened lots of doors.

To Rachel Sager, my artist friend whose outstanding professional work certainly enhanced and enlivened an otherwise steady "just a collection of stories."

To Ralph and June Tippit, "What can I say?" Old and dear friends from olden days of my early childhood. With you in my corner, I couldn't lose. You guys are tops.

To Dr. Vivian Kelly Travis, a first grade classmate at Fairview who early on gave me inspiration and encouragement to begin the project.

To Harold Adams, an almost twin of mine from the old days in Drumright. A transplanted Okie in California who contributed some great memories.

To MaryAgnes Klock, a distant cousin who was so complimentary from the beginning. Although we never met there is a strong bond.

To Jean Moody Fischer, an e-mail friend and one who was always there as a source reference when I needed some facts about the old hometown.

To Robert Carriker, elder sibling, whose memories predate mine.

To the un-named and, as yet, unknown friends throughout the USA who subscribe to the *Drumright Gusher* and read the "Tiger Creek Tales."

TABLE OF CONTENTS

INTRODUCTION

The story of the oil strike concerning one of the larger oil deposits in the early part of the Twentieth Century took place in the extreme western section of Creek County, Oklahoma on March 17, 1912. This occurrence and information regarding all the personalities related to the exploration and discovery of the oil has been well documented in several accounts. The event, heralded on the morning of St. Patrick's Day 1912, for every intent and purpose could be considered as the date of birth for the community that grew to become Drumright, Oklahoma.

When Wheeler No. 1 came in as a gusher down in the brush strewn, rocky ravine, spewing liquid gold hundreds of feet into the air, it sent out a clarion call throughout the United States that here lay opportunity for wealth in yet another frontier.

Within a space of a few weeks people began arriving at or near the site, coming by horseback and buggy and even on foot. The nearest railhead was located at Cushing; a small hamlet located nine miles to the west.

Long before summer came to the area the land was teeming with men eager to join with the oil explorers in seeking a fortune with this new form of wealth. Dozens of oil companies from the very largest to the one-man 'ham and beans' operations descended on the private owners of the land. Every inducement was used, both legal and sometimes a bit extralegal, in trying to beat out the competition in securing the necessary lease agreements. Before any oil exploration or drilling could take place on private property an oil company's agent had to secure a "lease" or legal right to do so.

Many times part of the lease's full name would include the landowner's name. This brought about drilling sites known as Jeanette Richards Pure Oil Lease, Thomas B. Long Magnolia Lease and Jackson Barnett Lease named for the landowner who had signed over the oil rights. There were hundreds more leases such as these scattered throughout the oil patch.

Rag towns, dug outs and other temporary living quarters sprang up in various parts of the huge oil patch as drilling companies set up operations and began to hire the crews necessary to work on a twenty-four hour a day schedule seven days a week. These oil workers, known as roughnecks, worked three eight-hour shifts or "towers" as they were called colloquially.

Finding an acceptable place to live soon became a serious problem for the man whose wife and children accompanied him to the oil fields. This problem became magnified after an oil company had a large number of producing oil wells on several different leases in close proximity.

A ready source of dependable labor was necessary to insure help being available to work on short notice. The raw and loosely organized communities, such as Drumright and Oilton, were located too far away to walk to work. Transportation to and from the work site was unsatisfactory due to a lack of roads and ownership of cars.

The oil companies readily saw the problem as being theirs as well as that of their workers. The answer to this vexing dilemma was to have housing built, at the company's expense, and rent it out to the workers for a modest sum of money. In the beginning the houses were rather crude affairs built from green, newly sawn lumber for the difficulty wasn't seen as a long- range situation.

As time passed and the number of successful oil operations increased in the oil patch it became apparent that a better quality type of construction needed to be used. It became readily apparent that workers were going to be needed for years to come. As a result, large number of these company built 'lease houses' sprang up the entire length and breadth of the oil patch as dozens of people came to live as neighbors even though they worked for different oil companies.

In addition to providing the homes being built, in some instances the oil company provided the utilities. The larger ones provided free natural gas, cheap electricity and dug the water wells for the water supply. When an oil company built and operated a gasoline refinery there would be literally scores of houses with several hundred people living in them.

These social groups owed allegiance to the mother company who provided the wage earners salary but the individuals also aligned themselves with one of the towns that developed in the oil patch such as Oilton, Drumright or Shamrock. The boys and girls of the lease communities played together and went to school together in the schools erected nearby to accommodate the diverse communities.

If parents wanted their children to receive an education beyond the eighth grade they would be sent to one of the above towns for their high school experience.

This is the setting and social organization from which most of the tales in the book are drawn. Living in many different lease communities, attending five different schools as well as in the town of Drumright provided a rich and varied source of childhood memories.

PROLOGUE

Sometime during the lengthening days of early June 1926, an older model, faded red Dodge truck came wheezing east down Tiger Hill. Shifting down, it laboriously climbed the steep hill that overlooked the main street of Drumright, Oklahoma. The Creek County line had been crossed a mile back and these people were here to belie the advice of Horace Greeley who said, "Go West, Young Man" for they were migrants; eastward bound.

Squeezed into the slat-sided truck, along with odds and ends of furniture, were the three male children of Willard Samson "Jack" Carriker and his wife Melvina Adeline "Shug." The three warriors occupying the back of the truck, all under the age of six, were Robert E. Lee, Raymond R. "Rudy," and Willard Marvin. They were very sunburned and much windblown but were still a group you had to take into account.

Riding in the cab with Jack and his wife "Shug" was Frances, the baby of the family. She was petite and blonde with long Shirley Temple curls framing her face. She would always remain the only female child in the family. With her gamin face and big blue eyes she was the pet of everyone. Frances was a year and a half old but her place as 'baby' was soon to be usurped by the little one swelling Shug's stomach.

Jack was concluding a five hundred mile plus trip in bringing his family back from a less than profitable stay of several months in Las Animas, Colorado where he had been working on an unfamiliar job stringing a power line across the plains.

He had been working the Texas and Oklahoma oilfields since age sixteen, having been pulled from school and taken there by his father, Bent Carriker, who had a bad case of the wanderlust. In a word, Old Pap just wasn't a steady worker and lacked something in serving as a positive role model.

On this particular move, Jack was alone in his endeavor and was returning to his roots by coming back to the Drumright area. His fervent hope was to be successful in finding steady and profitable employment in the oil industry. After only seven years of marriage he was responsible for a wife and four children with another one knocking on the door.

Since oilfield work was about all he knew how to do, he was hoping to find something to do to earn a wage in the dwindling, played out fields around Drumright.

Good fortune smiled upon the small family almost immediately for an elderly gentleman they met quite by accident befriended them. Jack had stopped the man to ask for directions and struck up a conversation with him. He was known as Grandpa Ulrich and lived a couple of miles east of Drumright in a substantial oil patch company house. He owned or had access to another house right next door to them.

His offer was to let the family move into the house and pay no rent, just make it a home. So, within the space of two hours after arriving in town the family was on its way to a really nice house located on the brow of Rumpus Hill. The unusual name had derived from an earlier day when dozens of lease houses were located on the hill and constant brawling and fighting were the norm. The hill was well named.

The older couple proved to be sterling friends in many ways. Their car was always at the disposal of the large family. He became the mentor and surrogate father to Jack and assisted him in seeking work. As an extra bonus the elderly couple offered to take the family to their church, an offer, which in time, was accepted.

The remainder of the idyllic summer proved a blessing to the little family as all the young ones became acquainted with neighbor children and bonded well with some. The late term pregnancy went smoothly with Grandma Ulrich's help and advice and it appeared the decision to move to Drumright was a propitious one.

September brought the first year of school for the first born, Robert E. Lee. He manfully trudged down the hill with his lunch bucket, caught the big yellow bus that delivered him to Pleasant Hill School a few miles distant.

October brought with it cool, rainy weather and the due date for the baby was looming closer by the day. Finally, on a drizzly, damp Wednesday afternoon Shug told Jack she felt it was time to make the run into town and bring back Dr. Orange W. Starr, "The Cherokee Medicine Man" who was going to do the honors of birthing the baby.

The birthing process had heated up considerably by the time the doctor arrived and it was only a few minutes until the airwaves were punctured by the wailing, squeaking voice of child number five. (Boy-child number four)

The optimistic parents had launched a new generation child and as usual, great things were expected of him. The date was October 20, 1926.

FIRST COFFEE
The Town

The early morning rush in the Boomtown Café had died down noticeably with the crowd diminished by the nine o'clock hour. Tables were empty, but some still covered with debris from the large orders from the breakfast menu. Only two of the counter stools were in use while the padded booths lining one wall held a customer or two nursing a cup of coffee. The stool occupants were the local constabulary, Ben and Arky, who were making desultory conversation about some vandalism that had taken place the night before.

Those unfortunates whose work required them to be on the job at an early hour had come and gone. They had come hungry, but left satiated by the solid, wholesome food prepared by Marvin Cutler, owner, cook and manager… "best biscuits and gravy served …anywhere."

The wisecracking and well-organized Ivey Jones, longtime waitress, had started the departed customers day in an upbeat manner. The Boomtown was a low maintenance establishment that owed its continued and profitable existence to the friendly atmosphere, good food and efficient service.

Ivey, with the morning rush completed, began a task she secretly looked forward to each Tuesday morning. This was the day of the weekly meeting of the Old Toots Coffee group. That was not the name that was used when within earshot of any of the members, but had been tacked onto the old guys by other citizens of the town. Using it was considered derogatory and just might prove to be detrimental to your health. They considered themselves "experienced gentlemen."

Ivey's job now was to push some tables together, pour glasses of water, lay out a service or two and then wait for the anticipated bunch to arrive. If truth be known, Ivey, a widow lady in her early 60's, was a little bit a'twitter underneath a businesslike facade. Several of the old codgers were either widowers or otherwise single, and her juices still ran with green sap.

The group of a dozen or so retired guys who met for coffee each Tuesday morning at 9:00 was a mixed bag. They had been meeting for several years, and the makeup of the group changed with move-aways, deaths, etc. Most of the group had been long-time residents of the town and had known each other for most of those years.

It was a diverse assemblage at present time, and personalities ran the gamut of sophistication from suave Roy "Doc" Pringle, retired veterinarian, to the rough-hewn cowboy, Joe Bob Smith. It also was a most compatible group who truly enjoyed each other's company.

Probably at no time were all the members on hand. Other activities interfered, and anyway, it wasn't a command performance and roll was never taken. Several of the old boys had slight hearing losses that made conversation a little "iffy" from one end of the table to another. If you knew someone had a problem, you just looked directly at them and talked a little louder.

On this particular morning the front door opened and the first member of the gang, one Otto Irving, entered. His greeting was a terse, "Mornin', Marvin," as he took a seat at the table and made a brief nod in the direction of Ivey. For the record, this old boy was not one to excite Miz Ivey, who had busied herself at making fresh coffee.

Otto had been the town's handyman for many years and lacked many of the personal qualities to cause a feminine heart blip. He also chewed tobacco, *and for Ivey that was enough said. Besides, there was a Missus Irving who played piano for her local church flock.*

Harold Atkins and Cecil Damore entered the café in a heated discussion with arms gesticulating like a pair of windmills gone wild in a windstorm. Both Harold and Cece had been in the local school system for many years, Harold as an elementary principal and Cecil as a high school science teacher. Their retirements had taken place at the end of the same year, several years earlier.

The two educators had been popular with the boys and girls of the town, as well as the parents and the general population. Likewise both had moved to the same retirement community on Beaver Lake in Arkansas when they retired. The old red dirt of Oklahoma exerted a powerful pull, and it wasn't long before Cecil returned with Harold following soon after. Both had lost their wives before retirement, and their children all lived out of state.

The oldest member of the coffee bunch, Lafayette "Faye" Bucklin, came in the door with just ever so little help from his trusty hedgewood cane and another member, James Kinnamon's arm. Faye, at 88 years young, predated most of the other members, for his membership went back to when the old "Spit and Whittle" gang used to meet on the corner of Broadway and Ohio Street.

At that time the curb at that particular intersection was high enough to sit on the sidewalk and rest your feet in the gutter. It had been a favored corner since sidewalks were laid, and the older men had used the location as they gossiped and watched the changing scenes of Drumright.

The coming of a younger generation of guys with cars had made life a bit uneasy and miserable for the old guys. The young broncs and their flivvers had developed a sport of driving up Broadway, turning right on Ohio and seeing how close they could come to the feet of the old men. It became a running battle between them, as the men shouted invectives at the kids, and more than once the Police Chief had been called into the fray. He issued a stern warning to the young guys to swing wider on that particular turn.

The earlier arriving members had all taken seats as they came in, and Ivey had poured decaf for Harold and Doc Pringle. After finishing, she had made it a point to hang in fairly close proximity to make sure they were aware of her presence. At times she would join in on whatever topic was being discussed.

"Where do you reckon Phil and Harley are today?" asked Cecil. "I haven't seen Phil around town for some time but saw Harley just yesterday."

"I don't know about Harley, but Phil's visiting his son and family in Tulsa and will be gone about a week. Said he'd be back for coffee next week," said Otto.

"Better him than me," muttered Doc Roy.

Most knew exactly what Doc meant. They had watched his ne'er-do-well son grow up in the town and knew him as a loser who had married a loser. Doc tried to make his contacts with them as infrequent as possible.

At this point conversation bounced around the table like the handing off of a relay team's baton. Sick report was made, and anyone with an ailment was reported and properly discussed, undoubtedly with the smug feeling of "sure glad it's not me." Any scandal or even the potential of one received its share of discussion, whether true or not.

"Man, these old hills seem to be getting steeper every day," said Cece to the company in general. "I'll go to my maker continuing to question the intelligence of any man who would have the lack of smarts as to build a town on hills like these."

"Couldn't be you're getting a mite old, now, could it?" spoke up old Joe Bob laconically, in his slow drawl. There was just a touch of sarcasm in his voice, but the twinkle in his eye gave it away. Everyone knew what a dry sense of humor old Joe Bob had and grinned with him.

For a time the men took turns ragging on Cece about his complaint. He took it all in good humor, for his reputation was that of a laid-back individual who took a lot to rile up. The conversation then turned to Tiger Hill and how steep it was and how much fun they used to have with their cars trying to climb the steep hill to the west. Speculation then began about Cece's complaint concerning the wisdom of a town being put on a series of hills.

Old Faye Bucklin, who had been around during the boom town days of the early oil strikes, said before the bricks were laid on the streets when it rained it was impossible for a single team of horses to pull a heavy load up the hills.

It was finally agreed that not many towns could brag about being built on such steep hills, and much of the charm, style and uniqueness lay in the fact the pioneer fathers laid out the town on these hills. Since old Aaron Drumright owned a big share of the land, the town lay on that was probably just coincidental to the decision.

Some conjecture was made as to why they didn't go just a short distance north, east or south where they would have found much more level terrain. It couldn't have been to the west, for there lay Payne County and that was not even a choice.

"Yeah, I got lots of good memories of our little burg," said Elmer Butterfield.

Elmer had worked more years than he cared to remember in the local post *office, so he was somewhat of an authority on the downtown scene, having his finger on the pulse of the town so long. He took a lot of ribbing about his soft government job, but it failed to dampen his good humor.*

Ivey came from the kitchen and walked to the table to freshen up the guys' coffee. She expected to hear some complaints laid on her and accusations of goofing off, and she wasn't disappointed.

After getting his fresh cup of regular, putting cream and sugar in it, Elmer pulled forward and while slowly stirring the mixture said, "Boys, let me tell you some of what I like about our little jerkwater town. I purposefully chose to stay here after my retirement from the post office and haven't regretted one minute since I made that decision. I know all about the warts and knots on this place, but I still can't think of another locality in the US of A that I'd rather live."

ON THE STREETS

Many personalities and possibly even some characters walked the streets of Drumright in the early days. Most of you guys have heard of Police Chief Jack Ary and his deputy "Babe" Carnahan, Dr. Orange W. Starr, Sam Whitlock and other such notables. I'd like to tell you about some of the lesser known ones.

You all know about the Candy Soldier, but who remembers the guy who wheeled that heavy pushcart all over town selling hot tamales? To we young kids he was a mysterious person who sold unmentionable things from his wagon … we imagined his selling dope and other "sinful" things and would look fearfully at him as he trundled his cart up the hill and down. In truth, he was just some old Mexican guy who made and sold a great corn-shucked wrapped tamale.

I'm sure he had a name and possibly a family, but to my knowledge I never heard it mentioned.

Another person you may remember is Ernie, the paperboy. He was a profoundly physically handicapped man who sold newspapers. I don't remember if it was the *Tulsa World, Tribune* or the Oklahoma City paper. He could usually be found at his stand by the old post office located on North Ohio. Ernie didn't let his handicap keep him from earning a living and was a pleasant fixture for many years.

There were many people who would stop, talk to Ernie and buy a paper even if they already had one. It was difficult to understand Ernie's speech at times, but he was always a pleasant, friendly guy and deserved and appreciated the purchase of a paper.

Speaking of papers … my brother had a job of delivering the Tulsa paper in the morning. He would roust me out at 3 a.m. and we would walk to the bus depot, pick up his papers and deliver them all over the town. I remember the route meant walking from the Wayside Inn on the far north side of town all the way to the Fond du Lac Inn far out on the west side. Now, as you can see, we walked many miles to make just a few cents for a paper.

Here's another experience that happened on the streets of town. My sister and I had a run-in with the town drunk one Saturday afternoon. I guess he would qualify for that title. We were so naïve we wouldn't have known a drunk if we'd met one.

What happened was we had sold our scrap metal to get enough money to go to the show. Unfortunately, there wasn't enough to pay for our brother's admission, so he had to stay home. We were walking up Broadway to the Midwest Theater and met this old rogue who must have been pretty well loaded to the gills with some kind of rotgut.

My sister was a pretty little thing with long "Shirley Temple" curls, and this old guy was admiring her and saying how pretty she was. As we left, he gave us a quarter to spend, paid for by letting him give my sister a pinch on the cheek. Now, you'd think we'd have remembered our poor brother back at home just a dime short of the price of admission to the movies. Unfortunately, visions of candy and popcorn far outweighed brotherly love, and we spent the whole durn thing.

We paid dearly for it when we got home. We got properly blessed by our mother for not having some brotherly love and milk of human kindness in our hearts.

As pre-teens we had a lot of fun just running the streets. There was a free "weigh machine" outside the Marquette Drugstore, and we had to get weighed every time we passed it. We would weigh ourselves, run like mad all the way up the hill and back down and couldn't understand why we still weighed the same. No one had ever instructed us on calories and how they burned. Then a trip into the City Drug Store to see the old friendly parrot. Was it the City Drug? That old sucker had a pretty good vocabulary. He was an institution around the town for many years.

"Yeah, you can walk the streets today and ever so often you'll see the names of some of the old merchants still inlaid in the tile at the entryway ... Kraker Brothers, Eddie Shaddid, Saffa's Grocery east of the tracks ... lots of ghosts walk those streets today," spoke Harley.

Elias Joseph's dad had a fruit stand across the street south from where the museum is located. Several of us would go visit him when his dad was gone and he was running the store alone. I ate my first tangerine at the fruit stand ... and probably didn't pay for it. Wonder what I owe for it ... with interest?" continued Harley Sprague.

"Well, after all these years you know you're not going to pay squat for it, so what does it matter?" spoke up Phil Wiley.

The way he reared back in his chair, we knew he was about to regale us with one of his stories, so everyone just got comfortable to see if this was a new story or one he had told us before. Sometimes these yarns just happened to get told as repeaters if they didn't get shut down.

UP THE HILL AND DOWN

You guys who are graduates of Drumright High School can possibly remember this little fight song the pep clubs used. It started out something like this...

"Drumright, Drumright, up the hill and down"... These were the opening words of at least one of a high school pep songs, and I wonder if there is someone who might know some more of it. It goes something like, "Working together with all our might, we're loyal true and something." It was sung to the tune of, "Sidewalks of New York."

Along that same line, do you reckon there's any "Peppy Coyotes" still around? If you remember, they were a select group of high school girls who, in modern day, would be called a "Spirit Squad." I suppose if some of them were still around they'd be about as old as the rest of us and just might not be so "peppy."

The group was made up of high-energy girls, usually the prettiest in school, who wore daring short skirts and attended athletic contests, mainly football back then, and cheered on the team. It was considered a real honor to be selected as one, and many vied for membership. How do you suppose the old sneaky coyote's name got into it?

The hills of Drumright sure do make it picturesque and unique. Other than San Francisco or maybe Juneau, Alaska, where are you gonna find a town located on such steep hills? In all my adult travels I can't remember one that could match Drumright. Maybe a few gentle rises, but no serious hills.

Remember how these hills posed some serious problems for the people who were just learning to drive. Even some of the more experienced drivers had problems as well.

Before automatic shifting became so commonplace, the choice of parking was limited to heading uphill or down, leaving the neophyte driver faced with the same dilemma either way. When backing out, facing uphill, there was no problem in just letting it roll backwards. Now came the most challenging part. How to synchronize releasing the clutch, taking your foot off the brake and applying the gas pedal simultaneously was, to say the least, daunting.

All too often the driver would release one of them too soon, causing the motor to overload and die. Even worse, if the car continued to run, it might do so with great leaps and bounds and still die. This was usually accompanied with hoots of laughter and shouts of derision from onlookers who usually hung out on the street.

When facing downhill, the problem was the same, "getting your act together" on the pedals; only you had to back uphill to start. Many times this was done with the car shooting violently out into traffic, with horns blatting and drivers swerving to miss the amateur. If you made it without being hit, you were home free for it was all downhill from there.

In the early days the extra steep Tiger Hill was a real challenge. The old cars with gravity flow of gasoline from the tank to the carburetor would do very well on the down slope. But in climbing the steep hill the motor would starve for fuel since the gasoline couldn't flow up hill. They would be stranded several feet from the summit with some unhappy campers aboard.

This problem was solved in a unique way, adapting to the situation. All the driver of the cars without fuel pumps would do was turn around and back up the hill! This would ensure a gas flow all the way to the top when the driver would turn the car around and continue on toward Cushing.

With the coming of more efficient fuel pumps and automatic transmissions in automobiles, the hills of Drumright were somewhat tamed.

One other claim to fame of Tiger Hill. Most of the young guys who were fortunate enough to own a car considered it macho and a boost to their maleness to be able to climb the hill in the highest gear without having to shift down. Draggin' Broadway was **the** thing to do from the top of Tiger Hill all the way to the top of the hill at the east end of town about where the grocery Supermarket is located today. Remember how the old Model A's would "chuckle" their way to the top?

Early day service stations were always full service. You would tell the proprietor how much gas you wanted, he would pump the handle back and forth on the gas pump until he had brought up that much gasoline and then drain it into your car. It was gravity flow as it emptied out.

The old guys sat in silent reflection, each one wrapped in personal, private memories kindled by the story they had just heard. They were taken back many years to a time in their life that was simple and yet made complex by the day-to-day problems of growing up from adolescence to responsible adults.

Hank Blackwelder, down at the end of the table, spoke up for all to hear, "Sure seems to me a lot of you were a notch or two higher on the economic scale than our family. From the stories you tell, money seemed to be a tad more plentiful than in our household. I can remember when weeks would go by without my having two coins to rub together in my pocket."

"Agreed," said Cece, "but it didn't keep us from having some unforgettable times as I'd like to tell you."

WONDERFUL OLD BROADWAY

When my brother, sister and I were running the streets of Drumright, there was always one thing we looked forward to doing at the beginning of a new year and that was getting free calendars. When we were scabby-kneed kids living a pretty tough life, they were a total thrill to get. Since they were available from many merchants who used them as a form of advertisement, they were free. Now there's a wonderful word to children of lesser means … free!

Shortly after the first of the year, my brother, sister and I would whistle up our old family dog, Shep, and head for town to get our yearly supply of calendars. What did we want with so many? Actually we never tried to answer that question … they were free … and that's all that mattered …

free is good ... free is nice. Also, do you remember what beautiful pictures were on them? They could even be framed!

As we worked our way up Broadway, we would get our calendar from the store and then decide which of us would go into the next place of business. Merchants frowned on a troop of small ragamuffins tromping into their stores, so we took turns going in, one at a time. We knew our manners. They'd only give you one calendar anyway.

I was wearing my usual uniform of bib-overalls and had a supply of calendars stuffed behind the bib when I went in to the next store. Not too bright, or I'd have left the stash with one of my siblings. Anyway, when I approached the guy who must have been the owner of the store and asked for a free calendar, he eyed me up and down and said, "What are you gonna do with all of those," pointing down to where several calendars were showing above my overall bib. I was totally embarrassed and fled the store blushing furiously.

Being an antique buff, I know now what those 1930s calendars are worth in today's antique market. We were holding a small fortune and didn't realize it.

Another activity we spent a lot of time doing was collecting labels from cans of fruit and vegetables that could be redeemed for something. The desired labels were First Pick, White Pony and Cabro. First Pick had a picture of a baby chick picking a bug from a leaf. White Pony had a beautiful white pony on it, and Cabro was just generic something or another. Any of you guys remember what could be redeemed for these labels? I remember combing junk yards for them and having dozens of them all in their own stack.

While in the junk yards we also would find coffee can lids that had been cut from cans of coffee. They made excellent early day Frisbees, and we would sail them by the hour. We also were always on the lookout for junk we could keep in our salable metal stash at home.

We also prized discarded packs of cigarettes. The inner paper had a tinfoil layer over paper. The foil was practically weightless, but it you collected enough of them, you could form it into a ball that eventually had some weight to it. It could be sold to your friendly scrap guy. It was a slow, painful process collecting the foil, but time was our most plentiful commodity. We weren't going anywhere.

From a brand of cigarettes called Wings you could collect some really neat pictures of airplanes. Since flying and airplanes had only reached its adolescence and World War II was looming on the horizon, warplanes dominated the collections. We collected Japanese, German, Italian airplanes, as well as the Army Air Force airplanes. The cards showed several views of the airships, and the theory was you were supposed to be able to identify the airplane from its shape shown on the card.

Speaking of cigarettes, do you remember the brand called "Envoy Flats?" The individual cigarettes were rolled into an oval shape rather than the normal round. They supposedly were for the lady smokers, so they looked more feminine. They even came in a fancy, decorated tin box rather than a cardboard package so they wouldn't crush in milady's purse.

When I got to be a little older, I collected bread wrappers from Pan Dandy Bread, a local bakery. These wrappers were accepted as coin to get into the movie house. I have no idea how many it took, but would bet it was a bunch. I had my first date by taking my girlfriend to the movies on bread wrappers. Thank heavens, I don't remember who she was and would imagine she doesn't remember either, or would admit it if she did. I wonder if she furnished her own bread wrappers?

I do know that at one time we were admitted to the show (movies) by collecting a gallon pickle jar full of grasshoppers. I doubt that we reduced the number of the pests by any significant number, but I have a vivid memory of a huge box setting out in front of the Midwest or Rex Theater full of jars that were a writhing mass of grasshoppers. What do you suppose they did with all those rascals? No, I didn't take a girl to the movies on a jar of grasshoppers. I had my pride.

This was the middle '30s, and the entire part of the country was in the grip of a terrible drought in addition to some real hard economic times. To add to the misery, there was a plague of tens of millions of grasshoppers. I have a vivid memory of seeing grasshoppers lined up head to tail on every strand of a four-strand barb wire fence. The standing joke was that they had eaten all the vegetation and was starting in on barb wire.

It was a real booger of a time, let me tell you ...

"Well, I reckon since most of us were living here we can remember it pretty well, too," came from several of the guys.

"Yeah, it was just a fluke of economics that a serious stock market crash followed by a long, drawn-out period of low oil prices and world-wide depression came along," this from Doc Pringle. "Our parents were innocent victims with few well-paying jobs for our dads ... or anyone's dad's for that matter."

More discussion was held on how jobs were provided by the WPA, welfare existing through the American Red Cross and young men joining the Civilian Conservation Corp Camps for a bit of money, a job and some security. More young men of high school age went to Shawnee and other places and took part in the National Youth Corp camps learning a trade.

With no more discussion of interest on this subject, conversation began lagging and soon the guys slowly pushed back from the table and drifted out the front door.

SECOND COFFEE
Area Personalities

"Well, and a jolly good morning to all of you gentlemen on this blessed day," spoke up rotund Jim Kinnamon as the coffeepot made its rounds of the table. He'd ambled in slowly and was the last of the coffee group at the Boomtown Café on a beautiful "four star" morning. No one waited on him, for the standing rule was that the coffee flowed as soon as the first guy arrived and you just picked up your place as you entered the group. Ivey Jones, the waitress, saw to this. She liked to keep her men folks happy. If the truth were known, it would have been specifically Doc Pringle and Cecil Damore, but she would have denied that assertion on pain of death.

"Hey, guys," said Doc Roy, "I was listening to my radio last night instead of watching the TV. I get pretty burned out on watching that fluff they call entertainment on the tube. Actually you can run across some interesting stuff if you'll surf around the radio dial. What I was listening to was a documentary on we older males. It had to do with a new product for rejuvenating your manhood, and it got me to thinking. Remember that rascal we had yammering at our dads back in the '30's by the name of Dr. John R. Brinkley? We young boys didn't know what it was all about but just knew it was a real hush-hush bit of information."

Now, of course, all the guys who were old enough to reach a radio dial had some recollection of the guy, but they were ready to kick back and listen to Doc Roy tell about him but not without a verbal jab at him.

"Why, Doc?" spoke up one of the smart mouths at the far end of the table. "Was that old crook your inspiration for becoming a doctor yourself?"

As usual, Doc totally ignored this tired and shopworn joke and resumed his story. Besides, everyone knew he had been one of the best veterinarians in the area for more years than anyone really knew. In a pinch he had even administered to a few human beings, but always said he preferred animals. They knew when to keep quiet.

His basic sense of humor had been sharpened by years of listening instead of talking, making him a natural born storyteller.

DOC BRINKLEY'S VIAGRA

Early day radio takes no back seat to the modern versions of hyping various products to the point of nausea. In the 1930s a large part of the country was treated to the champion of charlatans and quacks as they listened to Dr. John R. Brinkley ... the Goat Gland King!

Throw away your powdered rhinoceros horn ... pitch out your ginseng root ... here was a surefire answer to the problem of virility, or lack thereof, and could be sent for by mail and received in a plain brown wrapper so friends and neighbors would never know. Even the "little woman" might never suspect ... eat your heart out, Bob Dole ...

When you sent in an order, you got a stimulating nostrum that came in liquid form or you could order a generous supply of pills. If you wanted the full nine yards of treatment, you made a trip to the Brinkley Clinic for the goat gland implant. Actually the patent medicine was his biggest seller, and much of it may have been no more than souped-up water at a big price. I don't know if he had a money back guarantee or not.

I can vividly remember the radio announcer intoning, "This is station XERA, broadcasting from Piedras Negras, Coahuila, Republic of Mexico, with 500,000 watts of power." The power was eventually upped to a monstrous 1,000,000 watts which meant the broadcasts could be heard as far away as New York, Philadelphia and up into Canada. The radio signal just blasted right over all other signals on the radio A M band.

I wouldn't be surprised if some "over the hill" Eskimos didn't order some of the life-giving pills. It may have been better than whale blubber.

As kids, we had no idea what all the to-do over Dr. Brinkley was about, but did catch enough adult talk to do a lot of rolling of the eyes, smirking and elbowing each other. We wanted to be cool and pretend we knew what the product was all about, but it was all posturing on our parts. We didn't have a clue. In later years I found that the old quack was transplanting some slivers of goat gonads into the patient and voila ... rejuvenation of youth. The power of mind over matter, huh?

The joke going around at the time was:

Question: What's the fastest thing on four legs?
Answer: A goat passing Dr. Brinkley's hospital.

Old Doc Brinkley got his start in the little town of Milford, Kansas, where his clinic was located. It was a real moneymaker, even by Depression standards, but apparently greed helped to eventually bring him down. He applied for a boost in power in his local radio station but was turned down.

He just shook off the defeat and moved his entire operation to a small town south of the border, across the Rio Grande from Del Rio, Texas, where he could ignore FCC regulations. He bought station XERA and built a transmitter with three 300-foot towers to send forth his message of rejuvenation to the North American continent. And did he ever send them!

We always liked listening to his station at night for it had a lot of country music with fiddles, banjoes and singing. Of course, a huge portion of the time was taken up with his commercials that extolled his "goat gland" product as a salvation to mankind.

At one point in his career he even ran for governor of Kansas as a write-in candidate. He got a large number of votes from the Kansas people, and it was reported that he even carried some counties in Oklahoma! He would have won, but the authorities threw out a bunch of votes on technicalities. Must have been the Oklahoma votes.

They finally got him for not paying back taxes and XERA was shut down, with the cooperation of the Mexican government. Old Doc had a heart attack in 1941 and passed away soon after in 1942. The town of Brinkley, Arkansas may have been named for him, for he had a hospital in nearby Little Rock at one time.

Doc Brinkley may have been the one whose treatment inspired the put-down when some wife yells at her husband, "Hey, you old goat."

"That's a great tale, Doc," several guys spoke up.

They had remembered the bare bones of the story and really appreciated Doc Pringle refreshing their memory with the entire story again. It was amazing what some people will fall for and spend their hard-earned money on.

"Speaking of local doctors in our town, I don't remember any quacks like that bird. We've had some great ones in our little town, haven't we," spoke up Faye Bucklin.

"I mean going back to the early days of the oil boom here in the bojacks, and none come finer than the old Cherokee Medicine Man, Orange W. Starr," spoke up Harold. "His career as a medical person actually pretty well paralleled the lives of many of the members of our coffee group."

Harold Atkins, speaking almost in tones of reverence, told of his feelings for Dr. Starr.

A TRIBUTE TO ORANGE W. STARR

It's quite fitting that a story be told of the country doctor who really had a lot to do with my life. I'm also honored to be the one who gets to tell it. He was a well-known figure to a bunch of people in the community for many years. He also made an impact on the civic life of Drumright, as well as being the only medical man for many of us.

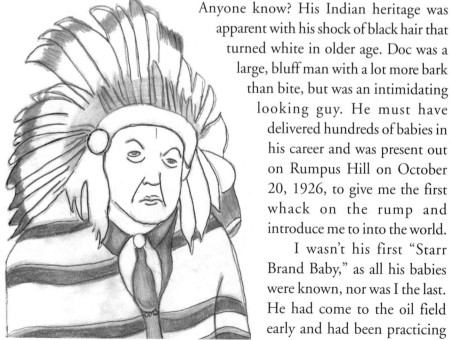

He was given the title of the "Cherokee Medicine Man" and well deserved. I wonder what the W. stood for? Anyone know? His Indian heritage was apparent with his shock of black hair that turned white in older age. Doc was a large, bluff man with a lot more bark than bite, but was an intimidating looking guy. He must have delivered hundreds of babies in his career and was present out on Rumpus Hill on October 20, 1926, to give me the first whack on the rump and introduce me to into the world.

I wasn't his first "Starr Brand Baby," as all his babies were known, nor was I the last. He had come to the oil field early and had been practicing his various skills for several years. In addition to "birthing babies," these medical skills were many and varied, for with all the dangers accompanying oil field work he was called on to tend all sorts of cuts, lacerations and other bodily traumas on a daily basis.

I've no idea what his standard fee was for delivering babies, but it couldn't have been much for we didn't have a large cash flow in our home, barely a trickle. He made house calls, and when summoned he drove his car out, and on a cool, rainy Wednesday afternoon in October, I made my appearance.

I never knew how it happened, but he listed my birth date as well as my birth name incorrectly. A Senior moment on his part? For whatever reason, many years later I had to go through official channels and get it legally changed to the correct one.

My next encounter with him was a year later in the winter of 1927 when I developed double pneumonia and diphtheria at the same time. Our old oil field shack lacked insulation, and the cold wind blew fiercely up on the top of the hill. I survived due to or in spite of the situation and became a hale and hearty "yard baby."

This led to my next need for Dr. Starr's services. I was playing in the yard with an older brother. He was chopping off roots while we built a road for our play cars.

I pulled up a root and he gave it a whack, and my middle finger on my right hand was in the way. The old chopping tool he was using cut the finger most of the way off, leaving it dangling.

My mother bundled me into the old car and took off down the sandy lease road headed toward town. She drove with reckless abandon in normal circumstances, but this time she broke all records and we got to his office on South Pennsylvania with me bawling like a banshee.

I don't know what medical hat Dr. Starr had on that day, but it wasn't the one for reconstructive surgery. He stuck the severed end back onto the stump, sewing it on with stout cord and called it a good job. The finger shows the result with a split nail and a huge scar to this day.

Old Doc took care of me later when, as a 12-year-old, I cut my left foot grievously while out in the woods cutting down a tree. His stitches weren't a thing of beauty, but they managed to hold flesh together, so what more could be asked.

Many years later I got a card from him announcing a "retirement celebration" being held in Drumright for all his Starr Brand babies.

Unfortunately it didn't mean enough to me at that time, and I've always regretted not going to pay him homage. He was a great old guy and a classic country doctor.

I believe most everyone who ever lived in our little town would have a "Dr. Starr" story if asked for it, for he touched most of the lives of those living here. He would probably have ended up a wealthy man if every one he treated had the means to pay him his fee. I know many times he'd just shrug his massive shoulders and say, "Pay me when you can," which was never, in many instances.

He was a staunch Democrat and would appear at political conventions in full headdress as a tribute to his Indian heritage.

"I remember him as being very involved in sports and was the team physician to the football team at Drumright High School," said Otto. "He also was a good horseman and rode a beautiful Palomino in parades and at rodeos. As I remember, he owned a horse farm out west of town."

"You know," said Harley, "when we were talking about listening to the radio awhile ago, it got me thinking. Remember the quiz show we had on the air by the name of Dr. I.Q.? I remember listening to it as a little kid. Some of the questions were real boogers, I thought. Sure would have been nice to have won some of that money."

DR. I.Q. QUIZ SHOW

I suppose you guys remember watching "Millionaire" with good old Regis. Makes us feel good to answer the first two or three dummy questions and sometimes being able to go way on up the line toward the million. It's not one of my favorites. Me ... I'd rather watch Vanna ... er ... ah ... I mean Pat Sajak on the Wheel.

Lots of you may remember that we had a popular quiz show back on early day radio ... we would gather around the old battery-powered table radio each week to listen in. It was called Dr. I.Q. and was an audience participating type of questions and answers. The good doctor would say, "For $2 can you answer the following question" .. a long way from a million bucks, but we were in an economic depression. Actually there were some four- and six-dollar questions and a few ten-dollar ones.

The broadcast would take place in some big city in a large theater with Dr. I.Q. acting as MC without the benefit of a beautiful girl in those early days. He would have male assistants scattered throughout the audience in strategic places, center aisle, lower balcony, etc.

As the program began, the Dr. would call on one of the assistants. The guy would have a mike and announce, "Dr., I have a gentleman on the front row, or I have a lady in the middle aisle." The question would be given, and if the person answered correctly he would get his two bucks and two tickets to next week's production here at the Rialto Theater.

It went on as different parts of the theater would be called on. I remember one week when the Dr. called on a certain guy, and he reported, "Dr., I have a lady in the upper balcony." It caused a roar of laughter, and the host was pretty well shook up for a bit. We were pretty innocent with our fun back then.

They repeated one type of tongue twister every week, and I don't remember anyone ever getting it right. You had to repeat a phrase such as this one letter perfect.

"My car is new, said Hugh to Sue … my car is new, too, Hugh, to him said Sue." They would invariably mess it up in some way. We practiced the type of saying, and at home we could usually say it. Didn't win anything but could be smug.

Another featured type of contest was a biographical sketch of a famous personality. If you got it on the first clue you got $100. The Dr. would start out by giving the contestant the first clue that was a rather obscure clue about the person. It would be next to impossible to know it on the first clue.

As the successive clues were given, the money amount would be reduced by $10 and the clues would come closer to identifying the personality. Finally, when the amount of money had dwindled to a really small amount, the last clues would be almost a dead giveaway. The last clue might be the first name of the famous person and the contestant would win.

At the end of the show they would announce that any person listening could send in a famous person written in the format of clues from difficult to easy, and if your biography was selected, you would win some money. I don't remember how much, but I thought I had a real winner.

I wrote a biographical sketch on Clark Gable, in my young kid scrawl, and sent it in. Cost me a 3-cent stamp, too … I waited … and waited … and waited and never heard a word from the sponsor. After about six months I had to give up and accept the fact that they hadn't chosen mine … an early day disappointment … it was my first lesson in the hard knocks of this old life ... "There is no such thing as a free lunch"... and ... "If it sounds too good to be true, it probably is," or "Don't count your chickens before they hatch" or something ... one ought to fit ... right?

"Yeah, yeah, life is tough," spoke up Joe Bob, "but you gotta roll with the punches. Sometimes you might think life wasn't even fair, but then who promised us a fair shake anyway? No one, that's who."

Talk slowed down for a pace or two as the old guys talked among themselves and tended to their fresh cups of coffee. Directly Elmer spoke up to get everyone's attention. "Now I know these guys weren't local people or celebrities, but they did make a big mark on our state and people. I saw a TV documentary the other night on the death of Will Rogers and Wiley Post. Since we were kids when they died, we probably remember them well."

WILL ROGERS AND WILEY POST

Any of you guys remember where you were on August 15, 1936?

There was no TV to make a 24-hour spectacle out of this event, but I would imagine there was some news flashes that came out over the radio on KVOO, WKY and other stations ... we didn't own a radio, so I suppose that we got the news when it made black, banner headlines in the *Tulsa World* the following day, "WILL ROGERS & WILEY POST DEAD IN ALASKA."

This stunning news shocked most everyone, for Will Rogers was one of Oklahoma's "favorite sons," and one of the most well-known people in the country. His folksy column appeared in many newspapers, he had made many movies and was a regular on Broadway, spinning his rope and cracking jokes. I've even heard he made a guest appearance in Drumright at the weekly "talent shows" at Way Memorial Park.

Will Rogers had become friends with the famed flyer, Wiley Post, and agreed to go with him on a fun trip to Barrow, Alaska, surveying a new airmail route to Russia. Will took along his old manual typewriter and continued pounding out his weekly column. Wiley was Texas born but moved to Garvin County, Oklahoma at an early age.

He had worked in the Oklahoma oil fields in his youth and lost an eye in a work-related accident. The small settlement he received gave him the seed money to buy his first airplane. Many remember Wiley wearing a black eye-patch as a dashing, daring young pilot who set many records in flying.

I remember the "Winnie Mae" as being the name of his famous airplane.

A different type of airplane was to be used on this particular flight, so Wiley had taken the wrecks of two other planes and put them together. The airship, named "Wiley's Orphan" or "Wiley's Bastard," was a conglomeration of the two wrecks, therefore the name. Will was a little skittish about flying in such an ungainly-looking craft, but was assured by his good buddy there would be no problem. With all the lakes on their route, the plane was fitted with pontoons rather than wheels.

They left Fairbanks, Alaska, to make the 500-mile flight to Point Barrow, far above the Arctic Circle, up on the North Slope. Flying was in its primitive stages, and without good radio communication they became lost in rain and fog.

An emergency landing had to be made in a lagoon just short of Point Barrow, and in trying to lift off, after getting directions, the engine quit. The nose-heavy plane fell back into the lagoon, shearing off the right wing, killing them both. An Inuit native saw the plane wreck and ran 15 miles into Barrow to report it.

Word went out over wireless radio from the Barrow Army base, and it soon became a sensational story to the entire world. The bodies were recovered and returned to Oklahoma as the people mourned the death of two men who were felt to be "bigger than life." They were our heroes, someone to look up to.

Ballads were written and sung about the life and death of the two men, and I remember a few of the words to one on a 78-rpm phonograph record we owned … does this ring a bell?

"A shining new plane shot into the sky and away for worlds of fun; Wiley and Will were riding the heights,

to the land of the 'Midnight Sun.' "

Soon after his death Wiley Post's widow sold his famous plane, "Winnie Mae," to the Smithsonian Institute in Washington, D.C., and it can be viewed there as one of our national historic treasures.

In 1982 the Will Rogers and Wiley Post Memorial Airport was dedicated to honor the two men. I assume this is the airport located in Oklahoma City, right? Also, monuments are located at the crash site and are on the National Register of Historic Places.

Things got real quiet around the table as each of the men digested the story and fell into a reverie of his own as they relived this memorable chunk of their past.

"I hadn't thought of those two old boys for years," Doc spoke up. "I always felt that it was fitting that they went together. They were a couple of great men and citizens to make us proud to be from Oklahoma. You sure did remember a lot about them, Elmer. How'd you get so smart?"

"Well," like I said, "I saw this great documentary on the History Channel last week and it sure brought back memories. Lots of good stuff on the tube, as well as a lot of trash. You just have to be careful what you watch. Since I didn't remember all I saw, I had to go to some search engines on the Internet to get some of the exact dates. I was a ten-year-old kid running the streets of Drumright when it happened."

Phillip Wiley spoke up for the first time in a long spell. "I've been listening to you guys talk about well-known people that have crossed our tracks here in town during our lifetime. I also agree that they have all the honor and glory we can give them, and I take my hat off to them.

"If you'll give me a listen for a little bit, I'd like to tell you my recollections of a group of people who made a huge impression on me. They are part of a lot of unsung personalities that walked these old hills that would make up a wonderful honor roll if they were so honored and named. I'd like to do that to one family of them."

DRUMRIGHT PIONEERS

In just a few short years our favorite town is going to have a memorable birthday. The City of Hills will be celebrating its 100th birthday. I would imagine that Drumright might settle on March 17, 2012, as the anniversary date, for that's when Wheeler No. 1 came roaring in, in 1912. It would be fun to be around for this celebration, but I'll probably be more interested in some WD-40 for my wheel chair.

This story I'm going to tell is about one of the pioneer families. It's not going to spotlight the movers and shakers like the Fulkersons, Drumrights, B.B. Jones and others, but will tell about a family who came early and stayed on to become the heart and soul of Drumright. Similar stories could be written about dozens of other families. No streets were named in their honor, nor does any building record their name. They made up the unnamed group of hardworking people who built the town.

In the early 1900s Allen and Elisabeth "Lizzie" McNabb were living on a hardscrabble farm near Clinton, Arkansas, with two boys and four girls. The boys were the first-born followed by six girls. Allen was a hardworking guy who spent long hours trying to squeeze out a living from the unforgiving rocks and hills of Arkansas.

News of the oil strike in Creek County, Oklahoma, filtered back to him, and the couple made a momentous decision. It was to pack up the kids and head for the oil patch in hopes of making a better life. They'd always farmed, but were intelligent and accustomed to hard work.

The year was 1916 and it was the first train ride for several of them. The settlement was a wild, raw conglomeration of tents and shacks, and they undoubtedly were wondering about the wisdom of their decision. They settled on a small farm near Happy Corner, and before long another girl baby appeared.

Allen and the two husky teen-age boys, Laurence and Virgil, went to work immediately in the oil field, while Lizzie stayed home with the girls. Since the girls had been raised to work, each one took her place as a contributing member. A sixth girl, Melba, was born in 1921, making a total of eight in the family.

They left the small farm and moved to Drumright, living on North Ohio and other places in town. Their final move was to 319 North Texas where Allen and Lizzie lived until their death. They are both buried in the North Cemetery in Drumright.

Allen was a robust, strong guy who was very health conscious. He was also a deeply religious man, being active in the Church of God. He was troubled by the rough ways of some of the oilfield workers  and longed to find something different to work at in better surroundings.

Since his roots were in the soil, he made a decision to find something along that line. He bought a large high-sided truck and became a fresh fruit and vegetable merchant. Some of you may remember him in his spot parked alongside the road on top of the hill in the east end. I remember it as being just east of Keeton's Service Station. Today it would be just west of the supermarket.

Allen would travel to Arkansas, Illinois, Colorado and southern Oklahoma for fresh fruit and produce. He was a friendly, pleasant guy and could always be trusted to give you full measure and weight for anything you bought from him. Several of the older girls helped out by working sales.

Allen and Lizzie McNabb are just one example of the solid citizens who came and stayed to make Drumright a prosperous town. Their offsprings total about 250 with eight children, 28 grandchildren, 72 great grandchildren, 128 great-greats and 11 great-great-greats and still counting.

Most have scattered all over the country, but there are at least one or two families still living in or around Drumright. I am proud to call these pioneers my Great Uncle and Aunt Allen and Lizzie McNabb.

"Hey, Phil," said Cece, "That was a pretty impressive story. Sounds to me if a Master of Ceremonies is ever needed to toss out the glorified words, we've got just the man for the job. I was ready to give three cheers and a hip, hip, hooray. Why, I've passed different ones of those people a hundred times in my life without a thought of their background. I also had no idea you were related to them."

Old Phil broke back in, "In a small town like ours it just doesn't pay to say anything bad about anyone, for you just never know when you're talking about somebody's kinfolk. If you got a little more time, I can tell you another quick story to prove the point of stepping on someone's kin."

THE COWHERD

Remember when we were talking about the fact that many families living in town kept a cow and possibly some chickens to supplement their diet and help with the family income? This was especially true when we lived in the east end of town. Many cows were owned and kept in a barn located on the property. Usually a garden and a chicken pen were nearby.

After the morning milking the cow couldn't stay in the cow barn, and the lot was too small for her to spend the day. In order for the cow to forage for food, from early spring to late fall, she was turned out to spend the day eating grass and other pasturage in the countryside. When the children of the family were in school or busy with something else, other arrangements had to be made.

There was an old guy who earned his livelihood doing the cowherding for those who needed it done. He endured some serious and disabling physical problems and was afflicted with a humpback but was otherwise quite active. His name was Phroney Klock and was well known to the people who lived in the east end of town. I remember him well as a guy with a grizzled beard painted well with tobacco juice stain and always accompanied by two or three dogs to help him herd the cows.

After milking time he had a schedule where he would pick up the cows in rotation and drive them down the various lanes, out from the residential areas to the countryside and keep watch over them for the day. The feeding place would be on east of town out on various oil leases where grass was plentiful and water in ponds available. Oil leases were open range so he and the cows could wander as they pleased. His dogs were ever present, for they were trained to ride herd on the cows and not let them stray.

I never knew anything personal about Phroney, but he was a friendly guy who provided this service for the people for the princely sum of $2 per month per cow. They were always delivered back to the home barn in the late afternoon in time for the evening milking. Each cow wore a cowbell with its own distinctive sound, and Phroney could recognize each cow by the bell sound. It was a really peaceful sound to hear all the cows coming down the lanes with the different bell tones sounding.

The only negative was that it was now just about time to go do the chore of milking the old cow. With several boys in the family, there was always argument as to whose turn it was to milk on any particular night.

In addition to just keeping an eye on the cows, Phroney also kept them out of the sludge ponds that were by each oil well. If a cow wandered out into the dirt-covered sludge, they would sink in and sometimes get their udders covered with an oily mess that had to be cleaned off before milking time. Folks were unhappy if he had let them do this, for it was a messy clean-up. Another duty of his was to keep the cows from foraging around oak trees, for if they ate the acorns, which they liked, it would make the milk bitter and undrinkable.

One other hazard came with milking. As the cows had grazed the countryside during the day, they were apt to have wandered into a patch of cockleburs. These rascals would attach themselves to the cow's long tail until it became a large, heavy matted club. While the milking was being done, the old cow might swing this matted club of burrs and whack the unsuspecting person alongside the head. When you sat down to milk, it was wise to part the long hair of the tail into two strands and tie the two around the cow's hind leg. This made it impossible for her to reach you by switching her tail. Milking was not my favorite sport!

"Yeah," said Harley, "but you sure liked to drink that milk and eat that butter and other good things that old cow gave you, I'd bet."

"You got that right," said Phil, "but you know, speaking of old Phroney ... he came from another long line of old Drumright pioneers. The Klocks were merchants and oil field workers from the beginning also. In fact, they married into the McNabb clan."

Old Faye Bucklin cleared his throat noisily and said, "Your talking about a clan reminds me of another bunch of people we all knew 'of' but didn't know personally or by any given names. As long as we're talking about personalities ... how about the roving bands of Gypsies that used to roam around the countryside? Seems like they had regular routes and would camp wherever they could."

GYPSIES

When I was a youngster living on an oil lease, there were two warnings cautious parents gave their children that would freeze their blood, cause instant terror and immobilize them with fear. This was before, "Don't get into cars with strangers" was the worst admonition a kid could receive.

The first warning was seasonal and would usually come on a typically cloudy, hot and humid day. When you heard, "A tornado is headed this way!" it was time to gather up the little ones and head for the cellar for a

26

long stay. It was a warning well heeded as many of us old Okies know.

The other warning wasn't necessarily seasonal but usually happened anytime from early spring to late fall. It also resulted in spine-chilling responses for a much different reason. When your parents called you together and in hushed tones said, "The Gypsies are headed this way!" you were usually wide-eyed and petrified with fright, although you weren't sure just why.

Just who the Gypsies were was unclear to us, but our parents assured us they were a dangerous bunch of foreigners. They were a swarthy, dark-skinned people with most of the men having large mustaches and the women dressed in bright-colored dresses. Many adults and children made up the clan and they roamed the country in old, well-worn cars. They would find some available land as a place to make camp and then proceed to rob and pillage the countryside. This was according to the stories we were told.

Especially vulnerable were hogs and chickens, for it was a "given" that the Gypsies would make off with the livestock in the dark of the night. Everyone who owned pigs and chickens would pen them up securely and keep a weather eye out. In all honesty, I don't ever remember knowing of anyone who lost an animal.

Sometimes the men would ask to do odd jobs for people. They offered to sharpen knives and scissors, cut firewood or do other paying chores you might have for them. The women would offer to tell fortunes by reading palms, coffee grounds or other mediums. They spoke with a heavy, foreign accent, which made them all the more mysterious. I have no recollection of them ever begging for a handout for they were a proud people.

They fascinated us and the boldest of the kids would slip out at night and go view the Gypsy camp. The viewing would always be done from afar with a clear field to retreat. The story was that they had sentries posted who carried long, wicked knives. The group could be seen gathered around the communal fire, eating and talking loudly. Sometimes music could be heard and they would be dancing.

According to my mother, who was a character with quite a sense of humor, the Gypsies wanted nothing better than to kidnap young kids and sell them as slaves. This always puzzled me, for I couldn't see why they would want more rag-tag kids when they already seemed to have more than they could provide for. Mother would let me know that you could be sold for a good price and she used the term, "White Slavery," which scared me witless.

27

But at the same time I wondered why she had me go out and sit by myself alongside the road. Life wasn't easy for one of the youngest in a large family.

After a week or so we would get up some morning and find them gone with no visible trace left other than cold ashes. They left the area of their campsite as clean as they found it. No one would have been kidnapped and life returned to normal.

Ivey Jones who had been hanging around listening to the stories bristled up to old Faye and said, "We know you're the oldest one in this group and we surely try to respect you, but I just gotta go to bat for your mother, with you telling tales on her, especially when she isn't here to defend herself.

"Several of us were well acquainted with your mother and knew her sense of humor. If she teased you about being kidnapped by the Gypsies, it was all in fun, for if truth be known she would have killed for you, if necessary."

As Faye looked around with the twinkle in his eye, everyone knew he had the same sense of humor his mother had, and he was way past "pulling their leg" … he gave them his widest, sunniest smile and said, "Peace, my children, I was only funnin' you."

"Back to the Gypsies," spoke up Otto. "I remember them camping in that large tract of land just behind Bill Andrews' blacksmith shop. He wasn't ever afraid of them or any damage they might do. He was another one of our personalities, and I've a story to tell about his place of business. It's about my turn, durn it."

THE VILLAGE BLACKSMITH

Regardless of how old we are, each of us has a special memory that we like to reflect on with happy thoughts of an earlier time. We can pull it out, polish it up and remember the happy things and times it represents. It might be a drive-in-theater of the 1960s, a special place we danced, a favorite car we owned, or just a place where we liked to "hang out."

Such a place for me is the old blacksmith shop of my childhood days. It was a magical place filled with sights, sounds and smells that have never been duplicated … another institution that should have been preserved for posterity.

The smithy was a man by the name of Bill Andrews. Unlike the poem by Longfellow the shop was not located under a "spreading chestnut tree."

In fact, there wasn't even a scrubby blackjack tree around. He also didn't possess arms of iron bands. I remember him as an average-sized guy who smoked a pipe and wore the necessary leather apron.

The blacksmith shop was a corrugated tin building located on a bald hillside, convenient to anyone needing his services. The dirt floor was covered many inches deep in very fine bits of burned coal clinkers, which gave off wonderful and distinctive odors of age. The equipment in the shop was a large forge, two or three huge anvils, and tanks of water for "tempering" steel and other machine tools. A bin full of "pea-coal" was nearby to keep the forge fed. A hitching rail was located outside for the animals.

The building was the local social hangout for the old codgers who would gather in the cool shade of the tin building, sitting on oil drums, broken-down car seats and large cuts of wood. The old "chaw-baccers" would congregate on a daily basis to swap yarns, tell lies and remember the olden days even further back in time. Sometimes, if we young boys were really fortunate, Mr. Andrews would let us squeeze the bellows that produced the air to keep the fire at the right burning temperature. This didn't happen often ... only on slow days.

Damp, rainy days were special with the low-laying smoke from the coal-fired forge bringing a pungent, distinct odor mixed with the animal smells of the horses and mules the smithy would be shoeing. An overcast day would produce special sights as the white-hot iron that Mr. Andrews would be pounding on, hammering into the desired shape he was after, gave off showers of sparks that flew hissing onto the floor. The hammering of the unfinished product on an anvil made a ringing cadence as the metal responded to the expert blows by the smithy.

Then, when the horseshoe or other item was completed, he would take it to the tank of water and quickly dip it in, knowing exactly how long to leave it in the water to get the proper "temper" to take.

Shoeing animals was always fun to watch. If the horse was a gentle, docile old farm animal, the blacksmith could simply take the hoof up between his legs and work until finished. However, if he had a skittish horse or stubborn old mule, there was a special stall used to tie the animal and work in safety. A large rasp would be used to smooth the horse's hoof, and a knife would cut off unwanted pieces. As the hot shoe would touch some of these hoof shavings, a very acrid, unpleasant odor like burning hair would waft through the air.

Farmers would bring in their plowshares to be sharpened, wagon wheels that needed to have a new rim put on them or the old one tightened. A one-of-a-kind broken piece of farm equipment would be duplicated by the smithy, if necessary. Bill, like most old blacksmiths, made many of the tools used to do his work.

"Way to go, Otto, I remember the place well," said Doc Roy. "You told it so I could actually smell the old coal smoke and the other dampish odors connected with the shop. I remember old Bill having his water jug wrapped in a gunnysack that was wet. You didn't ask him for a drink from his jug. You either did without or bummed from someone else."

"I remember a time or two when I was bawled out kinda strongly by Mr. Andrews," spoke up Jim. "My old dog went with me everywhere I went, and if there was livestock being shoed or otherwise taken care of, he didn't want an old dog around stirring up the animals.

"When that would happen, I'd normally just go on my way for Shep was as important to me as my right leg and we stuck together through thick and thin. Since we're talking about personalities, I'll tell you a quick story about my dog. He was not only a personality, he was a character."

TRIBUTE TO OLD SHEP

This isn't going to be a tale about an event nor will it give any mention to specific people or places. Instead, I would like to give a tribute to our old dog Shep in hopes that, as you hear the story, it will recall a special dog in your past and you will relate to some of the incidents.

When and how Shep became a member of our family is long lost in the mists of time and memory, but come he did and remained our boon companion for many years. He was loved by all of us and returned that love a thousand-fold.

Shep was a homely dog … no, he was an ugly dog. In any "Ugly Dog Contest" ever held, he would have won paws down. His color was a brindle yellow with one ear that drooped at half-mast and the other up at the alert.

There was usually a "doggy" smile on his face, for his was a happy life. He shared our bed and board with no complaint as to its quality or quantity, asking only for at least a pat on the head occasionally.

With six kids in the family, he had a lot of ground to cover, but as the older ones left home to pursue teen-age interests, he gradually gravitated to the younger ones for attention and adventure. He knew we were always good for a romp or a trip downtown.

When we would take him along on our trips to town, he would patiently lie and wait outside the business door until we returned. He just knew we would return and he wanted us to know that he was standing guard. The merchants were sometimes unhappy with this, I might add. His presence could be intimidating to potential customers.

Shep was a prolific lover, willing to share his affections with any female doggy, for he didn't have a prejudiced bone in his body. I would imagine if enough DNA testing were done on the canine population of Drumright today, you could find his genes in several dogs, especially the ugly ones.

For all his attributes, Shep had one vice that he refused to surrender. He loved to chase cars! No, he lived for it and had developed car chasing down to a science. We tried every trick to break him of this habit, but he must have felt that since he was such a great dog that he was entitled to at least one vice.

We always felt he must have taken a correspondence course from the Canine Institute of Technology. With the patience of the Sphinx, he would wait alongside the road, and as a car came whizzing by would make a ferocious lunge at the front wheel and with unerring accuracy swerve at the last nano-second to barely miss the wheel.

Of course, this bothered the drivers greatly. Some would actually try to run him down. On one occasion a guy ran his car down into the barrow ditch trying to hit him. Of course, Shep loved the challenge and grinned broadly. On another occasion when it was a slow old "flivver," Shep actually got out in front of the car and ran along looking back at the driver, grinning.

Not being perfect, Shep went to a neighbor house one time and ate up two pounds of fresh-churned butter left on the back porch. This made the lady angry and somehow was able to hold him and forced two tablespoons of arsenic of lead down his throat. This amount of poison would kill under normal circumstances. However, since he had just bolted two pounds of butter, the butterfat negated the poison and he up-chucked the entire meal. He was in the doghouse for a while after that

When Dad was transferred to Kansas in 1941, Shep went along and continued his escapades as a Jayhawk. When I went into the Army in January 1945, I bid him goodbye. Sometime during my army tenure old Shep passed away in his sleep.

I would hope that he had some little angels to play with and he could continue chasing some celestial vehicles.

"Well, getting back to human beings, although it was a great story about your dog, Jim," spoke up Phil Wiley.

"This story needs to be told for many and various reasons. First off, it's a good story and concerns a man who deserves all our respect and admiration. He was a veteran of World War One which means he saw some bad times.

"Some of you might remember him as the Candy Soldier for that was the name given to him by kids many, many years ago," continued Phil.

"Well, this I want to hear for I've never heard of him," said Hank Blackwelder. "I'm sure living out east of town several miles kept me from knowing lots of the Drumright citizens for we didn't get to town all that much. Mainly on Saturdays to sell the cream and eggs and buy groceries was about it."

"It's a great story," said Phil. "It will take me several sessions to tell it all. In fact, my whistle may get a little dry, so bring on the coffee pot, Ivey, my love."

Ivey snorted, "Since when was I voted in as 'your love'? I sure didn't get to cast a vote. I want to hear this story anyway. Sounds interesting."

That said, she brought back the hot coffee and even poured Phil's first.

THE CANDY SOLDIER

A friend of mine told me a story about this old boy who I'll refer to as the "Candy Soldier." It makes a great human-interest story and adds to the lore of Drumright. Having some time on my hands and a curiosity in my craw, I spent some time researching the facts of this story.

It is one of those mystery stories and hopefully some of you can add to what little I know or found out. I've talked with some other old timers and found some additional information, so we'll go with what I have and see what happens. Some of you have already told me you had heard of him.

According to one person I visited with, the Candy Soldier was a man who traveled on foot all around the oil patch, especially in the north part of the oil patch, selling sacks of candy and other goodies to anyone who might have spare nickels or dimes. He was also seen on the streets of Oilton and Drumright at various times.

A bit later I'll answer questions as to his family, his hometown and other important information. I just don't want to give the entire story away right here at the first. That's not the way the professional storytellers do it. They like to string you along with tidbits.

A distinguishing feature about the Candy Soldier was the full dress WW I uniform he always wore, including the stiff campaign hat. It had to be uncomfortable walking around in the broiling hot summer sun in full uniform. He was extremely neat in appearance, clean shaven and walked purposefully with a military bearing.

There is little doubt that he was a veteran of the Great War and had served his country honorably. It was reported that his face and arms were scarred from a mustard gas attack from the Germans while serving in the trenches in France. His niece told me this was not true.

He apparently was proud of his military service and was a real patriot. Reportedly, he would come to full attention and salute the flag when he would enter and leave the post office in both Oilton and Drumright. What else is remembered about him was his neat appearance and friendly attitude. Kids loved to see him come for the "goodies" he sold, and it was undoubtedly they who gave him the title as they would announce, "Here comes the Candy Soldier."

The country was in the grip of the Great Depression, and the rate of unemployment was close to 20% of the work force. Good paying jobs were almost non-existent, and men were doing whatever was necessary to earn an honorable living. The Candy Soldier was a good example of a man doing what he was able to do and not be a charity case.

I would imagine that when Social Security came into being in 1936 that he was eligible for and drew a modest pension. He is remembered as being in the area during the middle 1930s. His wares were carried in a 50-pound lard bucket, but when he would come to the door he would have a selection of candy in a tray to display to his prospective customers. One item remembered was peppermint candy canes, for a lady I talked with said her mother bought one cane and broke it into five pieces, one for each of the kids in the home.

His trips around the oil patch took place mostly during the week. He would walk from one community to another where there were always families with lots of kids. On Saturdays it was remembered that he would usually be seen on the streets of Drumright or Oilton, for this was the time the streets would be crowded with potential customers.

I'll continue to add to the information I gathered as my story unfolds. It will be nice to put a closure to this interesting man ... the Candy Soldier ... what a story ...

THE CANDY SOLDIER — Continued

I'll now let the cat out of the bag in order to continue the story of the Candy Soldier. I am now able to give you a much more detailed and complete story on this person, for I've had several letters and phone calls from a lady in Illinois, Patsy Morgan Hunter, a niece of the man! Can you believe it? She supplied me with personal stories, a picture, articles from newspapers and her uncle's obituary. This gives me information to complete the story of this guy who was, at best, unremarkable and yet a really unusual person.

The name, the Candy Soldier, as I told you earlier, came from his wearing a WW I doughboy's uniform and walking around the oil patch peddling candy door to door to those living in lease house communities.

He was John Henry Morgan, born 1894 in Indian Territory near Lebanon, Oklahoma in Marshall County. He was the second oldest son in a family of eight children. The family income came from operating a traveling sawmill that meant they moved many times and life was hard, and nice things of life were few and far between.

When John Henry was in his teens, the family located in the Oilton area for a short period of time, then on to Sapulpa before the final move to Drumright where they built a home located at 229 East Second Street. Later he came into possession of the family home and spent his entire life at this location.

During World War I he served his country in France under General John J. Pershing. This experience must have made a patriotic impact on John Henry, for he wore the uniform proudly and was remembered as saluting the flag in the post offices at Drumright and Oilton. Excuse me if I repeat myself sometimes.

From all accounts, as John Henry was growing up he heard his own special strain of music and marched to a different drummer than his playmates and peers. He was considered to be "different" and grew up with few friends. The other kids did as they have always done with someone different, teasing and poking fun at him.

He was able to overcome his loneliness and lack of friends by becoming an avid reader and would escape into a world of adventure and travel through the stories he read. His trip to France during his war service further added to his desire to travel and search for new and different places.

After being discharged from the Army, he went back to high school and was graduated from Drumright High School in the early 1920s. He then took a job with the Pure Oil Company for a short time. According to information, this was the only job he ever had other than peddling his candy. He drew a small disability check unrelated to his Army service. He never married, and this small check and a modest Social Security check was his only income.

Being both well and widely read, he was very aware of current events going on locally and around the world and was highly interested in them. He sent an airmail letter of congratulations to Charles Lindbergh for his successful solo flight across the Atlantic. His niece sent me a copy of the letter he received in response, signed by Charles Lindbergh thanking him for his congratulatory letter. He also received a signed picture of the famous aviator.

The *Cushing, Oklahoma Derrick* of July 1, 1927 had a front page story of his receiving the letter.

The group of men around the table sat in rapt attention listening to this riveting story, and other than muttered comments, the general consensus was to get on with the story. They were spellbound.

Phil took a long drink of water and continued. However, he couldn't resist a smart aleck remark, which was his trademark. "I don't know when I've been able to hold your attention for so long," he chortled.

THE CANDY SOLDIER — Concluded

All right, you characters, this is going to bring an end to the poignant "Candy Soldier" saga and the brief story of the life of John Henry Morgan, long-time resident of Drumright.

In March 1929 John Henry received a letter from the personal representative of Commander Richard E. Byrd. At this time Commander Byrd was in the Antarctic attempting to become the first man to fly over the South Pole. John Henry had written a letter of congratulations to him on his attempt. I have a copy of that letter, and the reply states that Commander Byrd was out on the Antarctic Ice Barrier and there was no way to contact him except by radio. The letter expresses thanks for his interest in the expedition.

In addition to being an avid reader, he loved to memorize poetry and could recite long poems from memory. His niece remembers him as having a photographic memory for facts, numbers and important dates in history.

She doesn't think he ever owned or even drove a car. He carried a magnifying glass at all times, for he was extremely nearsighted but refused to buy or wear glasses. He was a proud man and considered this a weakness.

As a younger man, John Henry did lots of hitchhiking and visited many states. His obituary states that he had eventually traveled to all 50 of them.

She tells of one scary hitchhiking experience he had. A man and woman driving a big car offered him a ride. They asked him if he was afraid to ride with them. John Henry said, "No, I reckon not." After a few miles they introduced themselves as Bonnie and Clyde, the infamous pair of bank robbers. Within a few miles John Henry allowed as how he had reached his destination and asked to get out. They wished him luck and told him goodbye.

As he grew older, his love of travel didn't diminish, but he continued his travels around the country by Greyhound Bus rather than hitchhiking. You could buy a $99 ticket that was good for a certain period of time. It allowed you to get off at any point, visit and get back on the next bus. The depot agent said he would travel by night in order to sleep.

John Henry lived frugally to have money to travel. He had no utilities in his home. He carried water from a neighbor's well, used a coal oil lamp and burned wood he scrounged up around town. He was seen carrying groceries home in a gunnysack.

He was a friend of Dr. Orange W. Starr who probably attended to his aches and pains. His niece sent me a copy of a 1957 Christmas post card sent him by old Doc wearing his familiar full headdress of a Cherokee Chieftain. He invited John Henry to come visit him in Spavinaw, Oklahoma any time. I like to think he got to go visit old Doc.

A highlight of his life came in 1968 when he flew to Hawaii to complete his tour of all 50 states. John Henry may have figured his life had come pretty well full circle with this goal having been attained. Being a romantic, I like to think maybe Dr. Starr paid for the Hawaiian trip. It would have been like him to do it.

The end for his travels and adventures came sometime during Sunday, February 2, 1975. Fittingly, John Henry died pretty much the way he had lived, alone and unattended. His body was discovered and reported later in the day.

Graveside services were held for him on the following Tuesday at the North Cemetery in Drumright, conducted by the pastor of the First Christian Church. No mention is made of those attending, but hopefully it was attended by some who knew him and cared for this old guy who had a lifelong wanderlust.

If you happen to be visiting in the North Cemetery in Drumright and see the headstone for John Henry Morgan, would you place a small U.S. flag over his heart and maybe drop some candy on his grave for me … maybe even give him a salute. He'd like that, I'm sure.

Several of the older men could be seen wiping their eyes and clearing their throats at the conclusion of this story. It was a quiet and subdued group that filed out of the restaurant and onto the street. The coffee session has broken up of its own accord with no farewells other than several, "Thanks a lot, Phil."

THIRD COFFEE
Landmarks and Special Places

Summer rain came hammering down on the hilly streets of the town turning gutters into torrents of water. The welcome rainstorm served as an excellent street cleaner as it gave the macadam a good scouring. All accumulated debris from the past several weeks was making its way rapidly down the steep hill of Broadway into the open storm drains.

The shower did little to deter the weekly gathering of the old guys who met at the café to drink coffee and exchange stories. Several were picking their way carefully around the puddles toward the door.

"The old Spit and Whittle gang would have had a sorry time meeting this morning," said Otto Irving, holding the door open to let in Pete Ledbetter and Elmer Butterfield.

"Yeah, they would have gotten their tails wet sitting on that curb, as well as wet feet," replied Elmer.

"And it's just as well we became civilized and moved indoors," spoke Phil Wiley. These chairs are a lot easier on the old rear end as well."

"Pete, what gives us the honor of your presence this morning?" asked Harold Atkins. "It's been a month of Sundays since you were here."

"Well, a couple of reasons. First off, I've been doing some remodeling in the wife's kitchen, and that's taken up more time than I wanted to give. Also I've been hearing bits and pieces of some of the stories that have been coming out of here, so I thought I'd better drop by to keep you guys honest. Some people tend to exaggerate just a mite as they get older," grinned Pete.

Before anyone could throw anything, Pete continued. "Naw, you know I'm only kidding. None of you guys would stretch anything but your fishing stories."

Desultory talk continued to go around the table as missing members were mentioned and local people who were sick or ailing were discussed. Ivey made her appearance with the coffee pot on schedule, and a cool, dampish morning became a warm, cozy retreat.

Pete spoke up, "You know, I passed by the old Ball Tank on my way into town this morning, and it made me kinda sad to see the sorry looking sight it has become. It's been let rust so bad you can't see any trace of the old Flying Horse on the side of it."

"Well, it's kinda like most of us," said Harley Sprague. "We're all beginning to show the years we've been around. But it's sure true that there are lots of landmarks, including buildings that have just plain disappeared since we were kids growing up. Schools, churches and other landmarks that have outlived their usefulness and have just been torn down or just plain wore out and destroyed."

"Well," drawled Joe Bob, " I for one miss the bright and shiny silver Ball Tank with the old Red Horse painted on the side. It was sure a unique sight coming into our town from the north on old Highway 33. I always knew I'd left the ranch far behind and was coming close to town when I saw it as a young cowpoke on my Saturday off. I used to walk the entire seven miles from the ranch into Drumright. Sure won't catch anyone walking that far nowadays."

THE BALL TANK

Yeah, St. Louis has its Archway, San Francisco has its Golden Gate Bridge, Paris, France its Eiffel Tower and London has Big Ben … but … Drumright, Oklahoma has its own monument and landmark, The Ball Tank …

Anyone who ever lived in the Drumright/Oilton area could relate to this huge orb and feel that as long as it stood all was right with the world. When it came into being pre-dates my memory for it, like the rocks, hills and trees has just always been there.

The landmark has always been a point of reference to anyone giving directions in the area. Located just off the main paved artery north out of town, as you were traveling old Highway 33 to Tulsa, it was right on your way.

All you had to say was, "Well, you go to the Ball Tank and then from there you just turn"… and having that as your reference point you could direct anyone to most any place in that section of the oil patch.

It must have been a magnificent engineering feat to build such a structure. Any of you guys know what its dimensions are? How tall is it? How big around? How many barrels of oil did it hold? Was it built for storage of crude oil or refined gasoline?

I've no idea what oil company constructed it or when, but it was there in the late 1920s. It must have been the Magnolia Oil Company, for it was painted shining, pristine silver. On the southeast side of the tank facing the curve in the highway and covering almost the entire side of the structure was emblazoned the fiery red emblem of Pegasus, the Flying Horse. It was one of my first encounters with Greek mythology ... a horse with wings?

It was a focal point in my childhood for many reasons. As a young boy starting first grade at Fairview school in 1932, it was a thing of wonderment and awe. From a distance it was impressive, and up close and personal to it was almost too much to take in. Living on Section 14, we walked daily to school, and as we topped that last hill, it was there like a huge setting sun to show that we had almost arrived at school.

My folks also attended the little white wooden church located just east of the Ball Tank across the highway, so it was part of my childhood each time we went to services.

It must have been a source of pride to the oil company that owned it, for it was freshly painted on a regular basis. We used to marvel at the daring of the men who swung from ropes, with paint buckets and brushes in hand to paint the horse on the side. It took many days to complete the job, and we watched the progress as we walked by.

I don't remember any of the older guys ever being tempted to climb to the top. The ladder spiraled to the top temptingly, but a huge iron gate with a monster padlock discouraged any attempts. If my older brother and his gang never did it, I doubt it was done. Besides, it would have almost been like defiling a shrine.

This is why it was so sad when I drive by it and see the poor old rusty landmark looking bedraggled and worn. It still stands, sad and neglected waiting for what?

I would suppose that at some point in the future a salvage company will come with cutting torches and it will be demolished, and like so many other structures from our past it will live only in memories and pictures. Such is life …

Wouldn't it be great if it could be listed on the National Registry of Historic Places and made into a park and monument to a great era in the history of Oklahoma and Drumright in particular? Unfortunately, anything like this takes big bucks that are not available. Maybe someone could write one of those government grants and get a couple million dollars … ahh, but that's just wishful thinking.

"I know I don't want to be chairman of the fund-raising committee to restore it," spoke up Cecil Damore. "Wouldn't a small acreage set aside around the Ball Tank look great as a museum to remember and honor the pool of oil that was so much a part of so many people's lives in the area?"

"Afraid it would have to be a project for a much larger base of people," said Doc Pringle. Seems like in Oklahoma oil field museums are a dime a dozen, but you're right, it would certainly be proper and fitting."

Phil Wiley spoke up, "There's already one landmark lost to the general public many years ago, and that's the old swinging bridge across the Cimarron River up by Pemeta. It was a really stupendous sight, and not too many existed. Some of you might even have had the chilling experience of crossing the river on it. It surely separated the men from the boys, or in my case the little boys from the bigger boys."

THE SWINGING BRIDGE

As some of you may know, several miles north and west of town and not too far from old Pemeta, high on the frowning, rocky bluffs overlooking the Cimarron River, are the remains of two large 10" pipes that served as the anchor posts for a humongous swinging bridge that crossed the muddy swirling water of the river. The bridge was used by the pumpers and other oil workers to enable them to service the oil wells on both sides of the river without going down to river level.

It was built by an oil company in the early days and stretched 600 feet across the river. On the east side the large cables were securely bolted to the pipes set deep in the living rock of the craggy bluff. The bridge was similarly anchored on the west side. About 3-1/2 feet above the bottom cables

were two more cables to serve as handrails when walking across.

Large wooden crossbeams were attached to the lower cables, and on top of the crossbeams was secured a 2 x 12 plank to make a narrow walking surface. Since it was a free-swinging bridge, it swayed in the wind and took a fairly good balancing act to walk at a steady pace.

By the middle of the 1930s the swinging bridge had seen better days. The maintenance workers no longer used it, for many of the wells on both sides of the river had stopped producing.

Through weather and neglect many of the boards had rotted and some had fallen to the depths below. There were wide gaps making it a really scary crossing. Warning signs announced that it was "Private Property" and to "Keep Off," but these were like engraved invitations to the adventurous boys of the neighborhood.

On this occasion I had tagged along after my older brothers and their friends. Usually something exciting happened when they all got together, and since I was all of eight years old I was ready to go through another rite of passage. Their object was to cross completely over the rotten old swinging bridge and back. Right on!

We scrambled up and out onto the swaying bridge, and immediately I developed a serious problem. I suddenly lost all my courage and told my older brother I didn't want to continue on. Since he was the leader of the pack and Alpha dog of the group, he couldn't have flesh and blood of his turning chicken, so he insisted I go on.

Using some bodily force, he hauled me out onto the bridge about a hundred feet and left me with this final injunction, "Walk back or else!" Staring down into the abyss, I could imagine what the "or else" could be, so I immediately lost all heart, flopped down on the rotten floor boards and clung to them like the coat of paint they never had.

The "or else" turned out to be some more horror for me. By bouncing up and down on the free-hanging bridge, the entire structure could be made to undulate in its entire length into waves of up and down motion. All of them continued to do this, and as I lay plastered to the boards bouncing up and down, I visualized a horrible death falling off the bridge into the bottomless void. It looked to be about a mile down to the water and riverbank (actually about 50 or 60 feet at the most).

After much caterwauling, bawling, pleading and begging, they relented. However, by that time I was too weak in the legs to stand, so I literally crawled like an inch worm all the way back to the east side. I lost a lot of macho coup points on this day.

"I, for one, never did cross that old bridge, and from the sound of your story I sure am glad I didn't get the opportunity to do so," spoke up Jim Kinnamon. "You know, fellows, just thinking about it, we're lucky so many of us survived to adulthood with all the dangerous things we tried, and there were opportunities galore in an oil patch. Maybe it made good soldiers out those of us who went to fight in World War II."

"You know," continued Jim. "As long as we're talking about things up in that neck of the woods, did any of you guys ever go to a picnic at a place called Texas Park? It was real close to Pemeta on the east side of the Cimarron River. Today's kids would say it was a really 'cool place.' Since we didn't know 'cool' from apple butter, we just thought it was a fun place to go."

TEXAS PARK

In the days of lease house communities in the 1930s, large oil companies had dozens of men working for them, and most of them had large families. Several of the companies provided recreational places for the benefit of their workers. This meant graded ball diamonds, playground equipment with shelters and tables for picnics. A place to relax and a chance to enjoy life after the hard work in the oilfield made for happier and more productive workers.

The one that really stands out in my memory is Texas Park. I'd guess it was provided by the Texas Oil Company that became Texaco in later years. The park was located on the east bank of the Cimarron River a mile or so north of Drumright near the small hamlet of Pemeta.

We'd go north out of town on Highway 33 toward Oilton. Somewhere around the little settlement of Crow there was a sandy road that headed west toward the river. I believe we crossed over the river on a narrow bridge.

Driving off down in the bo-jacks we'd come to a pipe fence with a big gate, and this was Texas Park. It was located in a lush green-forested spot and had hills to climb, trees to scale and more playground equipment that we had on our playgrounds at schools.

On top of one of the hills a rope swing was attached to an overhanging limb of a huge spreading tree. This provided a heart-stopping thrill as you flew out over the landscape high above the people and ground below. The swing was a gunnysack stuffed with straw tied to the end of the rope and made for a very safe ride. You just jumped up, gripped the sack in your legs and held on tight. In later years I heard such type of swing called a "pappy-dad," but we never referred to it by that name.

The Texas Company was most generous in letting people use the facilities, and it served as a picnic area for church groups as well as individual families. Since the pastor of our little church worked for the Texas Company, our flock always had first dibs on a spot when we picnicked.

I remember Fourth of July picnics best of all, for it always meant a belly full of food, firecrackers to shoot off and fun and games with scads of kids of all ages. It was the only time I remember us having a No. 3 washtub filled with pop and a 50-pound block of ice chipped over the bottles. We'd pry the cork from the pop lid, put the lid onto our clothes and press the cork back in the lid and had a dandy bunch of decoration to sport around. Aluminum cans don't offer much for creativity.

Nehi brand was the pop of choice and offered flavors such as Cream Soda, Strawberry and Grape. I don't remember any cola except some RC Cola at times. Never heard of Pepsi Cola. We thought we'd died and gone to heaven with all the flavors and the quantity of pop to be had. Of course, we had lots of fun with the pieces of ice to put down the girls back and hear them shriek.

The older guys would always get up a softball game, and if the teams were a little short-handed, we younger kids might get to play right field or some other non-essential position. There were several horseshoe pits around, and the older duffers would take part in this less violent game. H-m-m-m, I pitch horseshoes now!

A tired bunch of young and old would finally wind down and call it a day … Much fun was had by one and all …

"Yeah, that kind of entertainment was pretty innocent back in our salad days. I'm not sure just how it would be looked at today. It just isn't fast enough for the kids nowadays and I'm not putting them down, just a different age and time," spoke up Pete.

He continued, "Every generation has its own turn-ons and turn-offs. Now take swimming, for instance. Seems all our modern day smarts tells us we need clean, antiseptic swimming pools for our kiddies with lifeguards and chlorine in the water. Boy, is that a long stretch from the old swimming holes we used back when we were young shavers.

Not a one of them would have passed muster with the County Health Department but, man, didn't we have fun swimming in them?"

"This one was known far and wide and had a great reputation with a mystery attached to it," said Otto. "Remember the mysterious hole right in the middle of the deepest part of that was supposedly bottomless? I don't know that anyone ever made it to the bottom of the hole for the water got really cold when you blew out all your air and sank to the bottom."

THE OLD SWIMMING HOLE

Finding a good, clean freshwater swimming hole around our part of the oil patch during the 1930s was a real challenge for all of us young boys, and sometimes girls who wished for some summertime fun in the water.

With oil leases all over the country and oil wells dotting the landscape, it was difficult to find fresh water. The goal of the big oil companies was to make money, with conservation and the Environmental Protection Agency being decades in the future. As a new well was drilled, the salt water and other oil waste products were dumped indiscriminately onto the ground in the immediate vicinity of the oil well.

This drained into the nearest stream or creek and eventually into the closest river. Consequently, many potential swimming holes were contami-

nated with a high concentration of salt, making them totally unusable. All
marine life was killed off, so no fishing was possible in the contaminated
waterways. Tiger Creek, on the east end of Drumright, ran with salty water and clots of oil floating on the surface. Where Tiger Creek crossed
Broadway, it was called "Stink Creek" for the foul odor it gave off. Even
the Cimarron River was too salty to have fish.

There were a couple of exceptions where we were able to go swimming
if you were willing to walk several miles to get there. The favorite one for
our bunch was called the "Devil's Bathtub." This was a heaven-on-earth
place to a young boy wanting to go swimmin' in the broiling summertime
sun of Oklahoma. However, heaven wasn't easily obtainable. It was a long
walk to get there from most anywhere.

It was located on a farm several miles north and east of town, and you
usually were ready go back in swimming after the long, hot walk back
home from the afternoon spent there. The farmer must have a special place
in heaven for the goodness of his heart. He permitted anyone who wanted
to go swimming to walk through his farmyard and continue on about 200
yards down to the creek. Just be sure to close all the gates!

The Devil's Bathtub was the result of a tremendous river that flowed
there in prehistoric times. A huge waterfall had tumbled hundreds of feet
over a rocky wall and scoured out a large roundish catch basin probably
100 feet wide by 200 feet long.

By the time of this story it was a placid river flowing over a series of rock falls and dropping about 15 feet to the main body of water. The water flowed over two rockfalls that were usually covered by slick green algae and made a perfect "raccoon slide" to a bunch of devil-may-care boys and girls. It was normally a male sport, for swimming was usually done in the raw or "swimmin' nekkid." **No Girls Allowed.**

On one hot summer day that I remember, all the guys were sunning themselves on the rocks high above the water when someone yelled, "Some girls are coming." There was a mass exodus of skinny-dippers who leaped about 20 feet down into the water. This was in an earlier day when modesty prevailed.

In the middle of the swimming area it was rumored that there was a "bottomless hole" that might even lead off to other passages. Few of us were brave enough to let our breath out and sink down to the bottom to check the story out. Naturally, the hole got bigger and deeper with time and story telling.

The Devil's Bathtub had another name that was much less evil. At least one church that practiced "total immersion" as a baptismal rite used the place for the ceremony. Congregations would have a morning Sunday service and then travel by car to the place they preferred to call the "Giants' Bathtub." It seemed to be a more appropriate name to practice a religious rite.

This last remark brought a solid round of laughter from the group, and those who lived in the vicinity of this swimming hole all had stories to tell of their own boyhood and hair-raising tales of some brave thing they had done there. These stories and anecdotes were told and commented on for some time. Finally someone mentioned another kind of swimming hole that was definitely a unique kind of a place to swim, and it could only take place in an oil patch community.

SWIMMING IN A CIRCULATING TANK

A bunch of us took part in using these large wooden tanks as substitute swimming holes. Since their existence depended on the presence of an oil well or a cluster of them, many got to take advantage of them. For the one or two who might need a little information about what circulating tanks are, I'll give a bit of information to understand the purpose of them.

Each of the drilled and operating oil wells had a derrick to be used in maintaining the clean-outs for optimum oil flow and other repairs. In the teens and 1920s they were wooden structures, but by the 1930s most were built of steel and were about 60 feet high. Many of the wells were self-sustaining and pumped their oil independently.

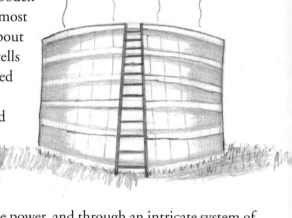

Power had to be furnished to pump the oil up, and an engine located on the site supplied this. It was usually a large Bessemer natural gas engine that produced the power, and through an intricate system of gears powered the pumps that sucked the oil to the surface. This huge gas engine was water-cooled, and so a large amount of water was needed to keep the engine cool as it worked many hours of the day and night.

To supply the large amount of water needed by the Bessemer engine, a large wooden tank was built adjacent to the engine shed and kept filled with water. This served as the cooling system for the power plant as the cooler water constantly circulated into the engine with the hot water circulating back to the tank to cool off. The tank was about 12 feet in height and maybe 15 feet across.

Since this was not salt water, it made a good swimming hole for those who didn't mind the inconveniences it took. A ladder was used to scale the vertical side, and once on top there was no "bank." You went right in, for the next guy was climbing right behind you. Diving was not advisable, and the insides of the wooden structure were always covered with a green slime of algae that meant it was very slick. You hung onto the sides to rest.

Another hazard was that you never knew what the temperature of the water was going to be. If the engine had been working long and hard, the water could be super hot. It was always wise to check it before jumping into the tank or you could face the danger of being boiled like a lobster. On the up side, with the water always warm, swimming could take place even in coolish weather. It was our early day spa and we didn't know it.

One of the workmen tried to discourage the boys from swimming in the tanks. He told them that occasionally the company put acid in the water to clean the engine. The boys found this a little hard to believe for one of their swimming buddies was this workman's son.

My first swimming lesson was taken in a circulating tank, and the teacher was an older brother. I'd tagged along as usual and had actually gotten into the water and was hanging onto the edge. He decided I needed to learn the art of swimming, so he pried my fingers loose and shoved me out to the center. Always one to encourage his younger siblings, his final admonition was, "Swim or drown." I was well on the way to the second alternative when someone towed me out back to the edge.

Two things need to be understood about being the younger one in a large family. One is that older brothers had a bounden duty to provide instruction to younger ones, done with the "tough love" philosophy. He was tough and loved it.

The second thing is that "Guardian Angels" were overworked in those days.

"Coming from a large family, I can totally understand where you're coming from," said Jim. "You have to grow up quick and grow up mean to survive in a big family, especially if you're one of the young ones. But it also has an up side," he continued. "In case you have some playground problems at school, you can count on some tough but loyal allies in your brothers."

"This is a little off the subject, but talking about places and things we remember that are disappearing, how about those little grocery stores we had back in the 1930s?" asked Henry Blackwelder. "I'm talking about the little Mom & Pop grocery stores that were located in the different oil patch communities. I know we had one out on the oil lease where my folks lived."

"I'd imagine they all went the same way as the dinosaur," spoke up Jim Bob. "They just disappeared but sure served a good purpose while they were here, though, didn't they?"

MOM & POP GROCERY STORES

Living in an oilfield lease house way out in the sticks could be a real pain when the grocery supply ran short. Saturday was normally "butter and egg" day to go into Drumright, Shamrock or Oilton to do the big shopping, but sometimes you ran out of something vital during the week and this was unhandy.

Scattered around the oil patch were various little stores that carried a limited supply of groceries. Some were of the "Mom and Pop" variety and were run many times right out of the front room of the home. Had

to make some money somehow for dad was probably out of work. Many things were done to beef up the family income and keep the wolf from the front door.

Since the demand was rather small, the variety and amount of stock carried was usually limited. The "Mom & Pop's" tried to carry some of the basic essentials, such as flour, sugar, beans and lard. Refrigeration was limited or didn't exist, so very few perishables were kept on hand.

One very small store was the "Pop" Greer Grocery located on the Jeanette Richards Pure Oil lease east of town. An elderly couple ran it, and both were really hearing disabled (they were deaf as posts). My older brother went in their store one day looking for his lost dog, Tunney. After repeating his story and getting louder each time, the elderly Greer lady said, "No, we h'aint got no sody." He left …

Some of the stores were free-standing buildings and could rightfully be called grocery stores. One of these was the Litchfield Grocery, which served the large Tidal community as well as the surrounding area.

Located on the highway between Drumright and Oilton was the Oil Field Grocery, just across the road from the Cities Service Camp. It was a bonafide grocery and was the largest one I remember. It even had gas pumps out front. They sold cold pop out of an icebox and some candy, along with a much wider line of groceries.

The Cities Service Camp was made up of dozens of homes with a large population and supported the Oil Field Grocery well.

Only problem was, few people would buy much at the small stores due to the higher prices they had to charge. Some people did run a bill there, making it convenient to send a kid to the store to pick up some needed item. Most people looked forward to the Saturday trip into either Drumright or Oilton to shop at the much larger Safeway and other markets.

Another small store was located on the east side of old Highway 33 just east of the ball tank across the road near the little white church we attended. Was it Tebbets who ran it? Their inventory was **very** limited. Sometimes we would go there after church to get a licorice stick or a piece of horehound candy (yuk).

A mile or so further north on the highway toward Oilton was the crossroads store of Crow. A grocery store was located there, but I was never in it. All of these stores had candy that was usually pretty old and shop-worn due to the slow turnover ... but we ate it anyway.

"We had one of them just down the road from our little old shotgun house," said Phil Wiley. "The store was in these people's front room and was just a family affair. I tried to make time with the girl who was near my age. I thought I might get a free jawbreaker or Black Cow for my attention. Must have been tried before ... didn't work."

Phil continued, "Changing the subject, but as long as we're talking about landmarks we remember, did you guys know we are sitting within a block or so of a famous one we all must have visited dozens and dozens of times growing up here? I'd kinda forgotten about it until I had the following experience I'd like to tell you about."

GHOST RIDERS AND GUN SMOKE

Remember the old Midwest Theater guys. I'm talking about the place where we saw all the wild rootin,' tootin' "shoot-'em-up" western pictures and hair-raising weekly serials when we were kids. You know that over the years it has been totally redone and you might not be able to find it. Anyone visiting the former Drumright Gusher office is in for a distinct surprise.

While chatting up the editor not long ago about her planned move a few doors to the east, the conversation came around to the location of her present place of business. I told her it seemed to be close to where the old

Midwest Theater was located back when I was a pup, trying to scratch up a dime to go to the movies.

To satisfy my curiosity we walked over to a back door in the office, and she threw it open. Lo and behold … it was easy to see that the back storeroom floor sloped downward to the north a whole bunch … She then said, "This **is** the old theater that we're standing in." Sure enough it was, and while it was too dark to see clearly, I could tell that indeed this was the hallowed hangout for a myriad of boys and girls from days long past.

The outer office must have been the lobby of the movie house, but little remained to identify it as the door to enchantment where we spent so many happy hours. I swear I could smell the aroma of hot buttered popcorn wafting through the air.

With very little imagination it was easy to conjure up the ghosts, images and auras of countless kids sitting with open mouths watching their favorite heroes and heroines get into impossible situations and wriggle their way out with bravery and fortitude. If you carefully sniffed the air, you might even smell the gunpowder from the endless bullets their "six" shooters fired. Remember how the good guy could fight like a demon with six outlaws and never lose his hat … and then burst into song when it's over …

Close your eyes and you can see Tom Mix in his white hat with horse, Tony. Here's Hopalong Cassidy with sidekick Windy. Hoppy is the only one of these cowboy heroes to wear all black. Wonder why? He was my favorite and I was always going to have a Bar 20 Ranch when I grew up … Ken Maynard, Gene Autry with old Frog and LulaBelle, Hoot

Gibson, Roy and Dale with Trigger and Buttermilk … Even the Cisco Kid with his buddy Pancho … A-w-w-w, Cisco … Bet you guys can name a bunch more of them.

All of these "bigger than life" movie star heroes rode valiantly across the wide screen each Saturday afternoon. Lots of us would go to the show early afternoon and sit through the entire thing several times until the lights were turned on.

I remember one time during a chase when the bad guys were going to waylay and ambush our hero. As our boy got closer to the ambush site, the music tempo picked up and tension ran high in the movie house. Finally some kid sitting way down front, who was totally involved in the plot, let out a yell and said, "They're hiding behind that big rock!" That's the truth if I never tell it again …

Somewhere, either before or after the main feature … I can't remember … there was always another chapter of the weekly serial. Whether it was Tarzan, Flash Gordon or Tim Tyler, we always had to get them out of the fix they had been left in the week before. Didn't do much good for at the end of this episode they'd be right back into another hair-raising, impossible predicament …

So … we'll hope when the move was finalized the staff was be able to get more work done without all the noise coming from the back room. We'll also hope the last one out closed the back door gently as they left.

"Good story, Phil," said Harley, "But a little sad the way it leaves me feeling. We all know that change is going to happen and there's no way we are ever going to hold it back. It still can't keep you from wishing you could hold onto some of the old things and never let them go."

"Yeah, said Doc, "that would be real convenient if we could pick and choose. I'm sure we'd all pick and keep good stuff and places and let all the rest of it go to eternity."

"It just doesn't work that way, but let me tell you of a couple of things I'd keep around," spoke up Pete Ledbetter. "One is a place I'd love to visit and take a long drink, and the other one is kinda special to me, for I romanced my wife there many a time long before she was my wife. One is the old artesian well out west of town, and the other is the Sundowner Drive-In Theater not too many miles from the artesian well."

ARTESIAN WELLS

Well, gents, after a long dry summer the fall rains have come blowing in. Living where we do, you don't question where the good wet stuff comes from … you just lay back and enjoy it. Kinda like the old sow that eats the acorns and never looks up to see where they are coming from.

With the road to Cushing being changed and made into a double lane, I've been told the old artesian well is no longer flowing. The ground water source was cut off and it isn't even there. I have no desire to even drive out there and look. I'd much rather see it in my memory as I remember it.

We didn't know much about them, but our dad told us it was an artesian well, but that's about all he knew about it. We were curious as how the water could flow up and out of a pipe without a pump to bring the water to the surface. Also, why didn't the supply of water run out? Remember this was in the dry and arid "Dirty Thirties" and water was a precious commodity.

It just seemed to be a magic source of water that came bubbling up out of the ground on it own free will. It was always icy cold and probably the purity was close to 100%. Lots of bullfrogs and other water animals always abounded there in a mass of always-green vegetation.

A whole bunch of years later I experienced another artesian well while visiting an uncle in Cleo Springs, Oklahoma … talking about them he said he would take us to one …I don't remember where it is now, but it was truly an oasis up near the Great Salt Plains. We stopped along the road and actually used an old-fashioned stile to cross over the fence to walk to the well … ever crossed a fence using a stile?

This artesian water flow was just bubbling out of the ground rather than coming out of a pipe. The constant flow had formed a huge marshy bog that abounded with all kinds of water plants and animals. We were introduced to watercress growing in the wild. If you haven't enjoyed a bunch of this in a salad or on a sandwich, you've missed out on a real treat. Sure wish I'd remembered where this was, for it's worth a trip to just eat some of the tangy watercress.

These are the only two artesian wells I've ever seen, and after some research and internet surfing, I was able to see what causes the water to flow on its own. For you guys with a personal computer in your house, the great search engine Google showed some clear-cut diagrams on what it takes for one to flow. Soil conditions and the "lay of the land" have to be just right for the water to flow. It's ground water only, and it can come up voluntary as a series of springs or you can sink a pipe into the water level and the internal pressure causes the upward force of the water.

The joker of the coffee group, Jim Kinnamon, now stood and loudly dinging a spoon on the side of his water glass got everyone's attention, "And now Pete will entertain us with some true confession stories about him and his beautiful wife at the old Sundowner Drive-in Theater."

Pete replied sharply, "Aw, shut up, Jim. These are tender memories and not to be made light of."

DRIVE-IN THEATERS

I heard some kids talking about going to the drive-in theater recently, and I felt like a goose had walked on my grave. I thought they had all gone by the way of the dinosaur, but come to find out there are some of them still around. If I were to tell you a bit about the old drive-in, it would possibly stir up different memories for several different age groups. Let's see what shakes out.

They became commonplace shortly after World War II and continued to grow into the '50s and '60s until TV came along and helped do away with most of them. While we 1930 models and earlier couldn't relate to them as teenagers, we still have vivid memories of drive-ins for several different reasons.

I've talked with several people of different age groups who lived or live in Drumright, and they all agree with me that there was no drive-in theater in the town ... a mile or two east of Cushing was one called the Sundowner which was about the closest one we could go to ...

Many of us were raising our families in the 1950s and '60s and went to them for a cheaper form of entertainment. The going rate for admission was usually so much for a carload, so you could load up the entire family and even include the family mutt and head out before dark. I believe they sometimes had a number limit, and then this led to some smuggling in, using the car trunk.

I was playing around on my computer the other day and wanted to learn more about drive-ins, so I surfed the 'net and found the first one actually started way back in 1933, in New Jersey.

Along old Highway 66, "The Mother Road," they were located from the Sooner Drive-in in Miami, Oklahoma, all the way west to the 66 Drive-

55

in in Elk City. According to the information there are some still in operation.

Some really fancy drive-ins were built that had spaces for hundreds of cars. The record one held 2,500 cars back east some place. The smallest one handled 50 cars. One was even covered.

Most had playground equipment up front to keep the kiddies entertained until the shows started along about dusk. In small towns they were social hangouts, for many people would come early, get out of their cars to eat and talk with friends.

In talking with my wife the other day, we agreed there are "drive-in" stories abounding in just about everybody's heads. We older ones used them in a rather boring, mundane way with our wife and kids as a cheap night out. However, I'd imagine the younger set have a whole different set of memories …

The drive-in theater was popularly called the "passion pit," for it was a favorite place to take your main squeeze and practice some "affaires de amore."

Regardless of how it was used, it served a good purpose while it was around, but like so many other things it finally just outwears its usefulness and fades away.

"Well, fellers," continued Pete, "if you'll take a look outside you can see the rain has stopped and we have little excuse to still be here. We've already overstayed our time and we're gonna have to start paying rent, eh, Ivey?"

"I'll admit you've surely killed a lot of time here this morning," answered Ivey.

"But before you go, how about listening to a story I'd like to tell concerning a landmark that was an essential part of our lives. Lots of the places you've been talking about are places of choice where you go to have funsies. How about this place which was an absolute necessity?"

THE OLD OUTHOUSE

Sitting majestically out in the backyard behind many of our homes could be found the little building with many names. It was called the "comfort station," "the necessary room," the privy or just the plain old terlet. If truth were known, it was also known by a few other names not suitable for a mixed social crowd. For our purpose it'll just be the humble outhouse.

Lots of you lived in the more developed part of town and had all that good stuff like running water, indoor toilets and such, but in the more rustic

parts of town and out in the country we made do with more rude facilities. I was 13 years old before my first bath in a full-sized porcelain bathtub.

Dad had found some worn-out belting from an old bull wheel, and we had a continuous foot-wide all-weather path from the back door to the outhouse. You could find it easy in the dark and avoid some of the scary things. Naturally, there were some downsides that always had to be reckoned with, but these you just took as part of life in the country.

In the summertime there was always the fear of creepy crawly things lurking in the hole below. One of the biggest horrors was the possible presence of a black widow spider. Don't know if I ever saw one, but we just knew they were so deadly poison you'd die quickly. I thought, how embarrassing to die in the outhouse. Just the idea that a black widow might be there really shortened a stay. You took it on faith that there were none down there rather than taking a peek down that hole. Another big drawback was the occasional wasp nest up in the corner. Those suckers would eye you constantly, and you just knew you were going to get dive-bombed.

And yes, we did keep a Sears-Roebuck or Monkey-Ward catalog, adjacent to the throne. There was usually a can of white quicklime with a dipper to use in spreading it around to keep the flies and the odor down. Just don't get it on the seat. Occasionally mother would buy an aromatic candle that could be lighted to make things more pleasant.

Having, and being an ornery brother, one of the fun things to do was to find the outhouse occupied and then chunk a big rock upside the wall. A rock or clod hitting the side of a toilet when you are deep in a séance of meditation was almost a sure bet for a near heart attack ... it was always done with the full knowledge that you would suffer the same fate at some time in the near future.

After an undetermined length of usage as determined by the laws of physics regarding mass, it would be time to move the site of the outhouse. No sanitation laws applied, and I've wondered since about the pollution of ground water, but in the 1930s the motto was, "Who Cares?" Dad would lay out the site, and the boys would dig a deep pit in the nearby vicinity, and the outhouse would be skidded over to the new repository.

Modern day archeologists love to find the sites of a primitive society's "midden" as the place of refuse is called. It usually yields a bonanza of information concerning the people who lived at that time. I wonder if the same guys, a thousand years from now, will be as elated when they stumble onto ours.

All who attended one of the Wing schools will remember having outside toilets. The one at Pleasant Hill was a goodly distance southwest of the school. Mr. Wright had a sure-fire method of making sure skullduggery wasn't planned. He had a ruler hanging with a string on it. If the stick was there, you could take it and go. If the stick was in use ... you waited.

The school toilets had accommodations for several people, but the ones we used at home were singletons and were for solitary use. And yes, we did do the Halloween prank of dumping the outhouses, and usually the neighbor boys did ours as well. And, no, I never turned one over with the man waiting inside it to catch the pranksters. That's one of the oldest myths in existence.

"Why, Ivey, my little cornflower," exclaimed Jim, "I didn't realize you were so observant and practical. I see you've got even more you could tell us about this 'delicate' subject."

"You old horned toad, you'd better shape up and mind that mouth of yours or your coffee is going to start tasting a little bit funny, Jim-bo." Ivey's brown eyes snapped with feigned anger as she continued, "And with that remark I'm declaring this week's meeting of the Gentlemen's (sneer) Coffee Club adjourned. Good-bye."

FOURTH COFFEE
Oil Patch Living

"*Shut the door, Pete, you're letting in flies,*" *yelled several of the guys around the table. The door had hung up and stood ajar after Pete had come into the café.*

"*Well, and how about you guys giving me a little hush and allow me a micro- second to close it,*" *replied Pete.*

Pete shot a glance at Marvin and said, "As the owner of this fine establishment, you're gonna have to break down and get someone to give that door a little working over. It's sticking and dragging something awful. I'd do it for you, but my union card doesn't cover that kind of labor, and besides, you couldn't afford my services."

This insult was directed at Marvin Cutler, owner, operator and chief cook of the Boomtown Café which hosted, or put up with, the weekly meeting of this retired bunch of guys, most of who had grown up in Drumright.

This drew a "Humph" from Marvin. "I believe I'll get someone a bit younger, for I'm afraid if you got down to fix it you couldn't get back up. No telling what my liability might amount to in that case."

"*Okay, Marv, you win, but only because you used a low blow remark to do it,*" *said Jim Kinnamon from the head of the table. "Now, why don't you do something nice and send that good looking waitress out here to put something in these empty cups, I'm needing my 9:00 eye opener.*"

Ivey was a spectator to all this and could hardly keep from bursting into laughter. Instead, she immediately bustled her way to the table and in very short order had everyone settled in, content and satisfied.

The talk around the table centered on the two families who had moved away within the past week.

"*Boys, it looks like our little town is going to dry up and blow away if we lose many more families like the Carter and the Blodgett bunch,*" *stated Doc.*

"They both had a whole raft of kids, which puts a hole in our people count here in town. We suffer the same problem most little rural towns do. How do you keep them in town if there's no job base for them to work at?"

"Well, hopefully the last one to leave the old burg will be nice enough to turn the lights out," spoke up Phil Wiley. "Boy, it sure wasn't like this in the old days with the town bulging at the seams and the whole countryside alive with lease house communities." There must have been at least 30,000 people living in the entire oil patch stretching from Oilton to Shamrock."

OIL LEASE COMMUNITIES

Anyone living in the Drumright/Oilton/Shamrock area during the 1920s, '30s and '40s were part of or witnesses to an American social phenomenon that had never existed before and has never been duplicated since. I'm talking about the clusters of people who lived in company houses all over the oil patch.

There were undoubtedly thousands of people living on hundreds of oil leases owned by dozens of different oil companies. These small clusters of society had a unique way of life as to their day-to-day existence. They worked, played, loved, worshipped and educated their children in close proximity. In most instances most of them worked for the same oil company, lived in company-built homes, and the children attended the same school through grade eight.

One fascinating thing about this rural life was the reality that people were living in the area before the oil boom became an actuality. Even before the coming of the white settlers, most of whom came illegally, it was the home of nomadic tribes of Native-Americans. Later, when the federal government began the forced removal, many tribes were assigned there by the government.

Later with the Land Runs of 1889 and 1891 subsistence farmers, such as the Fulkersons, Drumrights and Wheelers along with lesser known names, settled the area. Many of these farmers or their descendants were living there during the oil boom time. This early history needs to be understood to set the stage for the coming of the exploration and successful drilling of the oil and the establishment of the lease communities.

Phil Wiley continued, "Fellers, I was born and spent most of my younger days living in one of those little old shotgun houses out on a lease five miles from

Drumright. I remember it most fondly and had great memories, although there were some tough times, too. I'd like to tell you about some of it."

AT HOME IN A LEASE HOUSE

Lots of memories were made while growing up in a modest oil field lease house, and I guess it didn't warp us too much. I suppose we were happy enough in spite of having next to no niceties compared to our present day comforts.

Insulation wasn't even considered, so the inside walls of these old houses were usually covered with tacked-on cardboard. Over the cardboard my dad had hung heavy- duty builders paper, which had a sheet of tarpaper between heavy paper, making a paper sandwich. Many may remember the large tin washers that were nailed through to keep the paper on the walls. We used to use them as targets when throwing homemade darts.

Some walls were papered with newspapers ... truly ... my mother would make a mixture of flour, salt, vinegar and water and apply this to the wall and put several layers of paper on the walls. I liked that, for then I could "read the walls" as I sat and churned the milk in the old five-gallon churn with a dasher that went ker-chunk, ker-chunk. It was a little unhandy when she would paste the paper on upside down ... had to stand on my head to read, and get thumped on the head for doing it.

The old cook stove was a wood-eating monster, which had other uses as well as cooking the meals. There was a copper reservoir attached to one end, which gave us our hot water. This had to be kept filled with water for washing dishes, cooking and the occasional bath. Seems like it held at least 500 gallons of water. A large wood box nearby had to be kept filled with cook-stove wood. It devoured wood like a fire-breathing dragon.

Remember how there had to be a bunch of kindling wood scraps to start the fire ... as a little tad that was one of your first chores. It took a lot of scrounging around the woodlot to come up with a basketful to use in starting fire.

Present day cook stoves don't have the convenience of the warming ovens, which were located above the stovetop burners. It was a great place to keep food warm until time to serve. Of course, ashes had to be taken out really often, and every so often the soot had to be removed ... a messy job.

It was amazing what great meals my mother could cook on the wood stove with such primitive accessories. No temperature gauge ... no mixer ...

no power anything. Like so many good cooks, she went with the "dump" method for recipes. I know we ate a lot of gravy and potatoes …

When the wooden icebox had to have a new hunk of ice, this meant a trip into town to Pat Badger's Ice Plant. The block of ice was wrapped in burlap and wedged onto the front bumper of the car. Everyone owned ice tongs to pick up and carry blocks of ice.

It was absolutely a must to empty the ice water pan under the icebox drain. This filled slowly, drop by drop, as the block of ice melted. When it was forgotten, you ended up with a mess all over the floor.

People living in town had their ice delivered to them by an ice truck. They used a card with different numbers of pounds of ice you wanted the iceman to leave. It was a heavy-duty cardboard square with a large 25 – 50 – 75 and 100 printed around the edges.

The iceman could read the number that was in the "up" position and brought that size block of ice in from the truck. He used large steel tongs to impale the block, throw it over his shoulder and muscle it into the icebox door. A large piece of fitted leather was used as protection on his carrying shoulder.

Sleeping arrangements in the lease house meant bedding down with at least two per bed and even more on special occasions. We kids slept on straw ticks … you know what they were … a large bed-size case of cloth filled with straw. It helped if you fluffed the straw up every few days 'cause it would get flatter'n a fritter otherwise.

I can't remember how often we changed the straw …. I do remember how the straw would poke through and stick you … and yes, we also used corn shucks for mattress filler sometimes.

When you turned over in bed, the crackling of the shucks would awaken the dead … if a corncob had been missed, you could always count on finding it or it finding you when it jabbed you.

I must not have been a reliable fire maker, for I don't remember ever having to get up on a cold morning and make one. It must have been one of the older ones' responsibility.

"I'd imagine that since you were one of the younger ones in the brood you did get pampered a bit," retorted Hank Blackwelder. "As the oldest in our bunch, Pop put me in charge of making the fire, not only in the front room heater but after getting it going I had to go to the kitchen and fire it up, too."

"You stirred up a whole bunch of memories with that story, Phil, for I lived many years in a lease house as well. First thing that comes to my mind is the old coal-oil lamp we all had to use to see by."

LIGHTING WITH A COAL-OIL LAMP

Old "Honest Abe" Lincoln wasn't the only one who could brag about his reading and studying by the light of the wood fireplace. For most of my elementary days the flickering yellow light of a coal-oil lamp was where we did all our school studies. We usually had about three lamps in use, and they were shuffled from one room or area to wherever light was needed.

The chimneys were fragile and broke easily, would smoke up and turn black if the wick wasn't kept trimmed. When this was necessary, the chimney would be removed, the wick ratcheted up too high and scissors used to cut the wick off in a straight line and then lowered to the optimum height for best lighting.

Chimneys came in many different styles, some of them being very intricate and highly decorated. We used the simple unadorned ones, which cost probably 15 cents. Someone always had to keep the reservoir filled with kerosene. The kerosene, or as we called it, coal oil, cost a nickel a gallon, and we bought it in a five-gallon can. It was kept out in the washhouse for safety. As we talked about earlier, it was also used for medicinal purposes.

The light given off was of meager candlepower, and you sat in the soft glow of a puddle of light and hunkered up close to read. It was a difficult chore to try to do fine work such as sewing. It did make a homey sight when you came home after dark and saw the light shining through the windows to welcome you home. It also caused some sibling problems, for a familiar exclamation was heard when someone passed between you and the lamp. "You're in my light!"

One ever-present hazard of using them was the possibility of the flame from a poorly trimmed wick traveling back down into the reservoir of kerosene with the distinct possibility of a fire. We had a drill if this happened. One would snatch off the chimney, an adult would grab the lamp, and with someone holding the front door open it would be thrown vigorously outside. In most instances it broke the lamp, but that was considered cheap compared to a house fire. It was a traumatic experience.

Our lighting situation improved tremendously when an oil company paid my folks a small settlement for an industrial accident that caused a younger brother to lose a finger. They splurged and bought one Aladdin lamp. It was the Cadillac of kerosene lamps at the time with its round wick and long tapered chimney. It would light up an entire room.

The beauty sat majestically on its appointed table, a thing of opulence like something out of the Arabian Nights. The light given off was almost blinding in comparison to its homely cousin and became the focal point for family gatherings around the battery-operated radio we bought in 1938.

One place we lived had carbide lights that burned with a mantle. I have no idea how it worked, but you had to buy a large can of carbide, and it would be mixed with water, which activated the carbide crystals, producing a flammable gas. This gas made a good fuel to light up the mantles. There must have been a generator attached to combine the gas with air. Someone with more knowledge than I have about the gas can straighten us out. I just remember the empty carbide can had a potent odor.

One enterprising man I heard of had a natural gas line running through his wooded pasture. The company gas lines were buried quite shallow. This guy just bought the proper "saddle" and tapped into the line. It was a simple matter to run his private gas line from the company line to his house. Since it was a leafy, wooded area, he covered his handiwork up with leaves and debris to conceal the "bootlegging" of the gas.

Attaching this to his already connected gas lines in the house, he was able to have gas for lighting as well as cooking and heating. Natural gas was so plentiful and cheap, I doubt if he was ever found out.

Illegal?? Probably … but in order to be a survivor, you have to sometimes skirt close to the edge of complete legality.

"Yeah, we'd better not go anywhere near that topic for everyone might be thrown into the hoosegow. One has to do what is necessary to make it, as we all know," said old Faye. "I reckon I've seen just about most anything you want to

mention, short of a murder and I'm not too sure about that."

Jim chimed in with this, " I'd like to share something with you of the Kinnamon family and its trials and troubles of trying to stay alive and keep the old wolf away from the front door. Seems we moved a considerable number of times. I started to school at Fairview, then went to Tiger, then Third Ward and graduated from eighth grade at Pleasant Hill before coming to town school."

"Ask me anything you'd want to know about living in a ramshackle lease house and I can tell you," Jim concluded.

DAILY LIVING IN A LEASE HOUSE

I'd bet a pretty penny that many of you guys either have lived in one of the oilfield lease houses or at least have visited friends in one and know what I'm talking about. Now I'm not talking about the fancy ones that some oil companies built for workers such as the Minnehoma Lease, but rather the raw, green lumber structures that were thrown together at the height of the oil boom and still in use many years later.

The old shacks were light years better than living in a tent, but were still a mean and humble structure to grow up in. In several places we lived, no electricity, gas or water were available so … stove wood for cooking and heating, coal-oil lamps for lighting and water from a bucket on the water stand carried from the common well.

Typically these houses were thrown up in a hurry to accommodate the large number of people needed to work in the booming oil fields. With the cost of finished lumber being kinda high, the material used was rough-sawn lumber from available sawmills.

I can speak with a lot of first-hand experience, having lived in one of these old "shotgun" houses on Old Highway 33 on Tiger Corner north of town of for about four years. As the oil boom dwindled, so did the number of houses on the leases.

There were less than a dozen in the entire neighborhood when we acquired ownership of one and moved there from town.

The more crude shacks were perched on native stone for foundations and sometimes just a pillar put up at strategic places. Our house boasted of large wooden supports imbedded in the ground and connected to the floor joists to help keep the floors on a somewhat even keel. We had scrap tin nailed to the uprights of the foundation to keep the area under the house as varmint free as we could … no, we didn't let hogs under there either. We did have our standards.

The houses were built with wide planking running vertically, and then where the planks came together they had nailed a four-inch-wide board to cover the crack and give just a teeny bit of insulation. The old rough siding had never known a paintbrush and with age had done a fair amount of warping and twisting. Knots had shrunken and fallen out, in many places and usually a flat fruit jar lid was nailed over the knothole.

Rolled roofing that had been overlapped covered the sloping part of the roof, and on the flat parts corrugated tin sheets were nailed, also over-lapped and tarred to keep out the rain. It was a real soothing sound to lie in bed and listen to the sound of a pounding on the tin roof, but when it hailed it was another story. It was deafening.

Inside the house the floor had been laid with wide planking also, and the same weathering had played havoc with the boards. In some of our rooms linoleum had been laid to smooth out the floor. After a period of time all of the seams, knotholes and other imperfections in the floor would show through the linoleum and the colors would begin to wear off and a new one would grace the floor. It was like having a new room.

One of my great joys was when we would buy new linoleum and take up the old one. You usually put layers of newspapers down as insulation and as a buffer against the splinters. We would have two or three layers of linoleum on the floor eventually.

Before the new linoleum was laid over the old one I would pull out a bunch of the old newspapers to read that had been there for several years. Since I was a history nut, I would read and remember a lot of the events that took place in years gone by. I was especially interested in reading of the events that led up to WW II about Adolph Hitler and Mussolini and the war in Ethiopia a world away.

Knowing Jim and his reputation for being a straight shooter, everyone just nodded in agreement. In fact, most of them had lived in the same kind or worse.

"Say," said Otto, "changing the subject to something a little lighter ... who remembers the Thursday night Amateur Night productions held at Way Memorial Park back in the '30s?"

This brought a round of assent and nods of approval from all of the guys. It had been a most popular evenings entertainment for kids of all ages. Older ones could take their lady friends and younger ones could go to rip and tear around for an hour or so. Adults also enjoyed the evening, and many came with small babies in arms.

It indeed was a gathering of the young and old and provided a couple of hours of free entertainment for people who were overworked and lacking in cash to go to more expensive forms of fun.

With no prompting or encouragement, Otto went on with his turn of talking.

FREE ENTERTAINMENT

Many of the things done in the name of entertainment and leisure-time activities during the '30s was of the free or inexpensive variety. Family budgets for such things were usually quite limited or non-existent, so it was up to the individuals or the family to provide what leisure time fun stuff there was.

Fortunately the city "dads" of Drumright realized the problem faced by many of us and came up with one unique form of entertainment. Who remembers the "Talent Nights" held weekly at the old Way Memorial Park? This was an event that was held on Thursdays nights and was a social outing that was really looked forward to by many people, not only in town, but on outlying oil leases as well.

I'm sure the term "talent" was very loosely applied, for many of the acts were of dubious quality. They ranged all the way from totally ridiculous to somewhat absurd on up to some rather sophisticated acts. I truly don't think anyone ever used the Talent Nights at Way Memorial Park as a stepping-stone to Hollywood. If they did, they took a totally different stage name.

But since the main purpose of this was to entertain a wide range of people, the artistic quality could be and sometimes was overlooked. Mainly it was, "who had the guts to get up in front of the crowd and perform."

The drill was this: Local talent was encouraged to submit their names to the person who was in charge of the recruitment, come to the evening show and "do their thing." Sometimes prizes were offered by local merchants for competition of acts.

No auditioning of the performance before the production was required so consequently, the show would sometimes resemble the TV listing several years ago called "The Gong Show." The only problem was no one was ever "gonged," which encouraged some really weird presentations. Few of us were real connoisseurs of the "arts," and all presenters were appreciated for what they did for the audience.

I remember the Williams sisters were into tap dancing and performed rather often. (There were no rules against repeat performances). There were soloists, family group singing and any other type, for generally all that was needed was someone to have the nerve to get up and perform in front of a large crowd.

I remember impersonators, impressionists, self-styled comedians, jug bands and stringed instruments of all kinds. The winner of all the acts for absurdity was an old boy whose ability lay in being able to "play" a variety of handsaws with a home-made bow and a wooden mallet. He would flex the metal saws and produce "music" (?).

It must have been a loud and raucous time down in the "holler" where the park was located. and nearby residents were well aware of it all … and probably not too appreciative.

The spectators were seated on backless benches mounted in large semi-circles in front of the stage. I don't remember if there was an audio system, but most of the acts were loud enough to be heard by all. Many of the families would bring quilts and spread them on the ground on the outer edges so the infants could be put to sleep.

After a couple of hours the evening's entertainment was over, and then the mass exodus out of the park would begin. If any money was available, a stop would be made downtown for an ice cream cone at either the City Drugstore or the Marquette Pharmacy. At a nickel for a large double-dip, it made for a tasty treat. Dairy Queen or Baskins-Robbins? Never heard of 'em.

"You guys don't know how close you came to seeing me and my brother Jim up on that stage one time," said Pete. "You gotta be kidding"… "no way"…

"sure a good thing you didn't," and other less than complimentary words came from around the table.

"Seriously," asked Doc Pringle. "What was your act going to be, Pete?"

"Well," continued Pete, "Mom discovered by accident that Jim and I had just a little bitty bit of musical talent on a harmonica, so she was going to put us on as the Ledbetter Duo. Luckily, she was too late to sign us up for that week, and the next week old Jim came down with the mumps, which laid him up for a month. After that he couldn't blow a tune to save himself, so that ended our musical careers."

"Now, I didn't personally see him, but I've heard tell that Bob Wills played for one of the Amateur Nights at Way Memorial at some time or another.

Harold spoke up saying, "Let me tell you we used to get some pretty fair country musicians in here with those Medicine Shows we had. Those little bands were Hollywood caliber, if you ask me."

MEDICINE SHOWS

Another form of free entertainment we enjoyed way back when was the Medicine Show. This was a homespun form of advertising and selling of a medicine that was most entertaining. It was purely American in origin and had been around since earliest frontier days.

I have always felt fortunate to have witnessed this special bit of Americana. We didn't realize that we were seeing a treasured institution in its twilight years. Regrettably, there were no camcorders around to have documented one of the productions.

There would be advance handbills placed around town for several days preceding the arrival of the Medicine Show. Usually, the Chief of Police or his deputy would be on hand to welcome the arrival of the troupe.

This welcome had a two-fold purpose, for the Chief knew from past experience that possibly one or more of the entertainers would be accomplished pickpockets and could use the large gathering to practice their art of "dipping." His visit just served to let the entertainers know they were under the surveillance of an eagle-eyed lawman.

The old trucks carrying the people and the paraphernalia for the show would drive up to the old ball field in the southwest part of town where the group would set up. The show normally was billed for a couple of nights, and the entire crew cooked and slept in the old converted trucks, one of

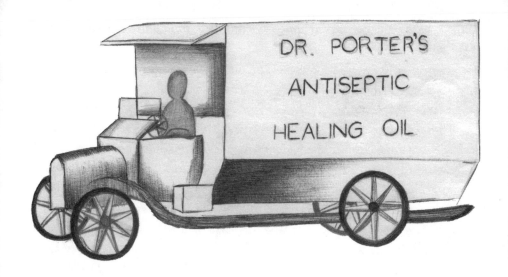

which would be painted with mysterious "mystical medical symbols." This was where the medicine was "manufactured."

On the night of the performance the show would open with a string band. After the musical number was played, the "Doctor" who was in charge of the show would come out on the makeshift stage and make a welcoming speech telling how glad they were to be playing before such a distinguished group of citizens. He was lavish in his praise of the town for he had heard what an upstanding group of people lived here.

Another musical number would then be played or possibly a comedy routine featuring Minstrel Show comedians. At its conclusion the "Doctor" would come out once again and start his talk on the product that he was privileged to bring to the people of this fine community. This "elixir" was always made from the secret recipe of a deceased Indian who had imparted his secret ingredients to the doctor just before dying to be used only for the good of humanity.

With this heavy burden resting on him, the good doctor was going to sacrifice any monetary gain and dispense the potion to the good folk for the low, low price of only 15 cents a bottle or two bottles for a quarter. A real bargain since it would cure anything from dandruff to flat feet. It was especially good for rheumatism, gout and other ailments that couldn't be seen. Naturally, it had a money-back guarantee if the customer was not fully satisfied (after they had left town).

If you weren't terminally ill, the stuff could make you feel better, for the recipe usually contained about 90-proof alcohol, and after several big swigs you would feel no pain.

The "shills" would then take several bottles and walk around the crowd hawking their wares. I remember one particular sales cry. The guy would yell out, "Honk your horn, hold up your hand! Anyone over in here?"

When the sales would cool down, the group would go back on stage, perform another musical number. The good doctor would make another speech praising the medicine. He would sometimes bring up a "plant" from the crowd who would testify to the miracles the medicine had wrought on him.

The "Doctor" was sharp enough to know when he had "milked" the crowd for the night, and after a closing number he would invite all the people to tell their friends and neighbors about the medicine and to come back the next night for the final opportunity to obtain this wonderful cure-all.

On some occasions the entire troop would do a midnight disappearing act and be totally gone by morning, especially if the local lawman was just a bit rough on them.

"Hey, just what is it we're talking about this morning, anyway," spoke up Phil Wiley. "This conversation is jumping around worse than a Mexican Jumping Bean on a hot stove griddle, but as long as we're just shooting the breeze, let me wander a little further out into left field and talk about another little bit of action that some of you may have engaged in, I'm sure. It was a sure-fire way to get rich. And as that guy used to say on that kid TV program, I'll say a rousing, NOT!"

Since the guys knew Phil as a big tease and an all-round comedian who could entertain them with a good story, they smiled in anticipation.

GETTING RICH PICKING COTTON

Yeah, and if you believe that heading, you'll also believe the moon's made of green cheese or that I've got that big old bridge back in New York that I'll sell you at a bargain basement price.

Raising cotton from planting to picking has gotta be one of the hardest ways in the world to make a dollar. After it's planted and has had enough time to come up six or eight inches, all hands have to go to the field to "chop" cotton. You see, it's over-sowed to get a good stand, then when too much comes up it has to be thinned by taking a hoe and chopping out unwanted plants.

This proved to be my undoing one time. As a young sprout about six years of age, I was vigorously wielding a hoe and made a mis-whack, taking off the top of my big toe on one foot. I still bear the scar. See a doctor? … no way … just wrapped a rag around it and back to the field.

In the fall of the year, sometime after school had started, the cotton would begin to mature and begin to spill out of the overloaded bolls, making the fields resemble billowing white clouds. Many of the older boys and girls would be kept home from school to help with the picking, for cotton was the biggest cash crop of the year, and much depended on the amount it brought in. In some areas the entire school would be shut down for the picking season.

Every able-bodied soul in the household was expected to pick their quota of cotton, for it was a small window of time to get it harvested and taken to the gin. Cotton sacks were made from heavy canvas material to be dragged along the dirt between the rows. For a small fry like me we usually used a gunnysack. Full-sized adults used much longer ones.

A wide canvas band on the upper end of the cotton sack hung around your neck, leaving both hands free to reach right and left to pull the fluffy cotton from the boll and stuff it into the sack. When it bursts open, the boll is razor sharp and a fast picker will actually have bloody hands to show for their superior skill in filling his sack so rapidly.

Naturally, the harder and longer you worked, the heavier the sack got to be, and at the end the adults would be pulling quite a load. You were cautioned to not get any clods or other foreign objects in the cotton, but it sure would add weight to my measly production. Had my ears boxed several times for that.

Normally a good picker had two rows assigned to pick, and ones like my mother could just make a blur with their hands picking so fast. When the mature cotton bolls opened, it was very sharp and the fastest pickers usually had torn and lacerated hands at the end of the picking season.

It seemed to take forever to fill a cotton sack, and the best I ever did was 22 pounds after picking all day. For my effort I earned two cents a pound. Simple math tells you I made the princely sum of 44 cents that day. Hope I didn't spend it all in one place.

When we were out of sight of our parents, we had some dandy cotton boll fights. When not opened up fully, they made a solid missile. This kinda helped break the monotony of the endless rows of cotton. Since it didn't all mature and open at the same time, it always took two separate pickings.

As the cotton sacks filled, they were taken to the scales, weighed and dumped into a high-sided trailer or wagon. I have no recollection of a cotton gin in Drumright. We took our cotton to the Oilton gin since, at that time, we lived on Section 14 several miles northeast of town.

"Somebody else's turn now," croaked Phil. "My throat is dry as a cotton gin and I gotta have a cold drink of sody rather than more coffee. I'm running my legs off with all this coffee anyway running to the bathroom."

Ivey was quick on the spot to see what she could bring Jim to wet his whistle and anyone else who might be in the mood for something else. Since the lunch crowd hadn't started, she was still able to hang around the table and listen in on stories and as shown before, could spin a fine yarn herself.

This time, however, old Jim Bob Smith, of all people, unwound his long legs, cleared his throat and spoke up. "Well, I'm not the colorful story teller or windjammer that old Phil is, but I really do remember this little part of our growing up before I had to go to work full-time when I turned 16 and had to quit high school. I had become the only breadwinner in the family, and with five more at home someone had to bring in some bacon."

SATURDAY NIGHT SOCIAL

Saturday night in Drumright actually started during the middle of the afternoon. The cars started pulling into town fairly early as it was "butter and egg" day. Many people, even those who weren't full-time farmers, had some cream and some eggs to sell above that used by the family. Apparently laws and restrictions regarding their ownership were either lax or non-existent, for many of us had a cow and usually a flock of chickens.

This surplus was brought in to town and taken down to Jim Trout's store where some ready cash was made available. Trout's store was located on East Broadway on east from Ollie Saffas' grocery store during the mid-'30s.

As the afternoon progressed, cars would start lining up on the street for the ritual to take place later on in the evening. I remember the most popular places to park being on Broadway, mainly on the north side of the street. You always tried to park next to some friend or neighbor, for this

was "social hour" on a grand scale, and this is where you got all the latest news and gossip.

Grocery shopping was done at the Safeway store located on the corner of Ohio and Broadway and other grocery stores in town. Everyone looked forward to the drawing for the "Barrel of Groceries" which took place late evening before closing time at the Safeway. For families that were "economically challenged" (politically correct term for dirt poor) as many of us were, the idea of winning a barrel of groceries was like hitting a winning ticket to the lottery today.

The Salvation Army band would play on the street corner at Broadway and Ohio, with trumpets blatting and tambourines shaking and jingling. Later money would be collected after a short sermon was delivered. No one cat-called, for they were a respected group of people. Some of us couldn't relate to them but were still respectful.

During all this time people were walking up and down Broadway shopping at the numerous stores that were open until late. I remember few, if any, stores being vacant, and the number of people was mind-boggling!

For the moms and dads it was a time to go out, sit on the front fender of the car and talk — and look — and be looked at. People spoke to each other that they hadn't seen since *last Saturday!!!* Sometimes, someone, if the season was right, would even cut a watermelon and the group would stand around and eat it on the hood of the car.

Those kids who were fortunate enough to have a dime or could wheedle one from mom had already headed out to the Midwest Theater. This was known as going to the "show" and usually meant going to see a good old western starring Hopalong Cassidy, Tom Mix, Gene Autry or other favorites. Usually we were at the movie house as soon as we could get to town, and we stayed until the "lights came on." There was no way a dime could be wasted by leaving after seeing the film once.

I probably owe part of my hearing loss to the fact that we always tried to sit in the first row gaping upward toward the screen. We usually got involved with the movie, especially after seeing it once, and would talk along with the cast, warning our hero when an ambush was going to take place.

The weekly serial was always a highlight. It could be Flash Gordon or Tarzan of the Jungle, but each week it always left the hero or his lady in a most tenuous position where it would be next to impossible to escape. Old "Ming the Merciless" was a vicious foe.

When the movie lights came on, it was stumble out, find the folks and we were on our way home.

"As long as I'm wound up, I want the floor just a little bit longer," said Joe Bob. "I just want to tell how us folks with shallow pockets provided for ourselves as far as money was concerned. No welfare, food stamps or other government help came our way, so we used old Mother Nature."

Most of the boys had never heard Joe Bob put this many words together before, so they were very interested in hearing what he had to say.

ROBBING A BEE TREE

Many families in the Drumright area got lots of their "sweetener" from this source.

Locating and robbing a bee tree was a real boon to the families struggling to eat during the Depression, plus giving them some "sweetening." However, it was a job that was difficult to do and led to a lot of discomfort. The bees were tracked back from their feeding sites until the source of the honey was found. It was a difficult job following the bee until you lost it and then waiting for the next one to lead you further on until the "honey tree" was located.

The usual place for the hive to be found was in a hollow post oak or other tree about two feet in diameter. It could be fairly close to the ground or up 10 to 15 feet above ground. The activity of bees and the honey spilling out of the entrance hole was a sure sign that here was a source of some really good eating.

The exercise took place early in the morning, usually in the fall of the year when the hive would have the most honey stored for the winter survival of the bees. The protective gear was rather primitive, consisting of mosquito netting draped over a hat and down over the face and neck. Long sleeves and possibly gloves covered as much bare skin as possible, for some very angry critters would attack as soon as the action began.

Before leaving the house, torches would be made of rags tied to the end of wire. Once on site, they were soaked in kerosene and used to produce smoke and hopefully stun the bees while the robbing was done.

Not having chain saws, sharp axes and crosscut saws would be wielded and a hole would be chopped in the tree, hopefully below the hive. Sometimes it would be possible to make the hole large enough to complete the job with the tree standing. Other times it was necessary to chop the tree completely down to get at the honey.

Once the honey was exposed, it was gathered in buckets and tubs to be taken home and processed. Occasionally a bee would get under the netting, and much slapping and yelling would ensue by the victim. The coal oil torches would be lighted and lots of smoke used during the entire process to calm the bees down. Along with the honey would be huge slabs of honeycomb filled with some delectable eating.

Sometimes, if a professional beekeeper was present, it was possible to locate the queen bee. If she was found, the beekeeper would put her in the temporary hive he had brought along. A large number of the bees would follow into the hive and the guy would have another hive of bees ... for free. Trust me, it wasn't all that simple.

Other times the bees would leave to swarm elsewhere. If the tree was still standing, enough of the honey was left to give the bees food to last through the coming winter. This would make it possible to return to and get more honey the next year.

The collected honey was stored in jars and eaten as raw honey. It helped to go through the honeycomb and pick out the young bee larva. The honeycomb was drained and the honey strained to get out dead bees and other inedible stuff.

Chewing on a great wad of the sweet honeycomb was almost as good as having some chewing gum to munch on.

"I remember making some poor trades for some of that stuff when we were in grade school at Lincoln after you came in from Tiger and you were the 'sharper' that skinned me, Jim Bob, although back then the teacher called you just plain old James Robert." This speech came from Harley Sprague, who'd been sitting quietly down at the end of the table.

"Now you know I would never do that to anyone, Harley," said old Jim Bob, which immediately drew hoots of derision from around the table.

"But anyway," said Harley, *"Now that I'm awake and have your undivided attention, I'd like to tell you of a sad happening in our family one time. No one died or anything like that, it was just a thing that happened to an innocent bunch of people in a family project we were doing. It'll also show you how ignorance will do you in regardless of how innocent you are in your planning.*

"Looking back over all the years since it happened, I still feel sorry for my mother. She tried so hard to do the right thing and was still the victim of something she knew absolutely nothing about. It could'a happened to any of us and we'd been just as mystified as she was."

"Well, come on and tell us what this big old thing was, Harley. You got us about to fall off the front edge of our chairs in suspense," said Harold Atkins.

AN UNWANTED SWIMMING HOLE

Several weeks ago we talked about the adventure of going to the cellar when a bad storm was brewing. Now some people called these storm shelters "fraidy-holes," but in our household they were considered the difference between life and death, according to my mother. She had a deathly fear of being caught in a bad windstorm.

When we moved to the Thomas Long Lease in 1936, we found there was no cellar and the closest neighbor with one was several hundred feet away. Mother considered this much too far, so the first order of business was to dig one. She figured it could double as a fruit and vegetable cellar.

When Dad came home from work for the weekend, she had him stake out a large 10' x 12' rectangle very close to the back door for quick access. Having no engineering skills but knowing the hole in the ground had to be over six feet deep, she called on her heavy, earth-moving equipment to begin the dirt digging. Unfortunately, the equipment operators were the children in the family, and we turned to the task with a will. This was indeed something different to be doing. Truthfully, it was our mother's will, fueled by her storm fears that provided the push.

Our equipment consisted of picks, shovels and a mattox to cut roots, and we started in to dig this humongous hole in the ground. The first part of the digging was easy, and we swung the tools with vim and vigor. It looked like a snap. Dirt was piled alongside the hole to be used later in covering the top with a thick layer of protective soil.

About two feet down we were horrified to find that we had struck solid rock! Not just in one spot, no, the entire project was underlain solid with Oklahoma sandstone. We all breathed a sigh of relief, for we thought this would sink the project, but Mother, always the optimist, buoyed us up by saying how much safer the cellar would be dug in living rock. She reinforced this with the command **"dig,"** and so we dug. You don't fight City Hall.

Fortunately for we tunnel rats, the sandstone was dampish and flaked off in great slabs as we drilled down with a crowbar and then pried. So the work continued on as the hole deepened to four feet, then five feet, and then to the depth that was considered the perfect one for a good hole. It was formed in solid rock, too, at least the last four feet.

With Dad's help a super strong roof was constructed from sections of a curved "bull-wheel" from an abandoned oil well. Stringers were run the length of the cellar connecting the curved arcs. Corrugated iron was nailed over the stringers, and then a two-foot layer of dirt was shoveled over the entire structure. A vent pipe was put through the roof at the rear and a solid door hung on the front lying almost horizontally.

The final construction was shelves for the canned fruit waiting in the house, and the cellar was a snug retreat and a great peace of mind structure for Mother.

We soon found, however, there was a snake in our Garden of Eden. Early on, we had noticed a little seepage on the floor of the cellar but took little notice. It soon became a major concern for our happy home. Since no hydraulic engineer lurked in the family background, we soon concluded that we had dug our beautiful cellar in permeable (someone told us the word) sandstone, meaning it permits the seepage of water.

Adding to this, we had undoubtedly dug directly in an underground waterway, so it didn't take but a heavy rain or two and our cellar had become an outdoor, underground pool about three feet deep. It was a family disaster, no less. We even did the old bucket brigade trick to little avail.

Dad brought home a centrifugal pump, ran a pipe down into the water, and we took turns turning the wheel to bring the water level down. We brought up many hundreds of gallons of water, probably enough to float Noah's Ark. But alas and alack, we were shoveling sand against the tide, for it was hopeless. It would fill back up shortly after we stopped pumping. Mother Nature is a vicious foe.

We needed to get to all those shelves filled with canned goods, for that was our winter fruit and vegetable supply, so we needed a way to get to the jars. To solve the problem of water, we anchored our oblong zinc bathtub at the bottom of the cellar steps. It was then my job to get in the tub, paddle out to the shelves and bring back whatever was needed.

"But, Harley," chimed in Henry. "Think of the prestige you could have claimed. First off, you had a covered, fresh water swimming pool and you could claim to eat only 'imported' foods. They all come by water."

"Not funny, McGee," spoke up Elmer, "and when did you get to be such a comedian, Henry? That had to be a really disappointing happening to your ma, Harley."

"No offense," Henry retorted. "I guess I was thinking that the only way we make it through this old life is to look on the bright side when things don't turn out right, if you can, and if there's not one you gotta fake it."

"But let me tell you all about me and my squirrel hunting experience," he went on. "You who know me know that I'm not much on sport hunting and probably wondered why. Anyone who grew up around here just naturally is supposed to be a regular Dan'l Boone."

GOING SQUIRREL HUNTING

Won't be too long until it's time to be getting the .22 rifle polished up, the dogs readied and heading to the woods for some serious squirrel hunting. The leaves will have pretty well fallen off the trees in the creek bottoms, the nuts and acorns well matured and ready for all the hungry little varmints to start storing away for the winter.

It may be looked on as a sport nowadays, but when it was sometimes the only meat to put on the table it was serious business. Nothing is tastier than some yearling fried squirrel or some squirrel and dumplings if the rascal is a little long in the tooth. They are fat and sassy by now and all resting at home in their brushy nests high up in the trees.

I'll confess to not being an avid hunter, and it took some time for me to find the cause. I was always a lousy shot with a .22, and after blowing up several boxes of shells never improved much. I found out many years later the reason being that I'm right-handed but am **left-eyed**. Don't laugh too hard, for there really is a small breed of us who suffer that condition with a hunter's shame.

Unfortunately, we live in a right-handed world, so we "weird ones" have a lot of adjusting to do. Try taking a picture with your camera looking through the viewfinder with your left eye. It can only be done by mashing your nose flat against the camera.

Back to squirrel hunting … try aiming a rifle or shotgun from the right shoulder while looking down the sights with your left eye … it's next to impossible and gets you into some strange bodily contortions. Everybody in the world made Marksman when I was in the Army … but me.

Since I wasn't a crack shot like my dad and a couple of brothers, I tried to opt out of going hunting. There was a small matter of ego involved. Dad, on the other hand, was the worlds "mostest" when it came to shooting a rifle. He claimed he shot them in the head so as not to ruin any of the meat. I believed him.

One time, as a budding teen-ager he felt we needed to bond as a father and son, so he talked me into going to the woods with him. In the first place you have to get up before dawn cracks so you can be in the woods and ready to hunt before Mr. Bushy tail wakens.

So … at first light we're sitting on a log, well hidden, when the squirrels get up and start their morning romp through the tree tops. Anyone who has hunted them know they are distinguished by their barking at each other. Since Dad could hear a squirrel clearing its throat three blocks away, he would use sign language to point out the location of the little rascal.

Now, it's a fact that squirrels are among the most intelligent of animals in the entire animal kingdom and also the most inquisitive. The little buggers would usually spot us and come around the tree to check us out. They knew when the rifle was raised and pointed there was danger and would scurry around to the backside of the tree making a shot impossible.

It was at this point that it dawned on me what the catch was about this bonding stuff that Dad had in mind for me. He would signal me to be his dupe or decoy, and it would be my job to circle the tree and show myself, with the squirrel going back around to the other side of the tree where Dad would bring him down with a well-aimed shot.

Well, I went ahead and played "Old Rounder" for him the rest of the morning, but this ended my bonding experience of hunting with my dad for I refused to accept the role of an old hunting dog again.

I decided that if bonding was going to take place it would have to be on some level other than hunting. I figured I had to keep **some** dignity and self-esteem.

Cecil, the retired schoolteacher, now spoke up, "That's the gospel truth about that business of left-eyed and right-eyed people. I know, as one who worked in schools there are kids like that, and in the first grade it makes a problem for them in learning to read. But changing the subject just a bit I'd like to tell you of a little different kind of family experience I had."

He continued, "I see lots of people living in big fancy homes in the new additions around bigger towns. There are also country homes that burn lots of wood in the cool and cold weather. The smell reminds you of rustic places and that's the impression it's supposed to make.

"It has brought about a new industry to lots of guys who aren't afraid of hard work. And believe you me, it is hard work. I been there, done that, and don't care to do it again.

"Trees to cut into firewood back in the '30s came from many places. Local farmers would let you cut dead trees or ones they wanted eliminated from their fields and pastures. Mainly it was post oak, elm, hickory and blackjack, but we'd take any kind, as long as it was free.

"I'd like to tell you of the woodcutting our family engaged in as I remember it. We didn't burn it for the romantic atmosphere it created, but rather to keep warm and to cook our meals."

CUTTING FIREWOOD

Not one of our homes in lease house communities provided us with the luxury of gas heat or electricity for lights. Running water happened if we took the water buckets and ran to the well where we got our water.

With wood being our primary source of heat it meant a large supply had to be available at all times. A wood stove in the living room provided heat, if it was in a central location. Back in the distant bedrooms it became pretty non-existent. When you got up in the morning, you made a mad dash to get to the stove. That big old fire-breathing dragon of a heating stove took an unending supply of wood. Added to this was the cook stove in the kitchen, which needed its share if we were to eat.

With five boys in the family, Dad led the troops out to wherever he had permission to cut firewood. Most all trees made great firewood if they were stacked in the backyard at home. Post oak split like butter, and the blackjack burned with a hot heat. We stayed away from walnut, for it left a lot of creosote when you burned it and was dangerous.

Finding the tree to be cut, Dad would use his razor-sharp double-bitted ax and cut a deep v-shaped notch on the side the way the tree would fall. He was a giant of a man in strength, if not in stature, and had learned the art of felling trees at a tender age in Arkansas where he earned money hewing railroad ties with a broad ax. On a bet, he could drive stakes in the ground about six inches wider than the trunk of the tree, cut the tree down, and it would fall between the stakes.

After the notch was cut, the two older boys would take the crosscut saw and cut horizontally from the backside toward the notch until the trees fell with a resounding crash. I liked that part for as a little kid, for I always screamed, "Timber," at the top of my lungs.

All work was done with hand tools; axes, saws, wedges, sledgehammers and gluts. Chainsaws? Never heard of 'em. There were two types of crosscut saws, ribbon and belly saws, both kept needle-sharp by Dad. Gluts are interesting, and if you don't know what they are, that'll be another story.

After the tree was down, Dad continued trimming branches with an ax while the older boys would begin to saw 15- to 18-inch-long cuts to be split into smaller pieces. Being a younger one, I was given the lowly chore of pulling out brush and limbs and piling them up to be burned. As I grew older, I developed the ability to use a crosscut saw.

This was an art in itself and called for teamwork and synchronization of effort by both parties using the saw. The stroke had to be done with a smooth pull and then released for the other guy to pull back his way. Any riding down on the saw, making it harder to pull, was cause for severe discipline on the part of an older brother who was on the other end of the saw. He kept a pile of good-sized chips handy right beside the log being sawed, and if you shirked, you could expect to have a chunk of wood take you upside the head.

I can hear him yet with this admonition, "If yer gonna ride the saw, at least pick up yer feet and don't drag them." A-h-h, yes, lots of family togetherness.

If the wood came together and pinched the saw, a wedge was driven into the top of the cut to release the pressure until the cut was completed.

As the cuts were made, they were stood on end and Dad would then show his prowess in splitting them into pieces. It took his tremendous strength and ability in swinging a mighty blow with the ax. He was able to "box" the cut in such a way that he would split it in half, sometimes with only one swing. I later learned to do the same thing to the wonderment of my son.

After a hard day's work the split firewood would be loaded onto a trailer and hauled to the house and stacked close by the back door. It was stacked in "ricks," which is a 4' x 8' amount or half a cord. If we had an overabundant supply of wood, we would sell it for $2 per rick, a hard way to make a buck.

Those were **not** the "good old days!"

Faye Bucklin roused up and said, "I think I, along with a few more in here, can relate to that wood-cutting, Cece, but you sure brought back some memories. I remember your older brother, too, and he was mean as a snake, at times.

"And you know, guys, all this time the men were working, the mothers and other ladies of the community were busy. One of their activities was to make the quilts that keep us warm in the winter. It was a fun activity for them, and Heaven knows fun for them was pretty limited back then."

"Yeah, I remember the quilting sessions by our church ladies at our house," spoke up Jim. *" It was quite a social event and more jaws flapping than you could put a rooster to."*

QUILTING BEE

As we'd move into yet another little oil field shack, my mother would start in on my dad's case to have him put up quilting frames in whatever room that was big enough. He'd screw four large hooks into the ceiling and attach the quilting frames to ropes that could be drawn up to the ceiling or lowered for the ladies to sit around and quilt on the workpiece.

Before the quilting could take place, the quilt top would have been sewn together using some favorite pattern. I believe this operation is called piecing the quilt. Many of these old patterns had been handed down from generation to generation. I remember a few of the quilts designs Mother used ... one was Wedding Ring, a pattern of interlocking rings, while two more were the Texas Star and Jacob's Ladder.

Our church ladies made a Friendship Quilt on one occasion where each lady member embroidered her name in a square. Made a wonderful keepsake quilt. Surprisingly enough, some of the old patterns are still used by the new generation of quilters ...

After the quilt top was pieced together and made ready with the cotton batting and the bottom sheet, it was tacked to the quilting frames. It was lowered to chair height and then let out full-sized so ladies could sit around the entire quilt and work on their particular square. The women took great pride in their sewing ability and vied with each other on making small, neat stitches ... from knowing where you sat at the quilt, everyone would know exactly who had made what stitches, so it was a matter of pride.

It was always a social highlight when the church ladies would come to the house to quilt, which was done on a weekly basis. Since several had quilts, the group would go to a different home each time to work on that member's quilt until they were all done. Some type of inexpensive refreshments, along with coffee, were served, and you've never heard the amount of talking going on. It was an old-fashioned group, and everyone was referred to as "sister" or "brother." Until adulthood I only knew them as Brother Pollard, Sister Nagel, etc.

As a little tad I enjoyed hanging around the women to get an occasional pat on the head, and besides, I enjoyed hearing the juicy gossip that would flow around the quilt. Nothing vicious, for it **was** a group of church women …

As the women would make progress on the quilt, it would be rolled up onto the frames the long way, and eventually the work piece would become more and more narrow. At the end of a work session the quilt would be pulled up to the ceiling, out of the way until next time.

When completed, the quilt was taken off the frames and finished off and ready to use. We'd chuckle over seeing quilt pieces that had been part of someone's shirt or my sister's dress. Sometimes the ladies would make comforters, which was a process quite a bit different and a lot faster to make than doing a quilt.

"After that gentle story," said Jim, "I so believe Mr. Damore has his hand in the air. Do you suppose he has a story he'd like to tell? Looks like it's about going home for lunch time. Where does the time go?"

"I'll tell you where it goes," said Pete. "We got a table full of old windjammers that all have diarrhea of the mouth and love to talk. We're gonna have to make a number board and take turns passing it around and talking when you get the board."

WAIT 'TIL THE COWS COME HOME

Several months ago I told of an old cowherd by the name of "Fonnie" Klock. Coincidentally, I heard from a lady whose mother had married his brother … then more strangely, I found that the lady who had married the brother of "Fonnie" (Alphonse) was a first cousin of mine. Her maiden name was Mabel McNabb, and her father was my great Uncle Allen McNabb! Hope you followed all that … I may be my own grandpa.

But to the story … and it has to do with herding milk cows. When we moved out on the Thomas Long Magnolia lease, we had the usual milk cow … like most of the neighbors. With no cowherd we just turned the cow out of the barnyard after milking and let her shift for herself during the day.

Being a social animal, all the old neighborhood cows kinda gravitated together to spend the day socializing and talking "cow-ey" stuff as they meandered over the countryside eating and drinking … you know how they are … discussing how much milk they are able to produce … and its butterfat content … how they dislike cold hands on their udders and other such bovine talk.

About five o'clock in the afternoon the summons would be issued to, "Go after the cows." Now was the time for the fun to begin. Since they were creatures of habit and usually predictable, they would be pretty much in the same locale from day to day. However, sometimes an adventurous cow might influence the entire group and suggest some greener pastures, and the hunt would be on.

Taking old Shep with us, and maybe asking a granddaddy longlegs first, we would head for their usual grazing grounds, and if they were there we'd just herd them home. As we trooped the herd along, we would drop the neighbor's cows off as we went past their house.

Sometimes it wasn't that easy. If they did come up missing, we would go to the nearest oil derrick, and one of us would shinny up the derrick and take a look in all directions.

If they weren't spotted, we'd walk to the next derrick on down the line, climb it to take another "look-see." Usually after a couple of climbs we would spot the herd, identify the location and go after them. Many times they would be standing belly deep in a pond just keeping cool. Other times they would be standing head to tail to one another swishing their tails to keep the flies off. As cows are, they would usually be together, peacefully chewing their cuds and gossiping about bovine business.

Each cow wore a distinctive cowbell that helped identify their location and that particular cow, usually before they were seen. Some of the rascally cows had to wear a large yoke attached to their neck. These yokes were usually homemade from a large Y cut from a tree and padded to fit the neck of the cow. If a cow tried to get into a fenced-in garden, the large yokes would hang up on the fencing and stymie the old cow brute. They could and would destroy a family garden in a heartbeat.

Occasionally the cows would have been wading in a BS, sludge pond, and if so, you only hoped yours wasn't one of them. These ponds were fairly full of oil sludge and would be covered over with a layer of blow-sand and vegetation that would entice the cow to walk out on it. If this happened, her entire undercarriage, including her udder, would be coated with a slimy, oily mess.

The clean-up job required some coal oil and a lot of wiping rags before the milking could take place. If you didn't want to be whacked in the head with a tail full of cockle-burrs, you could take the curry comb and remove as many of them as you were able.

If a cow had gotten in some barbed wire and cut one or more of her teats, then it required some Watkins Carbolic Salve to encourage healing. In the meantime, while it healed you would have to insert a catheter in the injured teats to get the milk. That was **not** a good situation, for it was painful to Old Bossy, and she could end up kicking the daylights out of you.

I actually got pretty good at milking cows and got to show off for my school kids at the State Fair one time

"I guess we've all 'been there and done that,'" said Pete. "However, it was fun listening to Cece remind us of where we came from, eh? I don't know of a single family that keeps a cow today nor doubt that many could milk one if forced to do so."

"After that 'cowabunga' little story," said Jim, "I'd like to hear Faye tell us once again about early day oil well drilling before it's going home time for lunch, which it surely is. Where does the time go?"

"Well, I for one really enjoy hearing and remembering all these stories whether they've been told before or not," replied Otto, "and as it was said, when we came in this morning, let's all give a little hush and hear Faye. We might learn something from him. I do believe we're about to strike oil again."

SPUDDIN' IN A NEW WELL

This was just a commonplace event when I was working in the oilfields back around 1912. It was no big deal, for it was just another oil well to bring in while putting a paycheck in our hands. Since I was just a young kid working in the oilfield, I never knew the 'big' picture of drilling for oil, so some of it might not be factually correct, but this is how I remember it after many years.

The early days of the boom with "wildcattin'" and oil-spouting gushers was still with us, and the drilling of a new well brought sights and sounds that gave a tingle to be a part of this great adventure.

When an oil company started bringing in all their drilling equipment in to a certain location, we knew we would have something to entertain us for weeks to come. How they chose this spot was a mystery. We heard talk of "domes" and "depressions" in the land, but we could only guess as to their meaning.

One of the first things done was the digging of the BS pond for the sludge. In an earlier day this was done using a horse and slip. For the uninitiated, a slip was an earth-moving piece of machinery. A horse pulled the slip, and the operator walking behind would trip a lever, which made the slip dig into the ground and evacuate a large bite of earth. Then came truckloads of equipment, and the site became a beehive of activity with dozens of men working at setting up the drilling rig.

There were two classes of specialized workers needed around each oil field. One group of men was called rig builders, and the other group was the tank builders.

Also, in earlier days, a wooden, and later, steel derricks had to be built to handle the drilling operation. It wasn't long and some inventive guy came up with the jack-knife rig which was portable and saved a ton of money, especially if a dry hole was hit.

Now, I'm not about to make this a technical story on oil well drilling for one simple reason ... I wouldn't know what I was talking about. I'd be shot out of the saddle real quick. I just want to relate the excitement that went along with it all. We who got to be witnesses to it were really lucky like seeing Medicine Shows, Talent Nights at Way Memorial, and such things ... poor modern day kids ...

When the drilling operation was in full swing, it was a sight to behold, especially at night. The entire area was lit up like a small city with bulbs strung up the derrick to permit working around the clock. Drilling was done in three eight-hour shifts or "towers" as they were called.

The bright lights and the noise that went along with the drilling could be seen and heard from a great distance and attracted us like moths to a candle. We would have to find a place to watch quite a ways from the wellhead; otherwise we were chased away. We'd inch close enough to hear the oil workers who were called "roughnecks" using their colorful language, and this increased our vocabulary and education a whole bunch.

An exciting time was when the drill was lifted and the contents of that load was spilled out. If it was just salty water, it was emptied onto the ground and found its way to the nearest creek to foul up the waterway. No one thought anything about this practice, for that's just the way it was. As traces of oil were hit, the sludge was emptied into the B/S pond to accumulate there.

We watched them collect samples of the core drilling and knew that it was analyzed by somebody to see how close they were from the oil-bearing sand they were looking for. Sometimes the old guy in charge of inspecting the sample would sniff the mud, and we swore he would taste it to determine the presence of oil … probably not.

There was always the hope that we would see the well come in as a gusher, spraying oil to the top of the derrick, but those days were gone forever and all we would be treated to was the bubbling up of oil which was quickly and easily capped.

In addition to the roughnecks as the laborers on the gang, there was also the boss called the driller and a tool dresser who took care of sharpening the dulled bits. Very little cleaning up of the site was done such as OSHA requires today, and as everything was hauled away, the well became another producer.

"We're fortunate, boys, to have someone in our bunch that was active in the early days of the oil boom and who still has all his marbles," said Doc Pringle. "Faye is kinda a rarity, and I for one enjoy hearing about the boom days around here. You realize we really ought to be putting all this jabber and nostalgic talk on a tape recorder?"

"I'll go along with a recorder, but deliver us from a camcorder," spoke Otto Irving. "Lawsy, it would show what we look like as well as what's being said. No one wants to see pictures of a bunch of old buzzards like us."

"Well, you just speak for yourself," Jim spoke up, preening himself as everyone gave hoots of laughter as they got up and left the table.

FIFTH COFFEE
Wing Schools

"Well, son of a gun," spoke up Harley Sprague. "Look who old Phil is bringing in with him. It's my new neighbor, Clyde Branson. What brings you here, Clyde, as if you had to have an invitation? Welcome to the Spit and Whittle gang, the bunch I've been telling you about."

"If you'll be quiet, I'll introduce Clyde to the group," said Harley. "Boys, I had invited Clyde before, but he was always too busy getting unpacked and squared away at home. So, it doesn't matter who brought you, we're just glad to welcome a new face to our little group and hope you will come back."

"Yeah," spoke up Otto. "We get kinda bored with the same old lies from this bunch, and just forget that 'spit and whittle' stuff."

Clyde actually was a new guy, not only at the coffee but also new in town. He had been born and raised in Tulsa and was trying to adapt to the pace of the small town. However, looking this group over, he could see the possibility of finding a compatible group of friends.

One of the guys asked the usual question as to what Clyde had earned his keep doing while working for a living. He told them he was retired from the Tulsa school system after 37 years of working there. There was a pretty good system of retirement benefits coming from the state, and Social Security checked in with a small amount that was sufficient to have a comfortable life in a small town.

Talk continued to center around schools, and since all but Faye and Clyde had gone to school in Drumright and graduated from DHS, there was plenty of common ground. When Clyde asked the guy across from him where he went to school, he replied, Pleasant Hill, the next one said Fairview, another Tiger ...

By now he was intrigued for he thought they were pulling his leg ... sure enough, when he finished making the rounds of the table, he had three guys who had gone to Pleasant Hill; one had gone to Fairview; three to Tiger; and four had gone to a place they called Third Ward.

The old fellow, Faye, said he hadn't had an opportunity to go to school past the seventh grade in Arkansas before coming to the oil patch in 19 and 12.

They had to explain to Clyde exactly what a *Wing School* was, for it was a new concept and term to him. In addition to Pleasant Hill, Fairview and Tiger wing schools, there was also Pemeta away up north and Tydol south of Drumright. Actually, Dry Hill existed at one time, but not in recent memory.

When the oil companies built the lease house communities around the oil patch, the workers who supplied the labor moved into company-built houses on the various leases. There would be the Magnolia Lease, Sinclair Lease, Cities Service Lease and scores more.

When the workers came to provide the work force, they were accompanied by their wives and numerous children. The lease homes were full of kids, and they had to be educated. Since a large number of children lived in one particular area, it was practical to build a school building housing grades one through eight, and all children in that geographical area would attend that particular school. The town of Drumright, many times with oil company help, had constructed these elementary schools.

When a student finished eighth grade, many considered that was enough schooling and went to work. Those wanting to go on to acquire a higher education went into Drumright if that was the closest town. Oilton was a choice further north, and Shamrock was located in the south part of the oil patch.

The Wing schools were under the guidance and direction of the Drumright City Schools, and one person was usually put in charge of all Wing schools. They were all organized in grades one through eight with the exception of Pleasant Hill, which had enough students to have grades one through grade twelve. A high school existed there until 1942 when the school was closed and the children were bussed into Drumright.

"Well, I sure can tell you anything you want to know about Fairview School," said Harold Atkins. "No one is going to dispute me, for I'm the only Fairview alumni here. I went there for eight years and enjoyed every one of them. I could write a book of my memories there."

Phil was grinning like a Cheshire cat when he said, "Remember some of those softball games when we really put it onto you? Beat the pants off you, eh?"

"Baloney, you're having delusions of grandeur," bristled Harold. "I'd imagine we came out about even over the years."

MEMORIES OF FAIRVIEW SCHOOL

Seems my most vivid recollection is that of my hair being about pulled out by the roots by my first grade teacher at the old Fairview School building. The old wooden frame building was torn down in the late 1930s and replaced by a strong and sturdy stone structure built by the WPA. Sadly enough, a year or so after the building was completed the school was closed due to insufficient pupils enrollment, and the new stone building was torn down and Fairview was no more.

It was the northern-most of the wing schools in the Drumright School System, located on a Magnolia Lease, west of the Ball Tank. The original building was a three-room, white frame building with two outdoor privies and a manually operated water pump. Now, manually operated is just a high-faluting way of saying some kid had to stand there and pump the handle up and down until all the kids had their drink …

This was at the depth of the Great Depression with failed banks, joblessness and homeless families begging. The student population represented homes with fathers employed by Sinclair, Cities Service and Magnolia Oil Companies combined with those of the unemployed, all coping in every conceivable way.

A few things showed how hard-up many parents were; children's clothing made from feed sacks, hand-me-down clothes and lunch carried in gallon-sized lard or syrup buckets.

Those whose daddies had good-paying and steady jobs wore store-bought clothing, boys sported ten-cent barbershop haircuts and wore aviator cap ala Charles Lindberg, while the girls were outfitted in Roman sandals.

Boys who owned pocketknives, marbles and string were "in," as were girls with jump ropes, jacks and hair bows. The real measuring stick was what was brought for lunch in brown paper sacks, bologna sandwiches with mustard and white bread being the gastronomical heights. Many went home for the all too familiar beans and cornbread.

Me and my brothers and sister went around behind the building and found a private place to eat our lunch which we brought to school in a one-gallon syrup bucket with our name scratched onto the lid. Whatever was in the bucket for lunch was pretty much what we ate at home meals.

"Long-handled" underwear was standard gear as soon as the weather got cold enough, and my mother was the determiner of when it got cold enough. I remember one time I was wrestling with a kid. I also had a large hole in the sole of my shoe. The bystanders pulled my long brown sock off through the hole in my shoe. I was mortified and lost the wrestling match.

Asafetida bags to ward off colds were social suicide. Teacher's pet was allowed to "clap" the blackboard erasers. Clapping the blackboard erasers took place out on one of the back walls of the schoolhouse. When the erasers filled with chalk dust, it was a high honor to be chosen to go whack them upside the wall until the dust was all knocked out of them. A high compliment was to be hit with an icy snowball or a small rock as a signal of a beau's interest, as were homemade valentines.

The teacher was a tough hand to draw to and was the sister of a local outlaw named Blackie, and she used forms of punishment that would get her fired in a New York minute today. She actually used hair-pulling, knuckle-rapping with a ruler, head-rapping with a pointer, corner-standing and confinement to quarters during recess.

I remember a girl, I believe her name was Vivian, who earned the teacher's maximum penalty by rejecting an assignment to draw a dog. After staring at her Red Chief Tablet, with her yellow pencil at the ready, she concluded that this worthless scenario was not to be endured. She held up one finger, the signal for permission to go to the girl's privy, left the room and headed for home.

She was caught at the top of a steep hill just south of the school and sentenced to stand on tiptoe with nose held in a circle on the blackboard for sufficient time to undergo an attitude change.

Even though we were poor as snakes in money, there was lots of fun to be had with homemade stilts, softball, "shinny," hopscotch on paved surfaces, mumbly-peg with pocketknives and roley-holey with marbles. Most of these required a minimum of cash outlay and provided us with untold hours of fun.

Other activities, usually done at home, included our comic strips with Buck Rogers, Tillie the Toiler, Boots and Her Buddies and Gasoline Alley and paper dolls. As kids, we played at being the cowboy movie heroes — Hoot Gibson, Hopalong Cassidy or Tom Mix. The outlaws Jessie James and the Doolin Gang were all influential in our youthful imagination as they were native or local outlaws.

"Boy, you sure know how to stir up the old memories, friend Harold," Jim spoke up. "I'd imagine most of us could say, 'amen' to the things you mentioned as we did about the same things at our country schools.

"I went to Tiger and could attest to most of those things. The Doolin Gang was located a little closer to Fairview than it was to Tiger, however, and we didn't know so much about them. You also had the infamous 'Bloody Bucket' roadhouse located up your way, too."

"Probably not too surprising that what you told was like a lot of the same things in our city school of Third Ward," retorted Pete Ledbetter.

Clyde held up his hand and said, "What's this Third Ward you keep talking about? Sounds like a prison."

Pete chuckled and said, "Yeah, I guess that is a bit confusing to a stranger. You see the city was divided into quadrants and each one was designated as a Ward. A school was to be built in each Ward and given a name. Actually, the formal name of our school was Abraham Lincoln, but most of the locals just called it Third Ward School. Second Ward was called Thomas Edison, and Fourth Ward was George Washington. First Ward School was never built."

Jim spoke up once more, "Well, Tiger School was supposedly named for an early day family of Cherokee Indians. The family name was truly Tiger, and if you check the history of the city, you'll find they almost called it Tiger instead of Drumright. All that got named after the family, other than the school, was the dirty little creek and that steep hill on the west side of town."

Joe Bob picked up the narrative: "Tiger school was in existence long before the oil strike and the oil boom. There were farmers and Indians living in the vicinity for many years before Drumright came into being. The brick structure that was there at the end followed several wooden frame buildings and all were called Tiger."

"But what a school it was," Jim concluded. "I believe there was more loyalty to Tiger School than any other one ... and I'm ready for the argument that I know is coming."

RECOLLECTIONS OF TIGER SCHOOL

I attended Tiger school for all eight years, so I consider myself an authority of that particular time frame. As I said, once you went to Tiger School you were an alumnus for life. I believe this is brought out a bit by the song the kids used to sing. Now, there's no way I'm gonna sing for you, but I'll at least say the words like a poem and you can get an idea.

"Tiger will shine tonight; Tiger will shine (repeat several times).
When the sun goes down and the moon comes up,
Tiger will shine!"

This was a portion of the Tiger School fight song. There may be people around who could give us the rest of it, but that's the most I know of it. I just know that school spirit abounded and we were competitive in softball, basketball and track with Fairview, Pemeta, Tydol and Litchfield schools.

Pioneer families with kids of all ages attended Tiger; some families had students there for many years. Some of the names remembered include the Powells, Bevins, Hoggats, Rhodelanders, Mills, Mansels, Kirks, Winklers and Tippits.

I recently saw a class picture of my combination first and second grades taught by Ms. Grimes. Man, I saw faces I'd forgotten for 60-some years. The guy who owned the class picture was kind enough to make a copy of it showing my very first love, dear Sally Jo. Of course, she never knew of my feelings for her ... kinda like the kid in Charley Brown who admires the little redheaded girl from afar.

Some of the teachers remembered were Orville VonGulker and his wife Gertrude. He was principal; Mable Grimes; Frank Haxell; Ms. Woodruff; Ms. Woodall and Schendel. Several of these teachers transferred to the Drumright system and made outstanding contributions.

Like most of the Wing Schools, Tiger's privies were two little white buildings east of the school and water was from a pump immediately north of the front door. We were taught how to fold a square piece of paper into a "soldier's hat" drinking cup and were not to drink from our hands. Apparently some of us didn't follow directions too well, for I have a chipped front tooth where someone banged my head down onto one of the bubbly water fountains.

No bus transportation was furnished, and this meant that some walked several miles to attend school.

Since no lunch program was offered, all students carried a lunch unless home was close enough to walk. A one-gallon syrup bucket made an excellent lunch box. Students ate outside and "wolfed" their food down, for as lunch was finished the noon hour softball game would begin. In fact, some of the guys would have used a trip to the privy as an excuse. They would then grab their lunch and gobble it down on the way to the privy. That way you were finished with lunch before lunchtime. They were ready to play ball immediately.

All players were chosen by the "captains" who were the best players or at least the biggest ones in the eighth grade. To determine who got to take first choice, one of the captains would grab the handle of a bat, and then he and the other captains took successive handholds until the top was reached. Last one with a full grip got first choice unless you were playing nibs. Remember nibs?

"I know I wasn't one of the captains," reported Jim Kinnamon. "When I was in the eighth grade, I was carrying around a little excess poundage, even back then. I did play softball, but usually got sent to right field, for it was figured I'd do less damage out there than anywhere else. I do have some memories of being a pretty fair country hitter, however."

"I'll check in as being from Tiger School, too," reported Jim Bob. "Old Jim isn't lying or bragging there, and he is even being a bit modest. That extra weight he carried around was used in poling softball into orbit around the moon 'cause, man, could he hit those hotshot pitchers. I remember one time when he hit a ball so far it probably hasn't stopped rolling yet.

Listen and I'll tell you what I remember of a swell wintertime activity at Tiger or summer as well, for just about the same rules applied an any season. I just remember winter because it was extra rough, but what great fun."

PLAYING SHINNY AT TIGER SCHOOL

This game we played, and one that separated the daring and foolhardy from the cautious and timid, was a game called shinny. I don't have any idea where the name came from, but it was appropriately named for your poor old shins took a beating.

It could be played either on a wide open field or, better yet, on the surface of a frozen pond. At Tiger, the guys would use the ponds inside the tank dikes, for the ice would have frozen nice and smooth. On land, any large, wide open field would do.

For the unknowing, shinny is a loosely organized game of killer hockey, not for the faint-hearted. A kid would go to a stand of timber, find a "sucker" growing out the side of some new growth. Best ones had a large curved knob on the bottom end of them. He would cut off a four-foot section above the knob and have himself a dandy shinny stick and be ready for battle. Carving designs and names on the stick gave it added character and personality. Names like "Widowmaker," "Lightning" or "Thunder" were good. Common wisdom told you this made you a better player

Goals would be set on opposite sides of a frozen pond or field, sides would be chosen and the conflict was ready to be joined. The object of the game was to whack a condensed milk can through the opponent's goal on the opposite side of the pond. The milk can very quickly got beat into a small wad of lethal metal and would fly with the speed of a 20 mm cannon shell when smacked mightily with one of the clubs.

The contestants would be scattered around the ice or playing field with some on the offensive side and some defending their goal area. Some guy with more courage than brains would volunteer to be the goalie. Now keep in mind that this was all played with no special padding other than regular clothes. If the game was being played on ice, no one had ice skates, so all players slipped and slid around on the ice.

To start the contest, the can would be placed on the ice in the middle of the pond equally distant between the goals. Two guys, the ones who had made themselves captain (usually those same two from softball) would face off with the can between them. It was absolutely necessary that they place their clubs on the ice on either side of the can, lift it and touch clubs three times counting slowly, "One- two- three." At this point all heck broke loose.

Whichever one was quickest to hit the can shot it to another guy who then did his durndest to advance it toward the goal with one swipe or shoot it out to a teammate who tried to keep it on its way. This was easier to plan than to execute, for there were some guys huffing and snorting to reach in with their club and take it away from you.

Sticks would fly, bodies would go crashing together and tumble to the ice, and many times blood would flow from cracks on unguarded shins and other body parts. Unwritten rules prohibited deliberate tripping of an opponent or whacking with a shinny stick, but accidents did happen. A cross body block by slamming into another guy was an accepted defensive

or offensive tactic. Referees were never used, so the game belonged to the quick and the dead.

When the can was knocked out of bounds, two opposing players would have a face-off like was used to start the game, so it paid to have a really quick-handed kid to perform that duty. He could "out-swift" a bigger guy on the face-off.

Each successful goal counted one point, and if there was a designated score to play to, I sure don't remember … the winner might have been the side that had the most guys still standing when it was time to quit.

I still bear a scar on my chin where I was slammed to the ice and hit it chin first. I don't remember any broken bones, ever.

*"Joe Bob, that couldn't be improved on by the guy who invented the game,"
said Jim. "And I don't think it was invented, it just kinda evolved. It was a
great description of our old game. We played it at Pleasant Hill and I'm sure
Fairview, Pemeta and all the other Wing schools."*

*"Yeah, that was where you guys had it all over us at Third Ward," replied
Elmer. "We had too many kids running around for that to have taken place.
We just plain didn't have the room. We did make up for that lack with a lot of
other stuff which we'll tell you about later."*

Phil Wiley spoke up, "I'd like to go back to those softball games that were so popular at Tiger. Remember we used to visit Fairview and Pemeta and play a boys' game and a girls' game. Had quite a rivalry with Fairview since it was just up the road.

"Times were too tough to be gallivanting all the way to Pleasant Hill or Tidal School. Besides, they were too big for us, although we would have never admitted it. It was a popular sport at Tiger, and if you didn't play softball, you just weren't in existence."

"Since the ranch my daddy worked on was in the Tiger district, I got most of what education I have from those great teachers," said Joe Bob. *"I know we don't sit around and talk about doing arithmetic and spelling. What we remember most about school is the recess activities, for that is where we bonded our friendships. I surely do remember playing Work Up."*

WORK UP ONE

When the recess bell rang and the boys and girls charged out of the building, many times they were yelling words in English that would be totally foreign to modern kids. You would hear somebody yell, "Work up one," or later you might hear, "Shinny on your own side." They had a definite meaning to the boys and girls of Fairview, Tiger and the smaller Wing schools. Normally there were too many kids in the town schools for them to be necessary.

Work up had nothing to do with physical labor. Instead, it was a manner to determine the softball game that most always took place on the playground at recess. We did this when there weren't enough players to choose up equal sides. The minimum number needed to play a softball game was nine plus three batters.

The first guy would yell out, "Work up one"... the second would say, "Work up two," and so forth until everyone playing would have a number. Your number determined where you started. One, two and three were the batters ... Number four was the catcher, five the pitcher, six was first base and so forth. Number nine was left fielder, and the larger numbers were just scattered about.

If your number was greater than nine, you had to stay scattered in the outfield until enough outs were made so when nine moved up ten would take his place and so on. We'd played it so long it was just automatic.

The game would start, and as an out was made everyone moved up one position with the catcher now becoming the new batter. It actually was a pretty fair way to organize unless the best and/or biggest guys got to be one, two and three, in which case you never could get them out.

Sometimes the rule was that if the batter hit a fly to the outfield and it was caught, the guy who made the catch and the batter traded places. Other times it was just an out and you "Worked up one." When recess was over, you lost your position, and at the next play period you began play with new numbers.

As with most playground activities in the small Wing schools, seniority usually prevailed and the guys in the eighth grade usually ran things and called the shots. If you were an underclassman, you knew your time would come.

"Shinny on your own side" was a dire warning that, if you didn't heed, could end up in bloodshed and cracked shins. Most shinny players were right-handed, and the vicious clubs used would be wielded from the right side. If you lined up, or came at the shinny can from the wrong side, you were in a fair way to get the warning. Whether or not you took the warning was determined to just how smart you were … or just how foolhardy … rhymes with dumb.

The Tiger kids also had their artistic side. Each May Day was celebrated with the "Winding of the Maypole." This was an elaborate and intricate dance done by equal numbers of boys and girls around the May Pole. At Tiger School the pole was a playground swing pole with the swings removed.

The couples would face each other with crepe paper streamers in one hand. With the May Dance music blaring over the wind-up phonograph, the couples would weave in and out as they made their way around the flagpole. This continued until the streamers were all wound, leaving a very colorful May Pole.

It was really a pretty sight with the boys and girls all dressed in their finest.

"I remember falling totally in love with a big eighth grade girl one May Pole dance. I can't remember her name, but I was just a little shaver in a lower

grade and you remember we sat on the ground and watched this," Jim said all this with a still dreamy-eyed look on his face.

After all, it had only been 60 years ago. "If we caught a nice windless day and the temperature was warm, it was just as good as a Hollywood show they put on TV nowadays," Jim continued.

"Well, Jim," said Phil Wiley, "you really got with the program, didn't you? I'll agree with you 100%, it was a most beautiful sight and our girls were beautiful. I had a moving experience with Tiger School not too long ago. I'd like to share it with you for what it's worth. Normally I'm not a very sentimental guy, but this experience really moved me. Now, I'm not one who believes in ghosts, but I'd swear I was visited by them by the dozens and it was in broad daylight."

RETURN TO TIGER SCHOOL

Not too long ago I was loafing around the house, poking around and looking for something to do. I decided to take a drive alone and just look at some old spots I used to haunt. I drove out the old highway that used to be Highway 33 to Tulsa. I turned off at what we always call Tiger Corner.

I drove a quarter mile or so east and stopped on the gravel road that ran in front of the site of old Tiger school. As I sat looking at a lone cement slab, the only remains of the school, time and mortality came crashing down on me as I sat quietly in the car. With just a little imagination I could see the small area teeming with raucous, yelling boys and girls.

Ghosts and auras of long forgotten playmates and comrades flitted across my vision. There! See the kid pumping up and down on the old handle? Must have been his turn to pump water for the rest of them ... Do those placid, wall-eyed cows know they are walking on hallowed grounds?

I'd like to return to old Tiger School again to dig up a few more of the long-dead memories. These Wing schools were really special to all of us who attended them, and most have a special place in our heart for the kids we knew and the memorable teachers who helped mold our lives. Many people have said that their all-time favorite teacher was Frank Haxel who taught the upper grades at Tiger. He truly was a giant of a man.

Old Tiger school was located next door to a large tank farm. Several of these monster 55,000-barrel storage tanks were located around. Each tank was inside a large, man-made 25-foot-high built-up circle of earth called a tank dike. Kinda looked like a reverse moat built around a medieval castle.

The purpose of the dike was to contain the stored oil if the tank ever ruptured. It was especially needed if the oil spilled and caught fire which it sometimes did.

Anyone remember Ralph Tippit who served as janitor of the school when he was in the upper grades? His job was to sweep the floors, carry out the ashes, bring in the wood and do other assorted jobs. For this work he was paid $4 a month … simple math shows this to be a dollar a week or 20 cents a day. Wonder what a kid would want to do it now?

A family of German descent named Winkler lived next door to the school and had three children who attended. Many of you will remember Gertrude, Maxine and Eddie. The girls were exceptionally bright students. Mr. Winkler spoke badly broken English and used to call his kids, Yata, Muxin and the boy, "mine leetle Addle-hoss." He farmed a modest acreage around the school.

Mrs. Winkler even prepared sandwiches and sold them to the school kids who had the necessary nickel or dime to buy … we walked home for lunch … no questions asked. We just plain didn't have the needed dime.

By the middle 1930s there were only three rooms being used for teaching. Grades One-Two occupied the first room on your left as you entered. On down the hall was a room for the Third-Fourth-Fifth, and nearby were grades Six-Seven-Eight. The teacher for the upper grades also served as principal and, I assume, had housing privileges.

At the far end of the hall was an auditorium complete with a stage. Kid productions were held here, as well as community social events such as box suppers and pie suppers. At Christmas a large tree was decorated on stage, and Santa Claus always showed up with some presents for the kids. A softball field was on the backside of the school as well as a "giant-stride" and other playground pieces.

I started my car and drove away with a warm feel of nostalgia and headed for the next place to visit.

"Phil, that really was quite an experience you had. Are you sure you hadn't fallen asleep and maybe dreamed all that?" said Clyde.

Doc, the vet, slowly spoke up and said, "Maybe you were on some weed or an hallucinogenic trip of some kind. He answered himself and said, "Naw, I know you weren't. Sounds like a 'day vision' to me."

"Well, whatever it was, I enjoyed his little story, and now if you guys will

stop trying to dissect him and his experience, maybe we can go on." Old Faye got them back on track with his dry, succinct manner.

"Long as we're re-visiting our Wing schools for Clyde, I want to give you a tour of Pleasant Hill, the only wing school with high school graduates." This all from Cecil, the guy at the end of the table. "I'm kinda a hybrid, as you will hear from my story. I relate to both Third Ward and Pleasant Hill, so I got the best from both of them.

"My folks lived on the east end hill, and my brothers and sister and I walked to Lincoln School for about four years. We then moved a couple of miles east of town to the Thomas B. Long Lease. We continued going to Lincoln until the school authorities said we would have to transfer to our legal attendance center which was Pleasant Hill.

PLEASANT HILL SCHOOL REMEMBERED

This is going to be a fun topic to reminisce about, for it was a memorable time of my life, bittersweet in part, but life-forming in another way. The years to be written of are the school years 1939-40 and 1940-41, which were my seventh and eighth grade years in school. When school authorities informed us that we could no longer attend Lincoln School but must go to Pleasant Hill, we were very unhappy, for it meant leaving all our friends. Having attended Third Ward for about five years, we didn't want to go to that old "country school."

Having no choice, however, we caught the school bus on the road near our home on the Thomas Long Magnolia lease and were driven about four miles to school. Riding a school bus was a new experience and a neat one for us. We didn't know the expression back then, but in today's lingo it was "cool."

I found myself in a combination seventh and eighth grade room upstairs in the building, and the teacher was a man, Clare B. Wright, who had a profound influence on my life. I'll tell you more about him at a later date, for he was the first hero of my young life. Fortunately, I got to tell him this before he passed away when I saw him at a Pleasant Hill Reunion several years ago.

This was my first experience with a combination room, and while I can only remember one eighth grader's name, Billy Harrel, I certainly can recall my classmates in the seventh grade. There were eight of them, and they were all girls! This was a "take-off" on the old song, "Ten Pretty Girls at the Country (Village) School," and they were all definitely pretty.

Pleasant Hill was a small, friendly school, and with the high school boys and girls in the same building it was like a family. There was a small gym located in the building, and both boys and girls played basketball there. I remember the girls having a really rough time when they played the Kellyville girls. The only seating was sitting tightly packed around the perimeter of the gym or through the open windows upstairs, looking down onto the game.

Who remembers the senior girl, Lila Waters, singing "God Bless America"? We felt she belted it out better than Kate Smith. With war imminent, patriotism was running high, and many of the older students undoubtedly served the country with some making the supreme sacrifice.

My sister was at dating age, and I remember the family teasing her unmercifully about a couple of guys with the macho nicknames of "Soapy" Roberts and "Dopey" Phillips.

Cecil continued, "Long as I'm up and got the floor, I'd like to continue with a tribute to a really great man in his little corner of the world."

A TRIBUTE TO CLARE B. WRIGHT

I consider it an honor to give a tribute to a man who impacted my life so strongly. I feel many other boys and girls who attended Pleasant Hill School while he taught there would echo this. He arrived in the late 1930s and remained until the school was closed after the 1941-42 school year. Mr. Wright taught grades seven and eight and also served as coach for the high school athletic teams.

His name was Clare B. and it was always assumed that the B. stood for Bell. However, his son, Harold, called me and during the conversation said that the B stood for a rather unusual name. Unfortunately, I don't remember what it was. Harold said his middle name was the same.

Mr. Wright was married to a very pretty lady, Louissa. They, with their son Harold, had living quarters in the "teacherage" located south and a bit east of the school. The structure was built to accommodate faculty members with a need for a place to live, since the school was several miles from Drumright. The youngest son, Kip, was born after the move to Stroud.

My first contact with him came when our family was transferred to Pleasant Hill from Third Ward, in Drumright. We'd attended Lincoln for five years and were not happy to have to go to "that old country school." I couldn't have foreseen the far-reaching consequences this would have on my life.

Class enrollment was rather small, and I was enrolled in a combination seventh/eighth grade class. I've mentioned before having eight pretty girls with me in the class. The eighth grade was just reversed. There was a slew of boys and no girls. Since I hadn't shared a grade for several years, this took some adjustment on my part.

Mr. Wright was unique in so many ways and was a natural born teacher. His dry wit and wry sense of humor made learning a joy. He must have been in his mid-twenties so was kid enough to relate to all students. He was also the principal of the elementary school, but since the school consisted of all grades, in one building, the title didn't mean much. Frank McCracken was the superintendent of the school.

C.B. was an intelligent guy and had so many stories to tell he could hold us spellbound during history class. He was well grounded in other subject matter, so we got our three R's and much more. But it was with his unique delivery and sense of humor that he really made an impression. He made school enjoyable and learning was fun!

An early encounter that I had with him was a lasting one. The eighth grade was studying the Civil War, a favorite subject of mine. They were discussing some battle, and I, over on the seventh grade side of the room, spouted off with a comment. I'm sure I should have been studying my own stuff, but my mouth always seemed to get in the way.

Mr. Wright stopped the discussion, things got really quiet as he walked over to our side of the room. He stood a bit and then in a low key way said, "There is a wall right here between these two grades. You can't see it or feel it, but it's there. Any questions?" I didn't have a single one.

Normally, a look or a few words was enough to solve any slight pupil problem, but if necessary he could and did mete out punishment. I really don't remember his using a paddle, but he may have. I do remember the infamous "Hot Seat." For some wrongdoing you were sent to the front of the room where you assumed a seated position, but there was no chair for support! It was mandatory that you hold that position for a given number of minutes.

The first 30 seconds were a snap, but as time dragged by every muscle in your legs began trembling and quivering with fatigue. You had to maintain a perfect 90-degree angle with your knees. When you had completed your "sentence," you kinda wobbled your way back to your desk. One thing was for certain … you tried to avoid doing anything that would merit that brand of punishment.

Strangely enough, it didn't destroy anyone's self-esteem or ruin any psyches the way present day philosophy would have you believe. It was just a great lesson in "accepting the natural consequences."

C.B. was a great one for giving "nicknames" to boys. I remember "Hambone" and "Weenie." I adopted this trick from him in my days of teaching kids and they loved it. If your name was Wayne, you automatically became a "Weenie."

As an eighth grader I won the honor to become valedictorian of the class. This meant giving a speech on the night of graduation. I had absolutely no idea how to write a speech, and my parents, with limited education, could offer no help. Mr. Wright came to my rescue and wrote an oration that lasted a total of about five minutes. I still have the original speech he typed, and amazingly enough can still recite it.

It starts out so typically like Mr. Wright.

> "When the smoke from our recent examination had cleared away,
> I was very pleased to find myself valedictorian.
> Then someone mentioned a speech."

The speech concludes with a poem called, "Today" by Thomas Carlyle and has a beautiful message so typical of Mr. Wright.

> "So, here hath been dawning another blue day;
> Think, wilt thou let it slip useless away."

In so many intuitive and subtle ways he was able to teach us things other than basic subject matter. Life-centered and character-building values were taught and exemplified that stayed with us. He modeled everything he said in the modern day lingo, "He walked the walk as well as talked the talk."

After Pleasant Hill school voted to annex itself to the Drumright school system in 1942, Mr. Wright was hired by the Stroud school system to serve as coach. He soon became a principal and after a few years became superintendent of school at Stroud. During this time he was continuing his education toward advanced degrees.

After earning his Masters Degree he continued on and received his Ph.D. in School Administration. He was content to stay at the smaller school system in Stroud, but became a respected educator of note in the state of Oklahoma. I would suppose that this was done in his old "down-home" country way. At one point he was offered a position in the State Department of Education but declined it. Taking the position would have required moving to Oklahoma City, and this was not acceptable to C.B. and Louissa.

After serving a long and distinguished career at Stroud, he retired. At this point he was still utilized by being asked to serve in a post with the State Department of Education.

I was fortunate to be able to sit and talk with Mr. Wright at a Pleasant Hill reunion several years ago in Drumright. I got to tell him of my career and how much of my success was due to his influence so many years ago ... we aren't always that fortunate to have that opportunity. He even asked me to send him a copy of that valedictory speech he had written for me so many years ago, and he got to see it before he passed away.

A fine man and a great educator ... Vale ... Mr. Wright.

As Cecil concluded this story, the men got up slowly and drifted away in a quiet atmosphere. It seemed the fitting thing to do.

SIXTH COFFEE
Lincoln School / Third Ward

The Spit and Whittle Gang was all "present or accounted for" at their table in the Boomtown Café ... "So it must be Tuesday morning," mused Ivey, the waitress. Even though they no longer whittled and were afraid to spit for losing their dentures, they still stuck with the name. There just seemed to be a decided resonance to it and who knows ... someone just might decide to whittle on something again.

It had been a long, hot summer and several of the men hadn't been back from cooler climes in Colorado and other summer retreats until recently. Coffee session attendance had been rather sparse for some weeks, and most of the guys looked forward to meeting and greeting their friends once again.

Cece and Harley had summer cabins on Beaver Lake in Arkansas. Both had bought a comfortable lake home when they retired, but later moved back home and just used the places for shortened vacations. They had made lots of friends in the lake community during the several years they had lived there, for they were naturally friendly, open guys. They normally spent several weeks on the lake each summer during the hottest weather.

The full attendance enlivened the waitress, Ivey Jones the ever present and cheerful waitress. She was keyed up and couldn't keep her eyes off Doc and Cece, her favorites. She didn't slight any of the others, but those two were so available and Ivey was willing.

She took extra special pains to ensure the guys getting the service and the coffee they wanted. She tried to sell some of the cook's specialty, which was a huge cinnamon roll covered over with creamy frosting. It was a no sale to all, for they knew the value of good health and tried to maintain good eating habits.

"Boy, it does take all my willpower to turn you down, Ivey, but do you know, I can gain five pounds just ordering one of those, much less eating it," said Otto. "That's just how fattening they are."

Harold broke in with," Do you guys know what day today is?"

No one spoke up with any bright suggestions, and all continued to look at their coffee cups as expecting some answer to present itself in there. There was a lot of negative head-shaking, and finally old Jim said, "Now, I know it's not some important person's birthday, so I reckon we'll just have to give up, Harold, and not win a cigar. I'll bite, what day is it?"

"I didn't expect any of you ignoramuses to know, but it so happens this is the first day of school," chided Harold Atkins, the former school principal. "Why did you think there were so many boys and girls loose on the streets this morning?"

Elmer said, "By golly, you're right as rain there, Harold, and you know, I was just wondering why there was so much more traffic this morning. Man, do I have fond memories of this day from many years ago. It was a red-letter day at our house, for our Ma was a stickler for us getting an education, but I also think she wanted us all out of the house after a summer of togetherness. We knew we'd better go there and learn something or we would answer to the folks at home. We trudged up the long hill to Third Ward with anticipation of a fun year. Some of us even got to go upstairs for fifth grader ... oh, boy."

DEAR OLD GOLDEN RULE DAYS

Who can forget the sights, sounds and smells connected with the beginning of a new school year? All these things were kinda intermingled with the exciting event that happened, usually around the first part of September. Most of us would have to admit to looking forward, at least a teeny bit, to starting school after a long summer.

We had "passed" last spring which meant a new teacher and maybe harder stuff to learn. All our friends had passed ... well, maybe with an exception or two. At Lincoln and other ward schools, it might even mean moving upstairs with the big kids ... wow ... look at those awesome stairs ...

School meant getting the necessary supplies, even if we had to share some of them with brothers and sisters. How can you forget the wonderful smell of a new box of Crayolas? We always got a box of the eight basic colors, although some of our more fortunate classmates could afford a box of 12. Shoot, nowadays my grandkids can get 48 different colors in every shade known to mankind. It brings decision-making to a new level having shades like puce, strawberry-lemon, black raspberry and the like. Enough to stress out a kid.

You could choose between paste in a jar with a small brush or a tube of it like toothpaste. It always smelled **so** good ... but you had to always be aware of our classmate who would catch you not looking and eat some of it. Old John-Boy always lurked nearby.

Other supplies would be the new pencils, a wooden ruler (plastic was far in the future), a bottle of ink and a pen and staff for penmanship class. A Big Chief tablet was a must with the paper so coarse you could see the wood chips in it. We normally had a writing book where we did writing exercises like push-pulls and ovals that were designed to give us a beautiful writing hand.

The pen-staffs and ink were usually taken up between uses and stored in the cloakroom for safekeeping. Otherwise, all our learning tools were kept in the permanent, screwed-down desk and it didn't hinge up for quick access. You just dug around in your junk. The well-used wooden-topped desks were scratched and marred with initials and other memorabilia from decades of students who had gone on before.

This was back in the days when all textbooks were owned by the family rather than furnished by the school district. Norwoods, up by the high school on South Pennsylvania, was the place to buy both new and used textbooks. The only time I ever got a new book was when it hadn't been used as a text the year before. Also with five kids in the family we passed books down just like we passed clothes. Since I was number four down the line, mine were well worn.

Sometimes there were family friends who had children about the same age as our bunch and we swapped books, saving both families some money.

So it was a great day when we all trudged up the hill to the doors of Third Ward to be greeted by Miss Head and the other teachers. The old building came to life with the hub-bub and buzzing of the scores of kids as they scattered to their rooms that were assigned. Lincoln had been built in 1916, so it was actually only 16 years old, a comparatively new building when I arrived in 1932.

The school served a large attendance area in the southeast quadrant of town and the outlying areas, so classes were quite large. At one time an "overflow" building had been built on the north side of the main building to accommodate two grades. I spent my third and fourth grade years in this building with Ms. Virginia Charles as teacher for both years. I still have my report cards for the two years in the overflow ... but in fifth grade I got to move **upstairs** ... with Miss Wanda Beasley, I think.

Getting re-acquainted with the kids we hadn't seen all summer was always a fun time. The playground bullies were the same and had to be avoided. We normally had gangs that we kinda ran with at recess and noon periods. Did any of you belong to the Purple Cross gang? I did and we had a special indelible ink tattoo we put on our arms to show membership in the brotherhood.

I'm pretty sure this gang came from Dick Tracy in the funny paper. So the problems of gangs existed even back then, but it was no problem for we were a peaceful bunch.

Elmer Butterfield took the stand and said, "I'd imagine those memories you talked about would fit just about any grade school kids memory in the country, Pete, and they sure do fit for me. Kinda strange that we don't have any members of our little coffee klatch from Edison or Washington. I guess we old Third Warders just can't get rid of each other."

"Well, we always used to think the Washington kids' parents were the ones with all the money, whether it was true or not," said Otto. "I guess it was because lots of the merchants' kids and other movers and shakers' kids in town went up there. I had some really good buddies who went there."

"Now, when you want to talk about tough. let me tell you something," spoke up Elmer. "Those old boys going to Edison or Fourth Ward could hold their own with Lincoln boys. I'd imagine in a 'knock down, drag out,' it'd be pretty 'Even Steven' unless we got to shove in one kid I remember from our school ... his last name was Allen and we called him 'Toad.' I have no idea of what his real name was."

THIRD WARD REMEMBERED

All of us who attended Third Ward or Lincoln School remember that we had some mighty tough hombres who went there. The one in particular who comes to mind was "Toad" Allen. He had a cute little trick of grabbing you by the shoulders and bashing you in the forehead with his forehead. His particular cranium must have been an inch thick and cast-iron plated, and while you were staggering around trying to remember what day it was he was off to another victim.

Lincoln School, if you remember, went from first through eighth grades until the late 1930s when the upper grades were removed to the high school building.

A majority of the families had moved many times chasing the oil field jobs, causing some students to have repeated a grade or two, meaning there were some adult-sized boys and girls attending. As was said in an earlier story, the city fathers had divided the town into quadrants. There was a Second Ward school named Washington High on the hill on the west end of town. Fourth Ward or Edison, out on North Harley Street, served the north end of town, and First Ward never came into existence. Third Ward served the southeast, east and outlying oil fields.

Growing up and attending Third Ward School in the 1930s was a lot like the words say in the song, "A Boy Named Sue," sung by Johnny Cash. "You grew up quick and you grew up mean, your fists got hard and your wits got keen." It wasn't a school with a playground for the faint-hearted, and survival many times depended on how many friends you had to run with at recess time.

I must have been good at recruitment, for I remember my ninth birthday. The Third Ward custom was to catch a guy on his birthday and whale the tar out of him by about as many as wanted to. Knowing all about this little ritual, I recruited a gang of my own for protection, and I went around the playground as safe as a babe in its mother's arms. Kinda like a mafia don. I said you had to grow up quick and mean earlier, but politics and a gift of gab also helped.

Even though the glory days of the famed oil boom had long since faded, the enrollment at Third Ward continued to be large and classes were overcrowded. The school served a large part of the southeast part of Drumright, and the population of the school ran from the upper-middle income kids to the lowest socio-economic group, with the majority being of the second group.

Many of us came from poor circumstances, and designer clothes were bib-overalls by Big Smith, usually handed down from an older sibling. Many of the clothes were designed, if you want to call it that, and sewn by the mother of the family. Shoes were a rare commodity to several of us until the weather got too cold to go barefooted.

Yeah, the principal of Lincoln Elementary School was a maiden lady, Miss Pearl Head, an imposing figure who wore tweed skirts, a suit coat and "no-nonsense" shoes. I remember her owning and driving a little early 1930s coupe of some make, which she always kept parked west of the school. She ran a "tight ship" and wasn't afraid to wield a paddle if the situation called for it. Her office was located on the ground floor on the south side of the hall as you entered the west doors.

She had a very capable staff of teachers who worked with kids from grades one through grade eight until the upper grades were moved out late in the 1930s. Kindergarten was a luxury not afforded by the Drumright School system and was far in the future.

We could spend a lot more time talking about the outstanding teachers that were doing an excellent job of coping with large classes and having many students who would be classified as "special education" types today. Their pay was meager, although I have no idea what it might have been, but they were working and that's a lot more than many were doing in the Depression era. My sixth grade teacher, Mr. Cletus Norton, supported a family on the salary.

The playground during recess and during noon hour was a real zoo. Since there was no lunch programs, everyone either went home for lunch or brought a brown bag lunch with whatever might be available to eat brought from home.

If you were fortunate enough to have a dime, there was a little cafe across the street to the west. Was it called Gobers Café or was that just the name of the owners? I'm not sure. Apparently there was no school rule against crossing the street to go to the café over there.

For your dime you could get a large hamburger and a 12-ounce bottle of Nehi soda pop. The only catch here was that dimes were rather scarce or totally non-existent. Above the counter was a punchboard that, for a penny, you could try your luck in winning a prize. I don't ever remember anyone ever winning anything of any worth.

Yes, there were playground fights … Omar Bohannan and I had a disagreement on one occasion, and after school was dismissed for the day, we went east of the school ground and decided to settle our differences "mano a mano." We made sure we were off the school ground, and then everyone expected that we would go through the rituals that were called for before starting serious fisticuffs.

It was an unwritten rule and included in a Code of Ethics that there had to be a lot of posturing done before the fight actually began. Sometimes one combatant would draw the actual "line in the dirt" with the toe of his shoe and dare the other guy to step across. Another piece of bravado actually used was to put a rock, stick or another object on your shoulder and dare the other guy to "knock it off" to start the fight.

I'd made up my mind that I wasn't about to go through all that pre-fight business, and as soon as our coats were off I charged and the melee began. The battle continued for a few minutes with the large ring of spectators cheering on their favorites, when all of a sudden someone said the dreaded words, "Miss Head is coming."

She ignored the line of demarcation since she was the power on the throne. She simply marched in, took Omar and me by an arm and was propelling us off toward the school. All at once one of the spectators by the name of Laverne "Red" Ridenour gave a loud round of applause and yelled, "Good fight!"

Miss Head dropped our arms, marched over and took Red in tow, and with Omar and me dutifully trudging along behind her we headed for the office to take our punishment.

Both Omar and I got a scathing lecture that curled our hair … Red got busted good.

"Well, now, I'd call that poetic justice," opined Doc Pringle. "But I don't imagine Mr. Ridenour appreciated it. As I remember Red from prior contacts, he just may have been guilty of other sins and transgressions at other times, and this licking he took was just interest on the loan."

"Sounds like you knew him pretty well, and as tough as he was he was just one of many guys who made our school such a great source of rough and tough football players when they started the grade school football program," said Pete. "But let me tell you about me and Third Ward and how I earned my spurs and right to be called an alumni."

GOING TO LINCOLN SCHOOL

I remember my experience of going to Third Ward School just like it was yesterday. I went there from 1934 until 1939, attending grades two through six. We had moved to town during my second grade year, and my first exposure to Third Ward was in Mrs. Eula's class. She had made me repeat first grade at Fairview, and my memories of her and what went on in her room aren't too pleasant.

She was a nice enough looking lady, but it was rumored that she was a sister to "Blackie" Thompson, who had shot two Drumright police officers in an ambush back in 1924. I don't know how much fact there was in that story, but it made good horror stories for us to talk about.

She had taught at several of the Wing Schools and had recently been transferred to teach at Lincoln One memory of her is that of her stalking quietly down the aisle behind me and grabbing me by the hair and using it as a handle, really giving me a shaking (I hadn't done anything wrong … heard that before?).

Things got better after that year, and I spent the next two in the white "overflow" building north of the main building taught by Ms. Virginia S. Charles for both years. She was from the Deep South and was my introduction to what a "Southern Belle" was like. She told us many interesting stories of plantation life and about the South in general. It was a totally new experience for me.

Ms. Wantland taught another third grade class in the main building. Ms. Wanda Beasley was my teacher in grade five, and then I had a man teacher, Cletus Norton, for sixth grade. I was recently looking at my grade cards from those years.

Some other teachers at Third Ward during this time were Ms. Woodall, Inez Slover, LouAnn Pinkston, Ms. Dyche, Ms. Anderson, Ms. Hornbeck, Ms. Dephine Jones and a petite and cute Miss Richardson. Several of these taught the upper grades and left when the seventh and eighth grades were moved to the high school. I'm sure there are those of you who will remember more names of this great bunch of teachers.

Yeah, and I remember another trick that good old "Toad" Allen had in his sadistic bag was to come up behind a guy and give him a karate chop on the back of the neck and then another chop on the front side. Surprisingly, no one ever got a crushed larynx out of the maneuver, but you couldn't talk for some time after taking these blows.

Remember the game of "poosh 'em out" that we played in a corner of the brick wall of the building? One guy would be the corner man, and then the other ones would try to root him out of the corner using just his shoulder so they could be the next person in the corner. One over-sized kid by the name of Melvin Cartwright was almost impossible to push out of the corner. The game got pretty rough.

Another game was a bit of mayhem we called "rooster fighting" where a guy would get a smaller kid on his back as a rider along with a dozen or so others. The battle would be joined with the object being to knock the other horse off his feet or pull his rider off, which put that team out of the game.

The game continued until only one horse and rider were left. This led to a lot of blind-side hits and a lot of clothes being torn, but I don't remember any broken bones ever occurring. It was a game of chaos with lots of bruises, but apparently the teachers felt it was a good way for a bunch of high-spirited boys to get rid of some aggression and permitted it to go on.

"It's kinda surprising that one of you guys wouldn't have blown the whistle on that guy, Toad. He was a menace to you," Clyde spoke up.

"Naw, I guess it was a macho thing, and the code of the playground meant not being a tattle tale, for that was one of the worst marks you could get on your reputation," said Pete. "You just took what you had to and bided your time until you got to be an upper classman. Remember, you grew up quick and mean … no joke. 'Course some of us had older brothers who made a big difference.

I can remember one kid who would deliberately provoke a fight and then beller out his big brother's name. The big brother would come a running and immediately settle things with his presence only. This big kid was new to Third Ward and was acknowledged as being as mean as a rattlesnake and being an eighth grader to boot; he had everyone's respect."

Otto said, "Now don't think that all we did was cuss and fight at Third Ward, for it's not so. Those teachers were a dedicated bunch, and most of us got a good solid foundation of learning there. At least, all of the ones who really cared. I'm kinda proud of my handwriting, and I owe a lot to the handwriting drills the teachers gave me."

MORE ABOUT THIRD WARD / LINCOLN SCHOOL

The teachers of Third Ward and all the other schools taught the entire spectrum of boys and girls who were enrolled in their grade. Special Education classes for the "gifted" and others needing special help weren't even dreamed of in those days. Everyone was in the mainstream, and the classroom teachers did the best they could with normal training.

For penmanship class we used a pen staff into which was inserted a pen. This was dipped into a bottle of ink and we were taught the old Spencerian method of handwriting. Does anyone remember the song we sang as we made our "ovals" and "push-pulls"? I can still sing the song after all these years. It was sung in a cadence to match your motion in making the ovals and push-pulls. The song went like this:

"Golden, crimson tulips; lift your bright heads up.
Catch the gleaming dew drops in your dainty cups.
If the birdies see you as they're flying by,
They may think the sunshine dropped, from out the sky."

It didn't do much for me, for my ovals looked like that toy that you play with on the stairs called a Slinky, and my push-pulls looked like the conversation by Alice the Goon Girl in the comic strip, Popeye. Does anyone remember Alice? Anyway, my handwriting has always been terrible.

Our pen staffs with the sharp pen in them were picked up after each Penmanship class and stored in an empty shoebox with the lid on which had holes punched in it for each individual's pen. They were lethal weapons and the teachers didn't want to take any chances. At the beginning of each writing class, a monitor would go down the aisles, and the owner of a pen would take it out for the class.

On one occasion when I didn't have a pen to use, I took a pen that belonged to someone else. The monitor was quick to rat on me, and I was sent to the office of Miss Head, the principal. She must have been a wonderful counselor for the skills she used. I was sitting there blubbering and said, "Well, someone took mine" (a blatant lie).

She took me over to the west window and said, "Son, do you see my car out there? Do you think that if someone stole it that it would give me the right to go steal another one?" What a lesson to have learned! I deserved getting busted, but her method was much more effective. This and many more episodes made me a better person in my adult life. She was quite a lady.

The teachers were not only effective in teaching us the basics, but were also concerned with showing us a more cultural side of life. We were shown art prints by the old masters and each painting discussed. They also had smaller prints for us to put into scrapbooks to take home to share with our families.

Near the end of school was a function called Exhibit Night. During the year the teacher saved our schoolwork papers in the various subjects. Early April we would start getting the papers back and organizing them by subject matter. The janitor would string wire along the blackboard in parallel rows so we could hang our work for display.

On a given night in the late spring, our parents would come to the

Exhibit and see our schoolwork that we had done during the year. It was a big social event for everyone, and the parents could beam with pride on the good work shown. I don't imagine they exhibited the poorer work that was done. It had to have been a tremendous task for the teachers, but it showed their accountability.

"I had forgotten those Exhibit Nights," said Jim. "We had the same kind of thing at Tiger School. I suppose it was only natural that we would since we were a part of the Drumright School System just like the three Ward schools."

"The thing that really impresses me about your Miss Head was the techniques she used which put her far ahead of her time in dealing with children." Coming from Harold, an old school principal, this was indeed high praise, who went on.

"I'd imagine Miss Head was making around $100 a month as principal, and the teachers were probably making do on about $50 per month. Now that's a pure-dee guess, but it was the middle '30s and money was real tight, especially tax money."

Phil Wiley spoke up, "You know, even with all the hard times, people loved to forget their situation by going to football games. They have always been a great diversion from poverty and hard times. From its 'boom town' days our little old town has been known for its rock 'em sock 'em winning football teams, and that's a fact."

"You sure got that right," spoke up old Faye Bucklin. "In the early days around here it wasn't unusual to have grown men playing for the high school football teams, and getting paid to do it. Rules were kinda loose and State Associations pretty ineffective. You could have an adult 24-year-old playing on your high school team. Since all the towns used the same practice, no one got all crossways with it."

"Thank goodness it finally took on a little law and order," said Doc Pringle. "It's surprising that some young kid didn't get killed by one of those adult players. But I remember by the middle '30s the quality was going downhill. Lots of families were moving away from Drumright, for the oil boom was long gone and so were a lot of jobs. Here's how I remember the high school coaches beefed up their football squads. I'd also like to tell you how we undersized little squirts made do on the playground as far as games were concerned."

GRADE SCHOOL FOOTBALL

The town of Drumright has had a long and storied history of great athletic teams, especially in football. Back in the boom days they even played large towns like Stillwater, Cushing and Bristow and won their share of games. Unfortunately the tradition has been let slip greatly, but the present program of starting the game with the very youngest grades will go even beyond what I remember as a great training program during our time.

Sometime in the middle '30s the high school football coaches hatched a plan to enhance the already formidable football teams at Drumright High. It was decided to introduce football in the three grade schools, Lincoln, Washington and Edison. It would involve the upper grades, be taught by regular coaches and give added years to the experience of the boys to prepare them for high school football.

It was met with a tremendous amount of enthusiasm by all schools, for it provided an outlet for the aggressive activities the boys already practiced, and it would be legal to smack somebody. What fun!

The name selected for the school team at Third Ward was the Lincoln Blues. I don't know if the other elementary schools were designated as "color" teams or not ... anybody remember?

Now that we had a name, the talented teachers at Third Ward put their creative hats on and produced a "fight song" to go with the warriors on the team. The words to the song went like this, and I wonder if any of you can sing along...

"B-l-u-e-s, Blues all the time.
That's the story you can hear,
Buzzin', buzzin', in your ear.
You can sing it, shout it, spell it,
Now you've got the rhyme.
B-l-u-e-s, Blues all the time."

The program was most successful for in the ensuing years Drumright did have some powerful football teams. In 1941 they were champions of two separate leagues of which they were members.

Meanwhile, on the playground the younger kids played marbles and mumbly-peg along with the other fun things I've mentioned before. Roley-holey was a popular marble game in which five or six holes would be dug in the dirt in a straight line with the holes being about three feet apart.

Another hole would be dug off at a right angle at the last hole another three feet away. It always had to be off to the right; it was an unwritten rule according to some old-time boys.

The object of the game was to shoot your "aggie" or "taw" into the first hole and then into each succeeding hole until you reach the one on the dog-leg. You then retraced your steps back to the starting line, then shoot all the way down to the dogleg hole and back to the starting line. If you were first … you won. Just winning was enough. There were no prizes, and Heaven Forbid, if you played "keeps." Ms. Head had handed down the answer to that on a stone tablet. She was the one who played for keeps.

Another marble game was played with a large circle drawn on the ground. Each player would take a designated number of marbles in his hand and drop them from a foot in the air. When all marbles were within the circle, the contestants took turns trying to knock the marbles out of the circle with their personal "shooter" or taw.

Sometimes a bigger boy, usually the bully of the playground, had a very disconcerting habit they had turned into a custom. If you were innocently playing a marble game, this guy could come along, reach down and pick up any marble, put it in his pocket and say, "Gray Mule." If these words were spoken, it made it legal and there were no complaints. I have no idea where the words came from or what particular significance they had. It probably was a case of "might makes right." Life was tough for the younger kids on the Third Ward playground …

"Pete, I remember you and Elmer were both products of that football program and went on to shine in high school," said Hank Blackwelder. "Since we didn't play football at Pleasant Hill, we occasionally came in to watch Drumright High School games."

"It really was a fine program and one that could stand to be revitalized nowadays," opined Jim. "I don't even like to go to the games anymore. What a shame to see a great tradition be dragged so low."

"Well, enough sad stuff, let me tell you guys how it was getting ready for school where I was a kid, said the newcomer, Clyde. "The big city of Tulsa had a whole slew of schools, and I went to one called Washington Irving. I think he made an exploration trip up our way sometime in the last century."

GETTING READY FOR SCHOOL

Okay, we're well into the old Dog Days of summer, and looming off on the distant horizon is an event that may bring a bunch of anticipation or apprehension, depending on your point of view. A new school year is approaching, and if the truth were known, I'd bet most everyone is excited. Even though some kids might not admit it, they are kinda looking forward to a new year. Vacations have been taken, the ball playing season is winding down and most all reunions have been held. Kids may even be a little bored.

In our household getting ready for school took on an entirely different meaning due to the concern our mother had regarding our health. She figured that we would do much better in our schoolwork if we were in the peak condition, so she used a traditional method.

Her feelings were that during the summer of idleness and playing that we had accumulated a lot of "ill humors" in our blood, maybe even a tapeworm. Therefore, it was her job to cleanse our innards so we would be in pristine physical condition to ward off the germs that would be encountered rubbing shoulders with all of the other unwashed classmates.

Do you remember a patent medicine called Black Draught? It was a concoction invented by the devil and sold over the counter at the local drug. It has to be the most powerful laxative ever created, and we were treated to a "round" of it along the middle of August. Black Draught came in powder form from a small cardboard box, and we were dosed with a spoonful of it for several days running ... pun is fully intended.

You had two choices in getting the stuff down. You could take a heaping spoonful dry and then washed down was one choice. The other was to mix the dry stuff with water and then drink it down. I preferred to do the dry bit, for it could be over and done with in a swallow or two while a glassful of the liquid elixir seemed bottomless.

How the cleansing of our innards related to our overall health conditions was knowledge that only my mother in her infinite wisdom knew. She had been well schooled by her mother and her mother ... aw ... you know the lore ... but she knew that the blood had to be cleansed.

After this purging process was complete, the next dietary supplement was several days treatment of sulfur and molasses. A bowl of sorghum would be combined with several heaping spoonfuls of Flowers of Sulfur and mixed well. She would even throw in some ground red pepper, for spice, and medicinal benefit. A bedtime ritual was one large tablespoon of this mixture … actually it wasn't bad.

Several standby remedies for ailments picked up in spite of this "gettin' ready" treatment were various liquid drinks. Sassafras tea was a favorite of all, and Watkins liniment was good for most anything that ailed you. In addition to drinking it, you could use it as a rub to take care of aches and pains. Of course, the tin of carbolated ointment was good for both man and beast. We always looked forward to the old Watkins man coming in his little Model A Ford coupe, for he usually had some licorice chewing gum for us … blatant bribery, but it worked.

I firmly believe that the water in the oil field area helped in reducing the causes of teeth decay. Many times the source of water was a local well and had a powerful smell of sulfur (rotten eggs), but it surely kept down the dental bills. A dentist never looked into my mouth until I went into the Army at age 18 … go figure.

"Well, Clyde, a lot of us didn't have much medical care until Uncle Sam took care of it when we 'jined' up or were drafted," said Cecil. "Now me … I was of the drafted variety which took place a lot later than some of you guys."

"It's amazing to think that medical insurance was an unknown term … good thing, for we couldn't have afforded it," said Harley. "We only went to Dr. Starr when it was either broken or blood was flowing. Poor folks had poor ways regardless of where they lived, and I'm sure your mother was doing the best she could under the circumstances. I had a shot or two of the Black Draught, and it's enough to make you get well in a hurry."

"It's getting close to the dinner hour," continued Harley. "Seems like we sit here longer each week, doesn't it? I will say this, I really enjoy our little old reminiscing parties. Makes me feel good the rest of the day. If I may, I'd like to ring down the curtain with one more short story of life on the playground of our elementary school days."

DOWN AND DIRTY AT THIRD WARD

The carrying of pocket knives was a common practice during our grade school days. This is an act that would result in sudden expulsion in today's schools. They were used for various activities, and I don't remember of an instance of their being used as a lethal weapon.

The game of mumbly-peg was a favorite game that required their use.

It was a game that required a knife with two blades. You opened the long blade up at a right angle to the handle. The smaller blade was opened all the way out. The player then stuck the long blade lightly into the ground and then flipped the knife up to turn several times in the air and then come back to the ground.

If the knife stuck into the ground straight up, it scored 100 points; with both blades imbedded in the ground it scored 75. With the long blade only sticking in the ground it scored 50 points, and if the long blade was in the ground and the knife handle was touching the ground it was only 25 points.

The game was played to a given number of points, such as 500, with the first one to get to that score being declared the winner.

The game got a little dirty at this point, for the winner got to take a match stick and hammer it into the ground a certain number of licks, and the poor sucker who lost had to retrieve it from the ground using his chin, nose, teeth or tongue with his hands behind his back. The winner was blindfolded during the hammering, and it sometimes wasn't too bad. If the ground was soft and he got a good lick or two, you literally "ate dirt."

Does anyone remember the beautiful murals the upper grades painted on the walls out in the halls upstairs? Ms. Woodruff or Woodall or some other talented art teacher used this as a beautification project, and the work was outstanding.

I remember my artistically talented brother painted a mural of the Taj Mahal, which was beautiful and covered an entire wall. Art appreciation was heavily stressed to the otherwise deprived kids of that era.

How about Cletus Norton? He was my sixth grade teacher and took perverse pleasure in embarrassing me. At least I felt persecuted. I was busily drawing a heart in a textbook one time, and he appeared behind me. Holding up the book he showed it to the class and said, "Now just who is this E.B. that you have in the heart with you?" I'll 'fess up after all these years and report that it was my "girl" of the moment who'll have to remain unnamed.

Another instance of his persecution ... we were supposed to write a short biography of a famous American and go to the front of the room and read it. Now it so happened that my mother had somehow scrimped and bought us a set of Book of Knowledge, and one of them was on Famous Americans. I practically devoured the book and knew all of the famous people "by heart."

When it came my turn to go up front and read, I had decided that I would report on Benjamin Franklin. Since I knew it word for word, I didn't see the necessity of writing it out. Needing a paper to hold in front of me, I grabbed an arithmetic paper and proceeded to recite the life of old Ben.

It apparently didn't ring true to Mr. Norton, for he strolled over and saw the arithmetic paper I was reading from and said, "What did you do, write your report in code?"

I was totally embarrassed and mumbled some incoherent words and fled to my seat. The class got a great laugh, and it took some time for me to live that down. Later, as a teacher, I knew it would be quite a feat for a kid to orally recite a biography with no notes ... Mr. Norton didn't see it that way. There's also the rule that you follow instructions.

How does that line go? Oh, what a tangled web we weave.

About this time Ivey strolled over to the table and said, "Now you guys just hold your horses, you're not going anywhere for a little bit. You haven't heard a female's story of some of these escapades, and it's time you listened to me telling you about some fun times I remember at Lincoln."

Ivey had a way of grabbing their attention and holding onto it. Not one of the old boys shoved their chair out an inch. They leaned forward, giving Ivey their total, undivided attention.

THIRD WARD OPERETTAS

I've heard you guys mention what a great job you felt the teachers did at Lincoln School working with a varied group of boys and girls. In addition to the regular classroom curriculum of the three R's, the staff did extra curricular activities to increase student interest and broaden their base of learning. I realize now that they spent many hours outside the classroom working with us. It is my belief that many teachers of the 1980s and '90s would have demanded extra compensation if they would have done it at all.

Each year at Third Ward the school presented at least one, if not more, operettas for the enjoyment of the parents and others. I'm sure many of you can recall several of the musicals that were staged in the auditorium on the first floor of the school. I remember them as being elaborately done with costuming and scenery of high quality.

Tryouts were available for all, and starring roles were highly sought. There were usually "mob" scenes so many of us would get to be a part of the production. Christmas programs were presented, and if there were religious overtones it was expected, and no one's "rights" were violated.

Who remembers the operetta, "Tom Sawyer"? I don't recall who the stars were but can sing along with some of the songs. In the finale when Tom and Huck are safely home the song went:

"We are happy that our boys are back again.
It relieves us of our sorrow and our pain.
Their adventures, we'll not censure, (repeated)
And their bravery we'll all acclaim."

Or how about Goldilocks and the Three Bears? Do you remember this song where Goldilocks knocks on the door of the three bears' house and no one answers?

"No one here, my, how queer, what shall I do, oh dear, oh dear.
If there're kind, they won't mind, helping me my way to find."

Or when the bears find their soup inedible.

"If some day your porridge seems a trifle hot,
And you dare not venture tasting it.
If your tea or coffee doesn't touch the spot,
Or if your sugar seems like grit" (lots more to it).

At home in my junk, I have an original copy of the program for "The Cobbler of Fairyland," an operetta presented, dated March 16, 1939. It starred a cat," Machiavelli," played by Jack Stephens. The head painter was Raymond Camden, killed at Pearl Harbor. Queen Monarchie was Irene Coffield, and the king was Kenneth Dose. The evil Vengefuletta was Gaynell McQuillen, and the wicked witch was Betty D. Lowe.

There are several dozen others in the cast including painters, elves, fairies, cooks and ladies-in-waiting. Lucretia Maggard, Vinita Curtis and Reba Stroud were some of the fairies.

Here is the song about Machiavelli, the cat. Remember the tune?

"Machiavelli's his name, he is a crafty cat,
And supernatural are his powers.
Now what do you think of that?"

Harold was a painter along with five other guys, and apparently we were strong union members, for one song went:

"A Union we, a Union they,
With little to do and plenty of pay.
A Royal job at the Queen's request,
And a union button pinned on each vest."

The director of this operetta was Miss Bernice Hornbeck, and the accompanist was Miss Dephine Jones. In charge of the properties was Melvin Cartwright, while Dean Barto handled publicity.

Harold spoke up and said, "Didn't really matter if you didn't have any talent … teachers would always find a mob scene to ensure that everyone was seen by their mommas and daddies on performance night."

"Yeah," Pete replied. "Those were the kinds of activities memories are made from. I haven't heard anybody telling stories of arithmetic or geography classes. Those were part of it, but the fun part was those extracurricular things."

"Well, I have one more little story to tell and then it's 'outta here' for me," continued Pete. "Naturally, it's school related, since it's that time of the year. Bear with me, boys, and I'll make it short."

ANOTHER YEAR OF BOOK LEARNING

"School's out! School's out! Teacher's had a blowout!"

Remember that little ditty we sang in the spring when we were dismissed for summer vacation and the long endless summer stretched wonderfully ahead of us. As kids, we actually thought we were putting something over on the teachers by getting a vacation. What we **didn't** know was … if we thought **we** were happy then, we should have known how elated the teachers were. I'd bet Ms. Head and all the teachers were turning cartwheels down the hall when the last kid left, or at least felt like it.

By the time Labor Day rolls around, I'd imagine most of the kids have made it back to school for another year of friendship, learning and fun. After three days of house arrest, I got to take off my leg irons; otherwise the old fire horse instinct would have had me bounding out the door and heading out the front door. Amazing how, even after all these years of retirement, I still miss the excitement, hustle and bustle of the first day of school.

The schoolrooms are sparkling, the books, maps and globes are shiny … even the kids are bright and shiny … A new year brings the everlasting promise that most **anything** is possible.

It makes it possible for me to want to share a few memories with you. Hope some ring a bell with you…

The Pledge of Allegiance is a hot topic now, and I wonder how many of you remember how we recited it back in our elementary days. All the boys and girls would stand and face the flag. We then placed our left hand over our heart and said, "I pledge allegiance" … at this moment we would then extend our right arm stiffly and point our hand toward the flag and say, "to the flag" … amazing. We looked like a classroom of boys and girls from Nazi Germany giving a "Heil Hitler" salute.

This old boogey man had been our worst nightmare for several years, and with World War II looming on the very near horizon and with Adolph Hitler being the nastiest of the Nazis, someone quickly determined that this was **not** the way the flag should be saluted, and so we didn't extend our hand toward the flag.

More grade school memories … remember how some teachers would read to their class, usually right after lunch? It was usually a chapter from a spine-tingling book. I remember loving to sit listening to the peaceful drone of Ms. Beasley or whichever one read while we sat in rapt attention.

Sometimes a co-teacher friend, Ms. Hornbeck, would bring her kids into our room, and we'd sit double in our seats and both classes would listen. It was kinda like a holiday when we had visitors … I remember one time one of the teachers was reading about the main character "knitting his eyebrows." The phrase must have struck her funny, for she looked at her fellow teacher and they both began to laugh.

Since my mouth had a habit of getting me in trouble at various times, I piped up and said, "How do you suppose he wore his old eyebrows out?" It wasn't very witty and was a whole lot smart-aleck. It's a fact of life that class comedians have most always been frowned upon by classroom teachers.

I never heard the conclusion of that chapter … I was standing out in the hall.

This concluded the coffee session, and the guys left reluctantly, looking forward to the next meeting of the group.

SEVENTH COFFEE
Kid Activities

The late August sun shone down valiantly, and while it had lost some of its mid-summer fierceness it was still nice to be inside enjoying the cool comfort of the air-conditioned Boomtown Café. Most of the regulars of the Spit and Whittle Club were present and gathered around the table for their Tuesday morning social time.

Doc Roy was absent, due to some family problems with his son who lived in Tulsa. Doc bore his cross of a wayward son and could only shake his head and wonder what new problems the middle-aged man could be in. Faye Bucklin was a serious health concern for the group. At 88 years of age he was, by several years, the oldest of the group and was still nursing a nasty case of summer pneumonia and had been missing for several weeks.

Otto was also among the missing, but the group figured he'd just drop in later. He had a rather demanding wife, and she was a force Otto had to reckon with.

After discussing the missing men, the conversation wandered around to the coming of another school year and what kind of football team they could expect. The once powerful teams of the past were just that ... in the past, and everyone awaited what the impact of the new program of starting football in the grade school and middle school would have on the high school varsity and how soon it would take place.

"Remember the fun activities we had during the summer months when no school was going on," remarked Jim Kinnamon. "We had to make do with a lot of simple things and modest equipment and also had to be creative."

"That we did, Brother Jim," spoke up Cecil Damore. "Ours was the simple life, but by golly, we did a lot of activities that were far beyond what the textbooks had in them. It was mostly due to a creative streak in boys with time on their hands. Remember the ants and spiders we fed? Now maybe the school board will finally wake up and get some hands-on activities in the school curriculum."

BUGS, SPIDERS AND CREEPY CRAWLIES

Some time back there was an article in the *Gusher* about a new curriculum or emphasis in a new science program for the kiddies in the Drumright schools. Sounds like a neat program and will increase the kids' interest in this subject. Right on ... school board.

It kindled a good story of something we did way back when in learning about bugs and other scientific things. All we thought we were doing was having fun ... maybe that's the best way to learn. Did any of you other guys do these kinds of things?

Around old buildings and in the foundations of the house were always found some really great spider webs. I mean they were huge and stretched out between anchors that made a large parlor for Mr. Spider to grab some free meals. He/she waited back in the entryway in the web just waiting for some unwary insect to stumble into the web, and zap, there was some McBug fast food.

We allowed as how we would give spiderkind some help and reduce the bug population at the same time. We would gather up flies, pull off one wing to slow them down and toss them onto the web. In a flash, out would come old spider, grab the morsel and zip back into his house. We soon upped the stakes by getting a big old horsefly, which had a lot more movement. Lots of excitement in the tussle, for the horsefly had no desire to furnish the spider his lunch.

We went further by getting small grasshoppers and used them as bait. Old spider would change tactics on the big stuff. He would spring out and using his web supply would quickly wrap the bigger critter up in a tight cocoon, turning him deftly with his legs. He would then leave it out on the web and suck out his juices at a later date.

I don't reckon we lessened the fly and grasshopper population by much and didn't get any appreciation from the spider, but we had a fun time.

We turned next to the lowly ants for entertainment and learning. One of us figured that if we would melt some lead or babbit to a liquid stage we could pour it down the ant hole, resulting in a model of

129

the den and reducing the ant population at the same time.

Scrounging around oilfield junkyards, we found a good supply of lead or babbit. We located an extra busy anthill and poured water down it for a day or two, forcing the ant colony to dig out their tunnels. Next step was to build a small dirt dike around the entrance hole about two inches in diameter. This was to keep the melted lead from spilling around.

Taking a coffee can, we crimped a pouring spout and then set it on the stove with the lead in the can. After 30 minutes or so the lead would be molten and ready for the pouring. We used pliers to carry the heated can to the ant den and very carefully poured the hot, molten lead down the hole.

On a hot summer day the ground wouldn't cool off the lead 'til it had gone to the bottom and into all the tunnels of the ant den. It was amazing how much lead it would sometimes take.

Now, naturally all the ants that happened to be home at that time were quickly incinerated. We always figured no scientific advancement had ever been made without some sacrifice, and this was just the price the ants had to pay. Besides, there were umpteen zillion ants running all over the world, and what's one little anthill.

Within a few minutes the lead would be cooled, and our next chore was an archeological dig. We would take spoons and dig up the ant den that the lead had formed. It was a perfect model of all the rooms and tunnels that made up that den. Not so surprisingly, we never did find two of them that were alike, and we must have poured a hundred.

Years later I helped a daughter pour some for a science project, and it was a real hit in her science class … might have even gotten an "A," I don't remember.

"Yeah, I can see you doing those things Cece," said Hank Blackwelder. "You were in training to be a science teacher even back then, and you were no older'n a young pup. I can remember how you would organize us into work units just like a cadet teaching team. You was a bossy little squirt at times, but we loved you."

"I think all of us were more of the outside type and wanted to do things with our hands and create something," spoke up Phil. "Nothing against the bugs and spider activities and they were fun as well, but digging caves and building tree houses were more up my alley … remember?"

A couple of guys spoke up, " Remind us how we went underground."

DIGGING CAVES

It all started when we would be in our favorite play area down in the hollow. Right next to a salt creek was a stand of blackjacks where our tree house was located. After wearing out our interest in tree houses, another urge would hit us and we would get the hankering to dig a cave and live underground like a mole. This usually was the result of reading some story or a book, like Tom Sawyer ... anyway, we wanted a dark, secret hideout.

While we weren't the sharpest knives in the drawer, we knew the dangers of just digging back into a bank, although some guys did just that. We went the more cautious route and made ours in a different manner. Finding a nice level piece of real estate, we would lay out the cave site. Seems like it would usually be about 25 feet long, and it called for removing many yards of dirt.

Many of you took part in the same activity and you remember how it was done. After figuring out where we wanted the tunnel to run and where the rooms were to be, we started in on the dirt removal. And what a monstrous chore it was. With little else to do, we made our own entertainment, and if physical labor was involved ... so be it.

I still bear a scar in my eyebrow I got when I peered over the edge of the tunnel about the time my brother pitched out a shovel full of dirt. Made a nasty cut as well as getting a face full of dirt, but no medical help was used.

We worked like Trojans, Turks, slaves or what have you and dug the trench about two feet deep by two feet wide. If we were lucky, we missed the old sand rocks, but if we hit one we just dug 'er out and went on. As we dug, we threw the dirt out alongside the trench to be used to cover the top of the tunnel when finished.

At times we got elaborate and would dig a dead end tunnel to confuse the enemy. Other places we would narrow the tunnel way down to have what we called "fat man's squeeze." We were all so skinny it would have taken three of us melted together to make a fat man, but we did 'er anyway ... never could tell when a fat kid would want to invade our cave. A room, maybe five-foot square, would be dug which was our meeting room.

What's that? You asked what our meeting room was for and what kind of meetings we had? Well, to tell the unmitigated truth I'm sure the forerunner of the CIA probably called on us for help and assistance. See what happens when you ask a loaded question?

When we were satisfied with the shape and depth of our cave, we found old timbers and laid them crosswise across the tunnel, covered them with scrap tin and sheet iron and then put all the dirt on the top of this. It made a really nice, cool lair to crawl into for secret doin's and other skullduggery. It was pitch black in the tunnel, and the meeting room and flashlights were too dear for us to own. We had to have a source of light ... so ...

We'd create some make-shift coal-oil lights by taking a pint fruit jar, cutting a slit in the lid and inserting a rag down into the oil and light the short wick that stuck out. It gave off a small amount of light with a whole lot of smoke. Hey, nobody told us that it could be dangerous ... besides ... remember those guardian angels? We had to give them something to do to earn their keep.

We learned early on that it was absolutely necessary to make a tight-fitting door at the entrance. Other creatures also loved our cool cave, and it was a botheration to find Mr. Snake or Mr. Possum wanting to share it with us. My old cautious brother would never be the first one into the place. He didn't care for creepy-crawlies at all ... as for my sister crawling in? No way, Jose ...

Faithful old Shep preferred the cave to that infernal tree house and after a little coaxing would go right on in. We'd try to have him go in first to check the place out for intruders.

I'm sure our old cave made a nice home for lots of skunks, possums and the like after we outgrew our boyhood games and started thinking about girls.

"We probably worked harder at cave digging and other things we did than we ever worked for our folks doing chores and never made a peep of a complaint," said Joe Bob.

"I can remember visiting a kid in town one time, and he and his buddies had built a cave on the order of ours," said Pete. "We were crawling back in it and his light was pretty good. When we stopped in a room, I asked him what they burned in their light."

He said, "Oh, it's a mixture of coal oil and gasoline about 50/50."

"Man," continued Jim. " I bailed out of there and scattered dirt on the way and never went back in. I may have been a kid, but I knew how explosive gasoline was in any mixture and didn't plan on having my head blown off. Amazingly enough, that character never had an accident, but every time

I saw him at school I marveled at his ignorance ... and luck."

"Where I lived I had the best of both worlds right at my fingertips," reported Jim Kinnamon. "I don't believe it was more than a hundred yards from our cave to my tree house. Now how's that for planning? I could satisfy either urge in a few minutes time"

Several of the guys nodded in assent, for they had lived in close enough proximity that they had probably played in both of the kid venues. It was a walk or a short bike ride to get there, but many happy hours were spent at each other's homes.

TREE HOUSES R-US

Most every kid from any generation has been bitten by the bug to build a hideout as high up in a tree as possible? After reading "Swiss Family Robinson," my older brother and I decided to build us a leafy home as a hideout. Out on the Magnolia Lease, east of town, we went scouting around the countryside. We were looking to find a suitable tree that would serve our particular need. We looked for something with spreading arms and level limbs so we could build a tree home just like the Swiss Family.

Well, not really, but it was to be our very own. The older sister, only girl with four brothers, joined us, although reluctantly. She had no other choice, but was a tomboy at heart.

Nowadays, I see dads building fancy-schmancy structures for their kids in the back yard located up on tall 4 x 4 posts with regular ladders to climb. We had to be a heck of a lot more creative when the urge hit us to build a sky home. With us, it was a total do-it-yourself project. Dad was too busy trying to put food on the table.

Around Drumright we weren't blessed with soaring oak trees with inviting limbs. We had to be content with full-grown, scraggly old blackjack trees that, while not soaring, offered us some good sites. You remember climbing the old black jack tree ... right? They are a dreadful mass of small dead limbs just waiting to reach out and grab you as you tried to climb ... would take off chunks of your hide if you weren't careful.

Our first chore was to clean out the trashy limbs, giving us a clear shot at two limbs that were growing fairly close together to nail on the foundation support boards. Lumber for these projects had to be scrounged from wherever it could be found. There were lots of scrap heaps and dumps around. Abandoned houses could be salvaged, and some could be gleaned from abandoned wooden oil derricks, so we didn't lack for material.

We didn't know doodly-squat about building, nor did we have tools other than a handsaw and clawhammer. But kids had to be resourceful, and we went at it with enthusiasm and ignorance. I'm sure that if a square had been put on it we would've failed to pass muster. It was a kinda ramshackle Urban Renewal type, but we loved it.

We nailed short sections of wood onto the tree trunk to make us a dandy ladder so we could shinny up and down the tree. After we got the platform built, we would sit and revel in the sights from our perch … but not too long, for it was necessary to get the sides and roof on, and before long we had our snug little house ready to use.

The tree house was a great place for sinnin', and we would take a stash of grape vines up and smoke them. Streets & Smith published great Western story magazines that we would take up and read by the hour. Remember their publication called, "Spicy Westerns"? It was strictly adult fare … but probably was still tame by today's standards.

On one occasion we attached a wire cable to our tree and ran it down to another tree a little lower and about 50 feet away. We found a large pulley and hung it on the wire rope with a straw filled sack tied onto the bottom of a short rope attached to the pulley. Now, hear me, straddling that sack and setting forth to ride the wire to the lower tree was a thrill you never forgot.

Since my older cautious brother wouldn't do it, I got to give it its maiden voyage, making sure to hit the lower tree with feet and legs extended toward the tree. Hitting that tree so many times with stiff legs may have stunted my growth, possibly.

This fun activity didn't last long, for when old Will, the cautious brother, came into the lower tree backwards he split his head open. After cleaning the blood off him, mother put the kibosh on that project by revoking our license.

We took Old Shep up into the tree house one time, but he let us know in no uncertain terms that his love and loyalty had its limitations and his contract didn't call for stuff where he didn't have all four feet on the ground.

"Boy, that sure brings back lots of pleasant memories," said Harley. " Remember the time we put the only door into the clubhouse on top. We were smoking grapevines, and some burlap we had on the walls for insulation caught

fire. It was every kid for himself in getting out. Fortunately, no one was hurt and the tree house wasn't damaged much."

"That was one dark, deep shared secret for a long, long time, I'll bet," spoke Clyde.

"Yeah, we had to build a fire on the ground for some reason to get an excuse to tell our mothers why we smelled so much like smoke," remembered Harley. "Also, guys, remember that it was right under the tree house where we found that nest of ground bumble bees that time?"

FIGHTING WASPS AND BEES

After playing in the tree house and in the cave and walking to the Devil's Bathtub for swimming, things got kinda dull and the summer got long. We looked around for some other activity to pass some time. Not that we didn't do the required amount of hoeing in the garden as needed, for our mother made sure we did.

In roaming around the countryside we sometimes would spot a huge wasp nest in a sheltered tree or in an abandoned building. Now **this** was something that got our adrenaline flowing, although we wouldn't have known the word. It was a challenge that we just couldn't pass up, so the battle was joined.

You may remember there was the black wasp variety and then their wicked, vicious cousins, the red wasp. The black ones were considered to be tamer, but those red ones! Now, there was a worthy opponent for us to join with in combat. They were aggressive, mean boogers who had a stinger about six inches long … well, it seemed like it.

Located up in a sheltered part of a tree, they would have a nest as big around as a large washbasin. I mean those nests were huge and provided a home to many hundreds of evil-looking red warriors always ready to defend the home fires. Our assignment: "take them out"… one way or another.

First thing we needed was our trusty slingshots plus a large supply of ammunition. We also carried our rubber band guns for close-in fighting. We had learned from experience that a close-up frontal attack was pure-dee suicide, so we stood back at long range and began peppering the nest with shellfire.

Now this bothered the wasp warriors a whole bunch, and a huge swarm of them boiled up and out, looking for the enemy. We usually left a clear path behind us so we could beat a hasty retreat, which we did. With their wasp radar the rascals figured out in a flash which direction the rocks were coming from and made a bee-line ... no, a wasp-line right to us.

Our normal garb in the summer was neither shirt nor shoes, so we boys had a lot of bare skin showing that was totally vulnerable to the attacks. However, it seems the wasps liked to go straight for our head. This brought about a version of a dance like you've never seen before. With arms flapping, hands swatting and legs pumping, we would try to outrun the insect bombers by zigging and zagging and flat-out flying.

If we were swift enough, the wasps would soon give up and head back to the nest to protect the home front. This gave us time to catch our breath and do some strategy planning before resuming the attack. The same scene was repeated, and the wasps were able to get in some good stings on us, especially in our hair.

We got **no** sympathy from mother in our stings, but we wore them as medals of honor. We used mud, a soda and water poultice and Watkins liniment to make the hurt go away, but actually we kinda took pride in exhibiting our wounds.

Normally, after several skirmishes someone would get in a lucky hit with a rock and the main support holding the nest up would be cut and the nest would come down. This victory might take two or three days to accomplish, and you can imagine the stories we told, bragging and showing how tough we were.

One time we discovered a nest of ground-based bumblebees right under our tree house. This bought about a whole new challenge. These big old yellow and black bees were formidable fighters, but we could take them out using our rubber band guns.

Faithful companion, Shep, was a determined fighter and would go into battle snapping at bees right and left. He decided he had enough though, when he got one down his throat. That devilish bee stung him pretty good all the way down. He decided to go home.

The guys sat in silence, digesting the memories they had been hearing. Some just shook their head in the total absurdity of the activities they had taken part in as youngsters, but a smile would steal over their faces remembering how much simple fun it was. They knew they had developed some solid friendships, and after a life's work in distant places were back to enjoy their sunset years with some of those very boys.

No television and very little radio demanded their attention. Sure, there was a war imminent with a little twerp named Adolph Hitler and a big blowhard called Benito Mussolini, but it didn't consume every waking hour of the day on the radio. Most would live to be an active participant in the coming war, and even some of their playmates would not make it back.

That's what made these boyhood activities being told and retold so dear to the guys and were precious memories to hold onto forever.

"You, know," said Elmer, "someone should write a book of all the things we did. That way we could share it with the entire world, if they'd believe some of the things we did. How about this one?"

DAREDEVILS OR DUMB KIDS

Climbing these sky-scrapping oil derricks was at once the most exciting and yet potentially dangerous activity we did when we were boys. I'm not referring to the earlier wooden derricks that were death traps with rotted steps and rusty nails. There weren't many of them around by the middle 1930s to even tempt us. I feel we were smart enough not to tempt fate by venturing on them. We weren't terminally stupid, but close.

The landscape was dotted with dozens of the later steel-built monoliths, each squatting protectively over their respective holes in the ground, which offered up the Black Gold. These metallic monsters, with an enticing ladder reaching up to the clouds, issued the challenge, "Climb me!" and we did.

It's truly amazing the number of us who made it to adulthood. There were so many activities connected with the maturing process, circulating tanks, swinging bridges that were chancy and some downright dangerous. They weren't spoken of as "rites of passage," for we wouldn't have known the term. Yet, as you grew up with older brothers and friends, it was a sign of your masculinity for you to take an active part in them.

The one exception to this macho business was one of my brothers. Will was always the timid, cautious one, and there was no way he could be bribed or shamed into climbing. He was adventurous, but always wanted to have one foot on the ground.

Climbing the derrick meant first scrambling up the girders to reach the bottom rung of the ladder, which the oil company had placed safely 15 feet up. Once there, it was with a knot in your stomach, heart in your throat, sweating palms and trembling legs that you started your torturous climb on your maiden voyage. The ascending ladder looked like a railroad track as it stretched endlessly up and up into the blue sky.

Beginning climbers were admonished to not look down but to keep the eyes focused straight ahead. As the climb proceeded, the view became astonishing ... you could see forever, or so it seemed. You were on a level with flying birds, and right over there might be a puffy white cloud. It was glorious! As you climbed you might, by listening very carefully, hear the rustle of your guardian angel's wings, for surely they were on duty on those trips.

One-third of the way up brought the arrival at the "tubing board." This was a wooden platform where workers stood while guiding the casing as it was pulled up from the well when cleaning was necessary. We would sometimes get out on the platform to rest and enjoy the view. Maybe even take the time to smoke a piece of dried grapevine during the break.

The climb continued on for many more feet, and finally ... you arrived. There was a huge crown block, a mammoth wheel, secured firmly at the top. This wheel was essential for guiding the thick wire cable to travel over in lifting and lowering the sections of casing as they were pulled from the well during cleaning.

We would then take time to sit on the top of the oil rig, brag about our feat and revel in actually making it to the top. Once again we would survey our domain, looking at cows and people down on the ground ... Sir Edmund Hillary couldn't have been any prouder when he sat atop Mount Everest chatting up his Sherpa guide. It was always necessary to take the obligatory spit down ... if you had any moisture left after the scary trip up. This was always done "downwind" out of courtesy.

After several trips to the top of the derricks, we became veterans and cast about for something more interesting than simply climbing up and down the ladder When several of us would climb the rig, it was proposed that we have a contest to see who could climb down the structure without using the ladder.

This added some spice, for it was then necessary to slide down a slanted girder until the next level was reached. The maneuver was then repeated until you had reached the bottom. With the derricks being made of steel, we were pretty dirty with the rust from all the sliding and got some stern admonitions from our mothers.

"And you know, fellas," said Elmer, after taking a long pull at his coffee cup. "Heights today just scare the pee-waddin' out of me. We visited the Royal Gorge one time, and I practically froze to the railing of the bridge looking down from where those bungee jumpers launched.

"And I was one of the first to make it down on the cross girders," continued Elmer. "I even tried to get into the paratroops when I went into the Army, but wasn't accepted due to poor eyesight and having to wear glasses. Something surely happened to me as I got older."

There were several of the other guys who said while they would use the ladder going both ways they refused to climb down the girders, so some sanity must have prevailed.

Otto, who had come in late, had been fussing and fuming to get his turn on the wheel of conversation. The guys didn't exactly take turns, and some of the storytellers were a little more boring than others.

Jim's stories were always animated and exciting with his delivery. Joe Bob, everyone knew, chewed his words slowly and they came out the same way, so his stories were a good time to kick back, have Ivey bring a fresh cuppa and enjoy his story. They were always comical, in his slow delivery.

Now Otto was ... well, I'll just have to let him tell his story and let you make up your own mind. Otto is Otto ...

1930s DESIGNER CLOTHES

My young grandson was over mowing my lawn the other day. We were talking about being ready for school, and he reported that he had paid 70 bucks for a pair of khaki pants, designer label, naturally. I was horrified and it made me remember the clothes we wore to Third Ward way back when.

We weren't too concerned with designer labels, were we? Unless it was having some Big Smith overalls bought from C.R. Anthony's, for that was about the height of our desires, if we had any. Being the fourth male down in the family, I had a large wardrobe of hand-me-down clothes. With hand-me-downs you hoped they had a minimum of patches and few rents and tears, especially in critical areas.

Remember the overalls where you adjusted the straps using two sharp points on the end that you attached to the button? I still carry a scar down the side of my face where I was deeply lacerated while wrestling some guy.

Looking back, I would tell you that, **yes,** we did wear designer's clothes and didn't realize it. Many of our shirts and some of my sisters dresses were designed and made by "Madam Adeline." This little known couturier (pretty fancy word) was none other than our mother! She owned, and had a passing relationship with an old treadle-type Singer sewing machine. An early memory of mine is of her sitting at the machine, treadling away, and lustily singing church hymns. Another vivid memory that was not so nice was the time she ran her finger under the needle. The momentum drove the sewing needle deep into her finger, hitting the bone and breaking off.

Material for the clothes occasionally came from 50-pound flour sacks, or chicken feed sacks, which were also quite colorful. Unfortunately, many of our peers also used the same cloth source, and the patterns were so distinctive there was no question of the cloth's origin. If you were a girl and found a person next to you in school with the same pattern, it was embarrassing. Boys didn't care, or if anything was said you just cleaned their plow.

With no flour sack material available, Mother would go to Anthony's and buy several yards of some hickory stripe cloth. This was really distinctive, for the pattern was just one bunch of old stripes of an ugly blue/green color, and it wore like iron.

On one occasion I needed a white shirt to wear to a church function. Having no white cloth, my mother used one of her white pillowcases and made me a shirt. A-h-h, yes, depressing Depression memories.

With no formal instruction on how to sew, my mother was self-taught and could become most creative. She didn't always need a pattern, and sometimes she would just "wing it." She also felt that the fastest way was the best way, and at times the finished product showed it.

She was pretty good on all phases on making a shirt with the exception of attaching the collar. I can remember some shirts having to be buttoned around on the side of your neck due to a slight miscalculation.

Shoes were not too much of a problem to many of us at Third Ward. We just went barefooted until the weather became too cold … and that was a very flexible date … depending on the amount of money available to buy shoes.

Our feet became as tough as a rhino's hide by the end of summer, and we'd brag about being able to "kick fahr out of a rock." This wasn't exactly true, for on several occasions, while barefooted, I would accidentally stumble over a rock and hit my big toe and knock a large chunk of skin off the end of it. Took forever to heal.

When it came time to buy shoes, they were usually of the old yellow brogan type or "plow shoes" as we called them. This usually called for a trip to Eddie Shadids' Shoe Store up the hill on Broadway on the south side of the street.

If the shoes lasted long enough to wear a hole in the sole, then Dad became a cobbler. He owed a "shoe last" and became quite good at putting on a great sole. The shoe sole material was some belting material from an old "bull wheel" found in the junkyards around oil wells. Belting material was quite thick and would add a half-inch to your height. It was also very stiff and caused you to walk kinda funny until your re-soled shoes got broken in and flexible.

So … our poor present-day kids … what would they do without designer labels on their clothes? However, I'm making no judgment calls on them … mine are pretty good…

"You know, I do believe I have something to finally add to this little kaffe klatch," said Harold Atkins. "I've really enjoyed listening, and what you don't know is I have some of the better ones caught on my tape recorder for the sake of posterity."

"Aw, you really don't," shouted several voices. "You'll be kicked out of the fraternity for taping without permission. We know our rights."

Old solemn-faced Harold snickered with laughter. "Guess I had you going there for a minute, huh? Nah, I didn't, but wouldn't it be a hoot to really tape some and donate them to the museum?"

"Probably the only thing that would hoot would be an old owl," said Harley, who had been tricked by Harold. "But let me tell you another little story about some more bugs we used as entertainment. We sure practiced some 'hands-on' learning, and today that's a real buzzword in education. Back then it was called playing."

DOODLEBUGS AND COW ANTS

Here we go again on Oklahoma bugs of 1935. Amazing that I didn't turn out to be some kind of "bugologist" the way we played with insects. We were experimenting and learning and doing things scientific and we didn't realize it.

Did any of the rest of your guys ever feed doodlebugs? This was the delightful little creature that lived at the bottom of a conical-shaped pit in an area of very fine sand. We didn't know it, but it was the larvae of a damson fly. We thought it was the end in itself.

These hungry larvae have a really curious way of getting their meals. They spend their larvae lives traveling backwards making doodle marks in the sand, hence the nickname. Coming to some especially fine sand, in its own way the larvae makes a conical pit in the sand. It then positions itself at the bottom of the pit with predator jaws opened wide.

Now here's what has to happen … an ant is hurrying and scurrying along the way ants do and accidentally falls into the pit. The unfortunate ant knows instinctively what has happened to it and tries madly to climb the sloping walls to get out. The rascally ant lion down at the bottom of the pit flips his tail and throws sand up on the ant, causing a miniature landslide that makes the ant slide to the bottom.

This is the end of Mr. Ant, for the jaws of the ant lion immediately grabs onto the ant. It injects its victim with a meat tenderizer kind of poison that liquefies the innards of the ant, which is then slurped up by the larvae. Scrub one ant.

We didn't know all this stuff. We just played with them, finding and dropping in wayward ants into the pit just to watch the larvae capture and pull the ant under the sand. We'd get bigger prey, but the ant lion knew when it was overmatched and would leave bigger bugs and grasshoppers alone.

They're really easy to capture. You find yourself a cigar box, fill it half full of sand, then take a tablespoon and scoop up right where the doodle-bug cone is and put that scoop of sand into the cigar box of sand. You'll never fail to catch several of the critters, and within a short time they'd have their cone built in the cigar box. You gotta keep them supplied with ants and a drop of water every three days.

It makes a great science experiment in school. We would do this when I was teaching seventh and eighth grade kids, and they were fascinated by nature's way.

The other bug character I'd like to tell you about is this beautiful critter we called the "Cow Ant" or sometimes "Cow Killer." Remember seeing it crawling along in its aimless way? It was beautiful with its coat of velvety hair of black and orange.

In my salad days of stupidity I reached down and picked one up in my fingers. Bad mistake! I received the most painful sting I have ever gotten. I mean it was agonizing and lasted for several days. Legend had it that the sting, therefore its name, Cow Killer, could kill a cow. Fortunately, not being a cow, I survived the sting, but you can bet that I never repeated that little exercise.

Needless to say, we learned a valuable lesson from my painful encounter with that little rascal and avoided them like the plague from then on. That was **one** critter that we didn't play with, but gave them the right of way. If we were wearing shoes, then we'd squish them. Revenge and retribution … how sweet.

Now I find that the cow ant is really a wasp, so small wonder that it could give you that injection from hell. The male of the species has wings and flies, so it's the female who stays on the ground and does the dirty work. Go figure!

When it came to painful insect stings, however, nothing came remotely close to the evil-looking stinging scorpion. Turn over an old board in a damp place and they will be living there literally by the hundreds. We gave them an extra wide berth in passing.

An even worse horror to avoid was the huge centipede. They grew to a length of a foot or more and were a horrendous greenish-blue color. My dad had a scar on his shoulder which supposedly was made by one of them just crawling across him when sleeping outside. Supposedly the ends of their legs had poison in them.

These centipedes were creatures of nightmares and we were deathly afraid of them.

"Oh, yes," said Harley, "I remember all the members of that little "house of horrors" story. However, I was never … ahem … dumb enough to reach down and try to pick one up. I just supposed everybody knew you didn't pick them up."

"Not funny," stated Harley. "Let's just say it was just another experiment that went wrong. You gotta have a failure every so often."

"Yeah, yeah," said several of the guys, but Harold broke in.

"I really did have a story to tell, but the hour is late and it's getting on to time to be eating lunch." He cleared his throat and said, "Boys, I'll make this one a short one, for if I wait until next week I'll probably forget what I was going to tell."

It's a lesson in stupidity by a bunch of young broncs that almost met their match in an oil field pumper whom they had bedeviled for a long time. In frustration, he felt it was payback time, and it ended up with almost fatal results."

HOW NOT TO MAKE GASOLINE

We were living on the Powell Lease, attending Fairview School in 1933. The Powell Lease was located down the hill west from the Minnehoma Lease. Don't know what oil company owned it.

There were many boys living in the neighborhood, and what one group didn't think to do wrong the other ones did. My older brothers ran mainly with a family of boys who lived about a half-mile away. Among the four of them, they invented the word "ornery" and were a particular nuisance to the oilfield worker called a pumper whose job it was to oversee all of the wells in the area and repair or report anything wrong with the equipment.

This was the same "Gang of Four" who had lured me out onto the old rotten swinging bridge across the Cimarron River that time.

Oil derricks were erected over pumping wells, and sometimes the "casing" had to be pulled to clean out the well. To do this, there was a cable left tied to the well floor and ran up through the crown block, a huge wheel at the top of the derrick, and back down to the floor.

One of their acts of vandalism was to cut the rope holding the cable and pull the cable up and over the crown block and then come crashing back down to the well floor. This made a terrible job for the pumper, for he had to attach the rope to one end of the cable, climb to the top of the derrick, run the rope over the crown block and back down to the well floor, and then pull the heavy cable back to the top.

On this particular day the pumper, who I'll leave unnamed, saw the boys out playing and said, "Hey, boys, how would you like to know how to make gasoline?" Well, this was a commodity that was very expensive at 15 cents a gallon and needed by anyone with an automobile, so they immediately said, "Yeah, yeah, tell us."

The pumper told them to get a 55-gallon steel drum and put in about five gallons of crude oil, being sure to screw the bung-plug in really tight. Put the drum up on rocks and then build a roaring fire under it until it got to boiling. After the oil boiled off, you would have pure distilled gasoline left.

It sounded logical to the boys, so they proceeded to get the entire stuff ready and built up the fire to a good blaze. They were down by the railroad track about a quarter of a mile from each of their homes. They kept the fire going, and it was bubbling away in fine style. What they didn't know was that it was also building up a huge head of pressure.

Mother had sent one of the younger kids to tell her kids to come home to lunch, but like any kid they were too involved and so they procrastinated. After another visit by one of us to tell them to get home, she sent an ultimatum that they knew that had better not ignore. They reluctantly left their refinery, telling their friends they would be back as soon as they ate. The other boys had decided to head home for lunch also, promising to be right back also.

The four of them hadn't gone more than a couple hundred yards toward their home when the overheated barrel went off like a bomb and shot a hundred feet or more in the air. It totally disintegrated the barrel and sprayed burning oil over a large area.

The boys were scared white and rushed to put out the fires before damage could be done. This ended their careers as distillers of crude oil into gasoline, and they gave the pumper a wide berth after that.

The poor old Guardian Angels went home with singed wings on this day

"Can you imagine the lawsuits that would be filed today," spoke up Clyde. "That oil company would never get through paying off the liability judgments for what that pumper did to those boys."

"Yeah," said Jim. "It surely was a different world we lived in back then. People did a lot more bowing and scraping to the big companies, kinda figured they could do no wrong. Of course, those who worked for the oil companies had to remain loyal to them, for they were the ones giving the paycheck, and since the Depression was still bad you were thankful for a job."

"This story here is another one regarding kids and their activities," spoke up Otto. "It wasn't dangerous like that last one and was actually very innocent, but we really got a kick out of it. C'mon, take just a few minutes more before we go."

MY FRIEND, DADDY LONGLEGS

Once again, I'll attempt to string together some words and tell you about one of my little creepy-crawly insect friends. This will be the last one, I promise. How did that oath go we used to make when we were kids? "Cross my heart and hope to die, stick a thousand needles in my eye." Now that was some kind of a powerful oath and not to be trifled with, especially when you put two fingers in front of your lips and spit through them.

Anyway, I'm out of bugs of interest unless I would consider the Black Widow spider, and she's out entirely. Only truck I had with her was when she lurked down below in the old outdoor privy. She was worse than a nest of wasps in the upper corner for speeding up a "go."

God must have been in a really comical mood when he made the Daddy Longlegs, for he is a sight to behold. The Daddy Longlegs is not to be confused with the Harvestman Spider. Granddaddy does have eight legs like a spider, but they all are attached to this one little pill-like body that only has two eyes. Actually he's more related to mites than he is to spiders.

You know the daddy longlegs I'm talking about ... sure you do. Probably seen one lately and even squished it with a fly swatter. They don't make webs, and in reading about them they don't even own a "silk maker." If they are seen in a spider web, it's because they are being used as the first course for lunch.

Old Daddy Longlegs lives in dark places, under logs and such, but will venture into the house in search of food. For defense against being gobbled up by bird predators they give off a really stinky smell when messed with. It's hard to describe it, but it is very distinctive. Only a daddy longlegs smells like that.

We were told that the poison of the daddy longlegs was the most deadly poison in the entire insect world. The only thing that saves the human race from being wiped off the face of the earth by them is that their little old fangs are too small and their jaws too weak to go through human skin. Saints be praised.

We used their knowledge and wisdom in doing our chores as kids. I've told you about having to go after the cows each evening. They were turned out to "open range" during the day and had to be brought back home for the evening milking.

Well, if we were lucky and found us a daddy longlegs before we left on our search, he would tell us where to go. You doubt this? It's a proven fact they can tell you. All you had to do was to get down close to it, avoiding those little fangs, and ask it, "Granddaddy, Granddaddy, which way are the cows?"

Sometimes you had to repeat the request, showing that you must have awakened an older one that had a slight hearing loss. But after repeating yourself a time or two, the granddaddy long legs would **always** lift one of those long spindly legs and nonchalantly wave it in the air.

That would be the direction the cows were located, and so, off we'd go. If we looked long enough in that direction, we'd eventually find them, proving once again that the Granddaddy Longlegs had supernatural powers.

As I got a bit older, I tried him on other questions of a personal nature, and he didn't know "squat." All he could do was point. I lost some faith in him.

"Well," grinned Jim. "Maybe you were just asking too much of the pore little guy. After all, he's not the "Oracle at Delphi."

"Wow, our Jimmy is really stretching our learning this morning," said Cece. "Never figured the Oracle at Delphi would come up in our conversation here at our little coffee klatch."

"Don't ever sell this little group short when it comes to 'l'arning,' whether it be 'book l'arning' or just plain old 'smarts,'" came back Pete. "Since we've all got such a sharp memory, try this story on for size."

ORANGE CRATES AND APPLE BOXES

If you have a good memory of these two items, then you have gotta be kinda like I am … older'n a sedimentary rock! I doubt that anyone under the age of 60 would have had first-hand knowledge of them and their value in enhancing the wealth of a scrounging kid.

When we were kids running the streets and alleys of Drumright looking for discarded treasures, we might, once in a blue moon or so, hit the mother lode and find an orange crate or a prized apple box. In those long ago days grocers got their oranges shipped to them in handsome two-compartment wooden boxes built from sturdy white pine lumber.

Apple boxes were even more prized, for they were made from solid pieces of nice, thin white pine lumber that just begged to be used to make all sorts of neat stuff. An added bonus to getting either of them was the wonderful aroma that stayed with the box for weeks on end. Taking a deep whiff could transport you to a sunny California orange orchard or a Colorado mountain apple orchard.

Competition was fierce to getting one or both of the boxes, and it always helped if you had an "in" with the manager of the grocery store. I remember Sam Whitlock as being more generous than the Safeway Stores. Besides, we "ran a bill" at Whitlock's and that gave us some extra points.

We would carefully take the boxes apart, saving all the nails for future projects. Sometimes a parent or older sibling would confiscate the orange crates. They made great storage boxes when stacked atop each other, and if you were a little short on furniture, they made do for storage shelves.

The orange crate sides were made of lumber that would split easily, and it would make dandy kite sticks. We always made our own kites by making a simple cross or a more complicated one using three sticks, and then we would cover it with newspaper. Remember how we would make paste from flour, water and a little salt? Not the greatest paste in the world, but you most always had the ingredients on hand.

With shallow pockets we had to make do with our home-made kites and string we saved up by scrounging, but by golly, we got 'em made and had lots of fun flying them. Remember how we used to "send messages" up to the kite using a piece of paper? We had to get creative or perish.

Apple box lumber was even thicker and could be used for bigger projects. I can remember making wooden airplanes complete with a carved-out propeller and mounting it on a spike nail for a pivot, and it would turn merrily in the wind.

I always wanted to make one of the action wind toys but never was a good enough craftsman to do it. You know the kind I mean … it might have Maggie hitting Jiggs over the head with a rolling pin as the wind blew.

Of course, birdhouses were always a favorite to build. I have a vague memory of Eula Melott requiring us to build a birdhouse when I was in First Grade at Fairview. Seems that was a requirement for "passing" on to Second Grade. I remember I didn't get it done, and so consequently I was held back in school. Naw, she surely wouldn't have done such a thing, but for some reason I did have to repeat some grade at Tiger with Ms. Grimes and was always a year behind my peers.

"Yeah, Pete, I've talked to lots of people who used those orange crates as furniture in their homes for a long time," said Jim. "They would give them a coat of paint, put a curtain on the front and you had a dandy dressing table for a young girl."

"They were sturdily built and looked great, especially if you stacked a couple of them on top of each other," reported Otto.

Jim came back, "Remember also while we were combing the alleys for 'good stuff' we were on the lookout for any kind of stuff we could sell at the junk dealer's place. Someone told me his first name was Harry."

KIDS SELLING SCRAP METAL

When we were kids, it was a rare occasion to have two coins of spending money to jingle together in our pocket. The same problem existed for many of our peers, and like us the word "allowance" as it related to a weekly stipend from our parents was never mentioned. Wouldn't have done any good.

The need for a little spending money ran the gamut from buying some "horehound" candy or maybe a "Black Cow" to the ability to go to the show on Saturday afternoon. Also, remember those nickel hamburgers and nickel bottles of pop at Gobers up by Third Ward.

Since we were left to our own devices as how to obtain ready cash, our older siblings told us selling junk was a good way. This junk was in the form of scrap metal that could be sold by the pound for cash, and so the hunt would be joined.

Metals we kept our eyes open for were zinc jar caps, any form of aluminum, brass fittings, copper wire and the foil to be found on the inner liner of cigarette packages. We would peel the foil off and add it to a ball of the stuff and watch it grow. We would heft our ball of foil and guess that it must weigh, oh, five or six pounds when it would only be a fraction of that amount. We were the eternal optimists.

The collecting would go on for several weeks, and anywhere or anytime you walked you kept your eyes always on the alert for salable items. Around an oil patch there was always debris left around the plugged wells and the junk piles. These were our gold mines, and we scouted them out quite often. Competition was stiff with all the other kids bent on finding the same type of booty we were, but it was an honorable competition. The item belonged to the first one who saw it, or which one could run the fastest to grab it.

Each of us had our own "stash" of metal, and when we had what we felt was enough we would load the accumulated hoard up in a wagon or carry it in a "gunny sack" and head out for the junk shop located on the north side of Broadway about where Texas Avenue is located.

I remember the old man who ran the shop as being an obese, grumpy old guy, probably from having so many dealings with kids like us. He had told us early on that he only dealt in brass and metal. Therefore, never knowing his name, we just called him "Old Brass and Metal." It was a dirty, dingy little hole in the wall with the floor and shelves littered with debris of all kinds. Out back was a large storage yard with old broken-down cars and other machinery.

We usually let my older sister, Frances, be the spokesperson in dealing with the old grouch, for we had learned earlier she could usually get us a better deal. Being a pretty, curly-haired petite blonde with big blue eyes, she could charm the old goat into a better mood. He always felt that he had to give you a hard time, but would eventually set the various metals on the scale.

This was the time for all of us to collectively hold our breath and hope for a heavy weighing. We were totally at his mercy and, after viewing the scales for what seemed like forever, he would pontifically announce its weight. Then, consulting with his chart of what the various metals were worth, he would tell us what he would give us for it. It wasn't a matter of bartering, for what he offered was what you took, without argument.

It doesn't sound like a lot of money to a present day kid, but if we got a quarter apiece for our effort we considered it a good day. On our way home we would, once again, keep our heads down looking forward to the next sale.

This is off the subject, but do any of you guys remember Wings cigarettes? They offered a picture card in each cigarette pack of a "modern" airplane as a bonus. They were mostly warplanes since WW II was right on the horizon. We had P-38 Fighters, B-26 Mitchell Bombers and the entire line of American warplanes. There were even pictures of the Japanese Zero and German Messerschmitts, the deadly fighters. Whatta you reckon a complete set of those pictures would be worth today?

"That kind of a memory makes you want to put your money deep into your pockets and keep it there," said Pete. "It surely did make us appreciate what we had as we were able to afford more.

"And on that note, I believe it's about time to shut 'er down for another week," concluded Pete. "So we'll see you guys in another week, if the old cow doesn't throw her calf or the crick don't rise."

EIGHTH COFFEE
Holidays and Special Days

Wisps of gritty snow sifted along the snow curtained streets of the town. The few cars in sight were laboring up the steep hill, while those heading down drove cautiously to avoid going into a skid. Remnants of the larger amounts of snow that had fallen earlier still hung on in sheltered nooks and crannies in the alleyways. The wind was blowing strongly enough to stir the Christmas decorations that hung from each lamppost and in the huge arch that spanned the entire street at the brow of the hill just above Pennsylvania Avenue.

Broadway reflected a festive air with the decorations gracing most storefronts on the entire main drag. Most merchants had enthusiastically bought into the mood of the season and it showed in their holiday displays.

In the area adjacent to the Boomtown Café, the sidewalk had been shoveled clear of snow, and a sprinkling of salt covered the area to avoid the possibility of ice forming on the sidewalk with a dropping thermometer. Marvin Cutler, owner of the café, realized the importance of getting his customers in and out of the café in all the safety he could provide.

The cars driven by the ones who had been eating at the café had parked along Ohio Street that ran north of Broadway. Since it was a level street, it was easier to negotiate rather than parking on Broadway and chancing the steeply sloping streets and sidewalks.

It was mid-morning and most of the cars that had parked close to the Boomtown Café were gone with the exception of those of the retired coffee bunch who had begun to gather. Cece and Harold had shared a car, as had Elmer and Pete.

They hurried briskly along the street in the biting cold wind and entered the warm confines of the café rubbing their hands and stamping their feet. Coats were shed and slung over the chair backs as they sat in their spots around the table near the large window at the front of the room.

Ivey Jones, waitress, came to the table and asked the same tired old question, "Well, boys, is it cold enough for you?"

Harold spoke and said, "A-h-h, you know it. With that north wind blowing, it's cold enough to freeze a brass monkey. Gotta keep moving or you'll freeze in your tracks. What do you say to some of the hottest java you can boil up back there, love? I need to thaw out these old bones with about a gallon of it."

"Second the motion," said Cece. "Today's a good day to give us those bottomless cups and just keep the nectar flowing, Ivey."

The same sentiment was echoed around the table as the guys settled in for an hour or so of good cheer and fellowship on a cold, blustery winter morning.

Harold Atkins spoke up from his spot in the group. His hands were wrapped around the warm cup of coffee, and he set it down gingerly as he began to talk. "Guys, since Thanksgiving was just a week or ten days ago, do you realize what is staring us in the face?"

CHRISTMAS IS A'COMING

Remember the Christmas tune that went something like this title? Well, I don't have to hear the music to know what time of year it is. It's a most favorite message and comes across loud and clear, in fact, so much so I can feel it as well. The electric atmosphere is everywhere now that Thanksgiving has passed, and the feelings I personally get are delicious, exhilarating and still exciting after experiencing as many as I have. Thanksgiving is wonderful, but to me it resonates on a little different level than the Christmas season.

We're kinda programmed that the holiday just past is more about blessings, both spiritual and material and the thanks we need to give and our need to share them. With our bunch it's always been a family holiday to join together in love and give thanks.

However, for as long as I can remember I get a warm, fuzzy feeling with Christmas. However, as with so many things the anticipation goes 'way beyond the actual event. Kinda like that saying, "The journey makes the destination worthwhile."

I never grouse and grump about how early the merchants want to put up displays or tout their new and exciting yuletide wares. Christmas is celebrated, observed and experienced on so many different levels of consciousness and this, to me, is just part of the entire season. Sure, I agree that the true meaning of the season should be a year 'round way of living, but that's an individual choice that is made. My personal feeling is that most people come about as close to the mark as they can under their individual circumstances …

Many years ago I heard someone say that it's wonderful to see so many people worshipping on special religious holidays, even if that's the **only** time they ever go. At least they are going on **that** day.

Whups ! I'd better change the way this story is drifting … no politics or religion is to raise its head in this group.

I've always enjoyed November and December for all the myriad sights, sounds and smells. I love getting the tangled strings of lights out and once again scaling the ladder to get them hung on the house … one of the grandsons will do the climbing from now on. I plan to get those blankets of lights and cover all the bushes in the front and perhaps string lights on the dogwood trees. In other words, I'm gonna keep both feet firmly on the sod.

One annual task is to load up the CD cassettes with Christmas music. I chuckle when I think of the evolution of Christmas music. First it was 78 and 33 rpm records. Then came LP's. Next was the big old 8-track cassettes. Smaller cassettes followed these, and now we have come to CD's. I can put six CD's in a holder, lay back and enjoy many, many hours of Christmas music.

I draw the line and will NOT go with DVD's. Don't even own one. Besides, they sound too much like my old BVD underwear. I'll admit we got one for our granddaughter, if you won't tell anyone.

"You got that right, Harold," spoke Jim. "We'd all better be good for someone is 'makin' a list and checkin' it twice.' At our ages it would be fun to be able to do something so we could get our names put on a 'naughty' list."

"But, guys," Jim continued, "speaking of what's coming, I'm sure we all have memories of some special Christmas in our past. Gosh knows we've had enough of them at our age. Sometimes I feel old enough to have made that trip to the original manger with those Wise Men. Since I got the floor first, I'd like to tell

you of one of my earliest Christmas memories and what made it so special.

"Bring that coffeepot over, Ivey and join us. There's not another soul in the restaurant and I don't see the big, mean boss, Marvin. I want to share with you a Christmas that was almost magical. I've never told this story before so hope it comes out right."

A CHRISTMAS STORY

At this glorious time of the year I am reminded of one of the most touching and inspiring events of my boyhood that highlights this wonderful season. As I grew older, it came more into perspective, but at the time was an awe-inspiring event for a seven-year-old.

Christmas of 1933 came as the country was sinking lower into the depths of the Great Depression. Our family was living on a small rented farm in a hilly, wooded area about four miles northeast of Drumright on what we called "Section 14," but was also called Devil's Run from a small creek that ran through the farm (ever wonder why so many places are named after the devil?).

It was a hungry time for our family of eight as we eked out a living on what little tillable land there was on the 60-acre farm. Dad raised and sold some cotton, had a small corn patch for livestock feed and a field of sorghum cane, which was processed into molasses in the late fall. My dad was a pretty fair shot with a rifle, and on many occasions our family meals consisted of rabbit or squirrel. The meals were supplemented with vegetables from Mother's garden, assisted by all the kids who hoed and weeded.

We had transferred from Tiger to Fairview School and were walking about three miles to get there. You've all heard the old cliché about our generation having to walk through snow for miles (uphill both ways). Well, that's what we did. Sure we did …

With Christmas approaching, we shared the excitement of every child who has counted the days and anticipated something a little extra for the holiday. We all knew our situation well enough to know there wouldn't be much in the way of toys. However, we could count on our dad to come through with something that he could make by hand, and Mother was quite innovative.

We attended the little white RLDS church located just east of the Ball Tank between Drumright and Oilton. At Christmas time there was always a religious program followed by a "doin's" where each child received a sack of candy and an orange. The boys usually got French harps as a toy, even though no one could ever figure out how to play a lick on one. About all we accomplished was to slobber around on it, and before long the cheap little thing was rusted out. Naturally, each of the little girls got a doll.

This year was to be different. With most everyone having a difficult time financially, the adults agreed to forego the gifts as there was just wasn't any money in the church's treasury. The program would consist of worship and praise and musical numbers by the kids. We were told that the spirit of Christmas was in the worship service, but this was a pretty tough thing for a bunch of little ones to understand.

I remember one of my brothers reciting a piece that went something like: "What shall I give him, as poor as I am? If I were a shepherd, I'd give him a lamb." It ended by saying, "What shall I give him? … I'll give him my heart."

After the evening services were completed we loaded into our 1928 Star car and headed for home. It had been snowing heavily all evening, and the ground was dusted with white and flakes continued to waft gently down the darkening night sky. It must have been Christmas Eve, for what happened next made it totally magical.

When we walked into the house, it was evident that someone had been there during our absence. Going into the kitchen we found a large dishpan on the table filled to the brim with candy and nuts. Off to one side was a toy for each of the kids. I'll never forget the mystified looks on Mother and Dad's faces, as we all just stood speechless by this wonderful Christmas surprise.

One of my brothers discovered footprints leading out the back door, and following them out in the yard found the tracks of a sled! We just knew who the visitor had been! Though it was hard to believe in miracles during these years, we knew that something very special had happened.

After we calmed down, Mother, with tears in her eyes, explained it to us in a way I've never forgotten: "It could only have been the spirit of Christmas, represented by none other than Santa Claus."

Years later we learned that Santa Claus was actually George Rogers, the owner of our small rented farm. Knowing we would follow his tracks through the snow, he had harnessed two of his horses to his wood sled to make us think that Santa's sleigh had been there. (Amazingly, none of us noticed that the hoof prints were much too large to belong to eight tiny reindeer.)

His wonderful kindness, generosity, and yes, cunning made this Christmas of 1933 a very memorable one for all of us.

Jim received a quiet few moments of silent appreciation as the guys absorbed his touching story. A couple of them even gave him a short handclap of applause. They usually expected some comical story out of Jim, and this one was so out of character for him it was hard for them to take him seriously. However, they could see he was dead serious, and it showed another dimension of their long-time friend.

Following along the lines of Jim's story, several others were moved to tell of similar Christmas happenings of their boyhood, for several of them had lived really close to the poverty line as well. It was a quiet, sober group who listened to each other's tales attentively.

Phil Wiley, who had attended Tiger School, spoke up, "Some of my best memories of Christmas have to do with how we celebrated it at school. Nowadays the public schools have to walk on eggshells concerning religion and Christmas. Not so in the '30s at Tiger school. We had religious themes, Christmas trees, Santa Claus and the whole nine yards and no one ever complained. We always got a good healthy sack of candy along with an apple and an orange, and I don't imagine our teeth were any worse than my grandkids are today."

"Same way at Third Ward," said Pete. "We most always put on a Christmas operetta, and it had religion in it as well as elves, fairies and boogermen. A different world back then, huh?"

After a half-dozen had shared Christmas memories of the close, personal nature as well as school, some being comical as well as serious, Ivey spoke up.

"Boys, I listen to your talk, gossip and your memories most every week. What do you say now to listening to a story from the ladies' viewpoint? You might remember seeing little girls around when you were kids, don't you? Well, that was us. As long as you're talking about holidays, I'd like to tell you a story about old-time Decoration Day."

DECORATION DAY / MEMORIAL DAY

Most of us know the Memorial Day we observe was originally called Decoration Day. A very practical name for it meant exactly what it said. It truly was a day that was used to decorate the graves of those who had fought for our country. Naturally, there is controversy as to who started it, where and when, and many towns take credit. It **is** agreed that it began

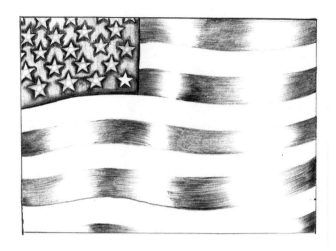

following the Civil War and honored those from both sides who were in the war. It really doesn't matter who started it.

During the Lyndon Johnson administration, the name was officially changed from Decoration Day to Memorial Day and honored the veterans of all wars, not just the Civil War. Now since this was well within the lifetime of many of us, we can be excused if we occasionally slip and call it Decoration Day. It seems much more fitting to call it Memorial Day and use it to remember the veterans of all wars as well as those loved ones who have passed on.

Choosing the month of May to observe this day was logical for many reasons. School was most always dismissed for the summer by the middle of the month. Makes you kinda wonder why the kids go so long nowadays. Apparently the teachers were able to pound enough education into our heads in a shorter number of days than today. Either that or we were just plain not as educated. Who knows? I do know that we were **always** out of school by Decoration Day. Today some of the schools are still holding forth until the middle of June.

The month of May usually meant the end of spring and the coming of summer to the kids. Swimming had usually started at the Devil's Bathtub or other favorite swimming holes. It wasn't too blasted hot yet, and so we looked forward to this holiday with anticipation of another year a'borning. We were eating sheep shower and poke salad and other greens to cleanse our bodies of the winter "humors," whatever they were.

Many folks did the traditional thing and went to the local cemeteries or traveled some distance to decorate the graves of their deceased family and loved ones. Many cemeteries didn't have perpetual care, so this was the time the graves were all cleaned of weeds, flowers planted and the site mounded up.

This was also the time for many family reunions, but like many of the people of Drumright we were kinda newcomers to the area, and few of us had family buried there and fewer still war veterans. The town had only been in existence a little more than 20 years, and the majority of the people living there were ones who had moved in from all points of the compass.

Only place we ever went was to Okfuskee where a grandfather was buried. He'd died in 1932, so we actually didn't go but a time or two. Our extended family, like so many following WW I, had become a fragmented institution. We'd scattered over the face of the United States like a covey of quail, and family ties became rather loose and close relationships became fewer. Many times this was due to the economic need of earning a living, for you moved to where the breadwinner could find work.

Decoration Day was a great excuse to have a picnic at Texas Park or some other good spot. It usually called for a freezer of ice cream along with fried chicken. I felt the people celebrated by eating heartily, being glad they weren't the ones who had died.

"And before I have to go back to work," said Ivey, " I'd like to finish up my little piece, then I'll let you fellahs get back to your 'remembering' times. I mentioned a freezer of ice cream in my story, so let me expand just a little on this topic. How about this little delicacy?"

A FREEZER OF ICE CREAM

Quick, what's the first thing that comes to mind when you hear the brand name, "White Mountain? Wouldn't surprise me much if a bunch of you said, "Ice Cream Freezer." That was the brand name of the wonderful piece of equipment that delivered a mouthwatering treat to us on many a hot summer day. Must have been a heck of a good product. for they still manufacture them in electric models as well as the hand-cranked kind.

Forget Dairy Queen, Braums and all the other soft ice cream places. This was "nectar of the Gods" produced right at home and done by a total family effort ... Our family didn't own a freezer, but our Grandma did, and it was ours to borrow any time we wanted it.

Making ice cream was an occasion that will forever bring memories of sitting on the freezer, licking the paddle, chunks of ice down unsuspecting backs and eating ice cream until we would deliberately get "frozen" headaches. Then rolling and moaning on the ground with the pain.

The decision to make a freezer of cream was not taken lightly. We usually milked an old cow, and Mother would save back enough cream to make the mixture very rich. Now, most every family had their own recipes for making ice cream. Some took eggs and others not. Some used store-bought ingredients, but Mother made 'er from scratch.

One of the first things to do was get a 50-pound block of ice. Dad would take the old family car and drive down to the ice dock at Pat Badger's. The ice dock was north and a bit east of the present location of where the Historical Museum is located today. The ice would be wedged onto the front bumper and covered with a quilt for the drive home. Arriving home the block of ice, rapidly diminishing if it was the middle of summer, was put into a gunnysack, tow sack or burlap bag, whatever it was called.

By this time the cook would have completed the ice cream mixture, and the completed concoction was poured into the gallon freezer bucket and set down into the wooden White Mountain freezer. Had to make sure the cogs meshed so the can would turn freely. Meanwhile, Dad would take a sledge hammer and bash the block of ice into small pieces to fit around the can in the freezer. Some people used the flat side of an ax to break up the ice.

The broken bits of ice were hand-poured into the wooden freezer bucket a little at a time. A layer of ice would go in, followed by a liberal sprinkling of salt. Next came more ice and then more salt until the top of the freezer was reached.

It was a real treat to have chunks of ice to suck on, and naturally we tried to sneak it down people's backs, which always called for retaliation. The family dog had no idea what to think of ice and would let it lie in the grass and lick on it.

Now came the wrangling over who got to turn the crank and who got to sit on top of the freezer. At first the crank would turn easily, and the sitter would have to get up and put more ice in the bucket as it melted.

As time passed, the turning would become more and more difficult as the mixture in the bucket began to firm up. Finally, it would become next to impossible to turn, and it was now time to remove the paddle.

Mother carefully cleaned off the salty ice and removed the lid to the ice cream. She slowly pulled the paddle up, cleaning most of the cream off. We'd already settled who got to lick the paddle, and the winner gave it a thorough washing by tongue and spoon.

The freezer bucket was then re-packed with ice and salt with blankets or rugs on top and left to cure until it was time to eat it.

"Okay, now, Ivey," said Pete. "You got our mouths watering with that story. Home-made ice cream, ummm. Now don't you think you'd better get back and see what kind of slumgullion the proprietor/cook has cooked up for lunch. There's nobody home at my house, so I'm just going to partake of whatever you have that's good to eat."

"Actually," reported Ivey, "you guys didn't notice, but Marvin has hired a full-time cook. He comes well recommended from a friend of Marvin's in Guthrie. He's been cooking in several places down that way. His name is Lefty Wells and swears he has no cooking specialty ... he can cook anything and cook it well."

"Well, rabbit me backwards," said Doc Pringle. "That's a real surprise. The quality of the food here will undoubtedly take a great leap upward, eh?"

"Back to the subject of holidays, let me tell you guys about a memorable Thanksgiving," spoke up the quiet Pete Ledbetter. It won't compare to the one we had recently, but this one is from my far distant past. Can anyone remember 1948?"

A MEMORABLE THANKSGIVING

Thanksgiving 1948 was a Thanksgiving to remember for several reasons. The main one being it was our first one since we were married in June. We were living in a basement apartment in Greeley, Colorado, where I was attending Colorado State College of Education on the G I bill.

We didn't own a car, and as the Thanksgiving holiday loomed, we were both just a tad homesick. We had a brainstorm and decided to invite my roommates from the year before. I had attended Colorado State College of Education while my wife finished Junior College. My former roommates were two brothers from Cripple Creek, Colorado, Dave and Charles Wilkerson, and a full-blood Navajo from Arizona named Keats Begay.

160

Keats, being a Navajo, had been a "Wind Talker" during WW II. Remember these were the men who would use their difficult native language in sending coded messages, for it was almost impossible for the Japs to understand. He'd been captured during the fall of Bataan in the Philippines and had survived the Death March of Bataan and four years of captivity.

Keats had taught me to play the game of cribbage, a favorite card game of mine. He was a "take no prisoners" teacher, and I was taught his brand, which was a cutthroat style. Simply stated, it meant you asked for no quarter and gave none. I had to learn fast or suffer humiliating defeats. I *did* learn to play a mean game.

Although we were living like gophers in a rented basement apartment, we managed to squeeze in the three guys. They really appreciated the invite for a home-cooked meal since they would be alone on campus during Thanksgiving break also.

Our landlady, who lived upstairs, used a floor furnace, which hung down into our basement living room. A week or so earlier some friends from home had visited us. They were sleeping on the floor in the living room when the floor furnace, right above their heads, came on with a roar, spouting flames. The man, probably a war veteran, leaped to his feet yelling, "My God, the house is on fire"…

But back to Thanksgiving dinner. Without a car we walked to our grocery store, located ten long blocks away. Actually, we didn't think anything about the lack of a car, and it was another year before we bought our first one.

With all the anticipation of newlyweds, we bought us a big old bird, and with no experience and little or no instruction but with plenty of enthusiasm and confidence, we proceeded to roast the turkey and make all the fixun's that go with a traditional dinner. Soon the guys arrived and the Thanksgiving spread was placed and ready to eat. All gathered around the small table, and I proceeded to carve the turkey. What a laugh.

I sliced, or rather haggled off a wing, and Keats said that was his favorite piece so he was served. The others of us took pieces and we started our meal. Good conversation went around the table, and my wife's cooking was properly bragged on. I noticed that Keats was gnawing on his wing a long time and offered him some different meat. He declined and continued wrestling with the wing.

Come to find out, the wings apparently didn't get properly cooked and were just as tough as old pieces of rubber. Keats never let on, but even today when my wife thinks of the way he gnawed that wing like an old hound dog, she gets embarrassed.

We still talk about that memorable meal we ate with some transient friends It was neat. Now the turkey is *always* done, even the wings.

"I heard from someone that they had looked Keats up on the Internet and found he was no longer living," continued Pete. "I wasn't too surprised for the Death March and four years of captivity in a Japanese prison camp had taken a terrible toll on Keats, and his body and he was just skin and bones in 1948. I'm sure he must have died young."

"Really neat story, Pete, and one about a true American Hero," opined Joe Bob, the lanky cowboy. "I would bet he was never awarded a medal. I see they have made a movie about the Navajo boys who used their difficult language to provide code. Yeah, they were called Wind Talkers. He must have been a defining influence on you and not just for the game of cribbage."

Jim Kinnamon spoke up, " I believe I got time to spin one more tale, and then it's time to hit for the roundhouse. Now this is going to be a religious tale, so if you want to remove your head covering you may."

No one made a move, so he went on.

OLD TIME BAPTISM

While going through a bunch of old pictures recently, I found one of the Devil's Bathtub that really jingles a memory bell.

It shows a group of people on the rocky ledge on the north side who are observing while the preacher and some assistants are performing a "total immersion" baptism. This was a rite practiced by the church we belonged to. I've mentioned that the church was located just east of the old Ball Tank, but no remains are to be found, neither building nor people. There is a small group that has been meeting in Oilton for many years.

I'd like to think the picture shows a group from my era as a young kid, but it would be wishful thinking, for old-time snapshots aren't very good and even with a reading glass it's guessing as to who's who.

The announcement of the baptism would be made a Sunday or two before the actual day so plans could be made and all would be in readiness. On the given Sunday all families brought a picnic basket, a bushel basket in the case of large families. It would be loaded with cakes, pies, fried chicken, and assorted other goodies. For a Depression hungry bunch of kids, it was "Gastronomical Nirvana."

Sunday services were held, and an appropriate sermon relating to baptism and its meaning was preached. We always seemed to have the most long-winded guys in the universe preaching for us. Our particular church used lay ministers rather than paid ones. To a bunch of hungry kids who were anticipating the basket lunch to come, it was painfully long.

So after a seemingly endless sermon followed by a closing prayer almost as long, we adjourned to the Devil's Bathtub. They may have called it by its other name for this particular service, which was the Giant's Bathtub. Be that as it may, everyone knew where they were going, and by dirt road it was only a few miles. You headed out toward Pat Badger's country place and then took the right hand fork at a Y and followed it south to the farm.

The Matherly family farmed the Devil's Bathtub land. I see the name continues to appear in the *Gusher*, so it must have been an extended family. They were a really nice bunch to permit all those cars and people to come into their farmyard and tromp the few hundred yards to the "Tub" site.

The men folks carried the heavy baskets of food, along with several oilcloths to spread on the ground where the food would be placed. Someone had to mind the gates, for livestock had to be kept in their proper place. We showed respect for the privilege.

At the site there was a fairly level and smooth sandstone area up above and back from the water. This was the place usually used to spread out the oilcloths. The ladies then opened the baskets of food. Potato salad and egg salads had been kept cool on ice, for we knew about salmonella back then even if they might not have known the name.

While this was going on, the boys of most ages were up by the swimming area telling lies. This included their prowess and exploits of "derring-do" in the pool and on the rocks to boys who lived too far away come here to swim. Rocks were thrown into the swimming hole and across the width of the pool to check who could throw the furthest.

When all the food had been spread, one of the ladies let my dad know. He had a piercing whistle that could be heard three counties away, and he would cut loose an ear-splitter. The boys were all at the food before the echo died, and everyone soon gathered around. One of the qualified men in the group offered a blessing on the food. We used to call it "returning thanks." Since it was kinda hard to prolong a food prayer while looking down at plates of delicious fried chicken and other goodies, this prayer didn't last as long.

Even as kids, we knew who the gourmet cooks were and whose food to kinda shy away from, for our mother was a finicky eater and had passed her word around.

In spite of any judgmental eaters, the food area soon looked as if Attila the Hun and crew had passed through. It was pretty well laid barren. Desserts of cakes, pies and cobblers finished everyone off, and everyone had a look of contentment on their faces and settled down for the words of the pastor relating to the purpose of our being there.

After a short sermon and another prayer, the preacher, his assistant deacons and the ones choosing baptism made their way down the rocks at the west end of the Devil's Bathtub. This was the outflow end and was a placid shallow little stream down here. This was an earlier time and all adults were addressed as Brother and Sister.

The head of our flock was a stern-looking gentleman by the name of Brother Pollard. His full name was Benjamin Franklin Pollard, and I remember the boys laughing at B.F. and calling him "Beef" Pollard behind his back … mortality hadn't caught up with us as yet.

Anyway, he would take the arm of the candidate, and together they would walk slowly out into the water. Brother Pollard walked with a staff in his left hand to feel out the bottom or the pool. He didn't want to be surprised by stepping into a chug hole. With his staff, I thought he looked kinda like Moses might have looked trudging across the Sinai Desert leading his flock.

When he and the candidate had reached a depth up to their chests, they stopped and faced the congregation on the north bank. All the people had gathered closer to the edge, but were still 10 or 15 feet above the water. At this time the song leader would lead the congregation in singing a couple of hymns appropriate to the occasion.

It was a rather solemn moment now as the ceremony was ready to take place. The congregation was as quiet as a pin. The minister had a snowy white handkerchief, which he kept in his hand to place over the candidate's nose during immersion. When all was ready, he raised his right hand and repeated the words as required by church doctrine.

He then laid the person back into the water in his right arm with the left hand covering their nose to keep water out. It was over in an instant,

and the person came up out of the water as a new member of the flock. They usually came up spitting and spluttering, but overcame it in a short time. The assisting Deacon was standing close by with a large dry towel so the person could wipe their face.

The song leader now led the congregation in hymns of gladness and joy as the little group made their way slowly back up the steep rocks.

A service was held that evening at church where the new member was confirmed as a member. This was a solemn occasion and usually the entire congregation attended. I just remember, as a young kid, that I had more "church" in one day than I ever wanted. Then we went back on Wednesday night for Prayer Meeting ... wow!

Jim said, "That's all she wrote, fellahs ... keep warm and see you next week."

The men, other than the ones staying for lunch prepared by the new cook, shrugged into their coats, donned their mittens and headed for their cars to a warm lunch.

NINTH COFFEE
Memories Good and Bad

The weather was an abominable mess of lowering clouds, low, moaning wind, and, while none fell at the present there was a sure promise of rain to come. This had been the weather pattern for the past several days and the gloom seemed to settle into the bones of the people, as they appeared to walk furtively along the streets.

Even though it was coming onto 9:00 in the morning the lights shone brightly in the Boomtown Cafe and most other places of business. Also, the streetlights that were set to come on with certain degrees of darkness had turned on. It was, in a word, one miserable, gloomy day.

This was further evidenced by the sparse attendance at the regular Tuesday morning coffee group of the retired guys. Normally by this time an even dozen could be counted, and on this dismal day the total muster was six.

"It's just as well," spoke Doc. "I've got some errands to run and so it won't matter to me if we make this a short session this morning."

"It won't hurt to sit and enjoy a cup or two of coffee before you go running off in the heat of the day, Doc," Jim offered. "A day like this one can sure get long and lonesome, and I sure don't feel like spending it at the house or in the pool hall."

"With this kind of weather a'brewing it sure makes for some stories that are miles apart from the happy memories we normally sit and listen to," said Elmer Butterfield. "Got time to listen to an old guy's meanderings on a doleful morning?"

NASTY ROTTEN APPLES

As you may have gathered, this is going to be a mixed bag of memories, some good and some not so good, but since they were realities in our lives, I'd like to share them with you. When we started talking about the good old days, we knew some of them were not all going to be of the happy, lighthearted kind. I said some of the stories would recall some incidences from our past that could be of the painful variety. We can be thankful for our present economic conditions and hope no one has to relive these times.

It's 1933 and is a hungry time for many of us trying to scrabble out a living as the Great Depression settles in. This would be the era when many Oklahomans were sold off their farms due to mortgages that couldn't be paid. In many instances they headed for California as related in "The Grapes of Wrath." I've often wondered what twist of fate kept our family from making that trek.

We were living on a small sharecropper farm out on Section 14, northeast of Drumright. Dad had small acreages of corn, cotton and sugar cane, none of which could support a family of eight with any degree of abundance, barely subsistence.

The Roosevelt administration was trying desperately to find the answer to the stagnant economy in the country, and in our little corner of the world it became an experiment that really made an impact on me, as a young kid. The scars of that period still remain with many of my generation.

Since the basic "Law of Supply and Demand" determines the price of most commodities, the government decided to reduce the supply of beef cattle. I've no idea what beef cattle were selling for, but it had to have been pitiful. The theory was that the reduced supply would increase the price of the ranchers' remaining cattle.

Agents fanned out over the country, checkbooks in hand, to pay the owners a given price for their beef cattle. I'd have to assume it was a fair price, but was also was a price you couldn't refuse. It was radical surgery for the economy, but the times called for radical measures ... don't mind me, I'm not being political

Accompanying these agents was another crew whose job was to destroy the cattle that were bought to lessen the supply of beef and get the price up. They literally went out in the pastures and ranges and shot the cattle down and let them lay where they fell. Guards were then posted to make sure no one carried off any of the meat.

I'm sure we, along with most other people, knew nothing of the theories of economics, but it was a cinch that **we** couldn't buy the reduced beef supply to raise the prices. We couldn't afford it at the rock bottom price. Yet here we were with dead cattle laying around all over the country, hungry for it, but couldn't touch it.

Several of the men, my dad included, decided this couldn't be tolerated, so a plan was hatched to get some of this beef. With needy family members at home, it meant taking a chance and probably skirting the law a bit, but had to be done.

A bunch of them went out late at night to the killing fields where the cattle lay. Some of the men created a diversion in one quarter, and when the guards went to check the problem, the other men pounced on the recently destroyed cattle and quickly butchered as many as they could handle. It's my guess that many of the guards looked the other way, for they knew and understood the plight the people were in and sympathized.

I have a vivid memory of Dad bouncing down the old rocky road to the farmhouse in our old 1928 Star car with the bloody half of a steer lashed to the roof. It was necessary to get it cut up and put away as soon as possible.

In other parts of the country shiploads of potatoes would have a blue dye poured over them, taken out to sea and dumped in the ocean. It was a contradiction of the times to be destroying edible products when so many in the country were actually going hungry.

We can only hope and pray something like this never happens again ... a happier tale to be told next week ... promise ...

Trivia question ... does anyone remember the name we called the NRA? The Blue Eagle emblem organization ... real name was National Recovery Act. It was called "Nasty, Rotten Apples." It was later declared unconstitutional. I have no idea why.

WE DO OUR PART

"That story does match the weather today," shivered Phil. "There is no question but I surely do remember most of the things you talked about, Elmer.

"It was on a day about like today that our family went through a trauma that could have proven fatal to some of us," Phil continued. "It was early evening on a stormy spring day, and you could almost smell tornado in the air. Dark rolling clouds out of the southwest had shut out the sun, and in the unsettled

weather condition you could feel tension in the air.

As the sailors say, "We kept a weather eye aloft" and were ready to head for the storm cellar at a moment's notice."

A WIND-CHARGER ACCIDENT

This is another happening of the not so nice variety, but I'd like to share it to show some of the bad stuff families survived growing up on the oil field leases in the 1930s. It could have been a major family tragedy

It must have been around 1938 when my dad and mother made a decision to go more modern with household conveniences. The most severe part of the Great Depression was letting up, and Dad was working steady for Sinclair Pipe Line, although it was still work away from home. We had used kerosene lamps, with their feeble glow, and had even bought an Aladdin lamp. They felt we could do even better yet, so they decided to buy one of those new wind-charger machines, make our own electricity and upgrade our standard of living.

They must have scraped up a down payment on one and felt they could swing the monthly installments. What an exciting event it was to the kids. The picture on the carton showed a tall steel tower with a device having a huge propeller on one end and a large tail fin on the opposite end. It stood about 10 feet tall on its tower, which wasn't high enough to catch the wind necessary to generate electricity efficiently.

My dad constructed a wooden tower braced alongside and against the house. The wooden tower stuck up above the roofline and had a wooden platform on top. The idea was to mount the steel tower on top of the wooden tower on the platform, and it would have the necessary height to catch the wind. It was a sturdy tower and with the wind-charger mounted atop, the platform was a magnificent structure in our eyes.

It worked like it was supposed to do, and we soon had a bank of DC storage batteries lined up against the wall in the designated room. There was an ampere indicator that told us how much charge was in the batteries, and we were enjoying our radio and other appliances as the DC voltage was converted to AC. Sure hope no one asks me how it was done, for I just plain don't remember.

Any of you who grew up around Drumright know that the wind does blow … and blow … so it was an ideal way to produce some free electricity with Mother Nature providing the wind. With the tail fin turning the

generator to face the wind, the huge propeller spinning madly, we were ready to
come into the Twentieth Century.

The charger couldn't be left turning all
the time. The DC batteries would get charged
up, and then it was necessary to turn the charger
off. This was done by going out to the wind-
charger and pulling on a chain that was attached
to the propeller and hung down to the ground.
By pulling the chain, it caused the huge blades to
turn up to a horizontal position when the blades
couldn't catch the wind to spin.

This was done when you didn't need any
more electricity and also when a storm was
approaching. With an extra strong wind the
blades would not be able to withstand the
force of the wind, and there was a danger of
it toppling the charger, tower and all. It was
absolutely necessary to keep a weather eye
open, and when the old black clouds
started piling up in the southwest the propeller had to be feathered.

On this particular night, it was after dark, storm clouds gathered and
Dad was working away from home. Along with the wind came a torrent of
rain as Mother and my oldest brother at home went rushing madly outside
to turn the wind-charger to the "off " position.

Unfortunately, they were too late, and as they turned the corner of the
house to pull the chain, a monster wind hit the wind-charger. With the
blades facing the wind, in the turning position, it was like wind hitting a
solid wall. There was just too much force, and the tower and wind-charger
came crashing down.

They were both under the structure when it fell, and not being able to
avoid it, they were struck by pieces of the wooden tower or the steel tower
itself. Rudy got a severe laceration and puncture wound in his shoulder,
and Mother had a terrible cut on her head, which ripped a large piece of
her scalp loose.

All this time it was raining torrents, but it was clear that someone had to do something to help. One of us went to get help from the family next door. The neighbor man came to the house, took charge, and soon the two of them were bundled into his car, and he made a very fast run into Drumright to Dr. Starr.

Both of them carried these scars to the end of their lives, and the windcharger was never put in service again.

"Something like that can scar a kid for life," opined Joe Bob. "To have a bad storm is bad enough and then an accident like that sure puts a strain on a family."

"I see in the news now that huge 'wind farms' are being planned for places with a strong and constant wind source. It's supposed to make a cheaper and cleaner source of electricity for all of us," said Doc.

"Well, they're building them in the right places if they pick the central part of Oklahoma and Kansas. We get more wind for the square inch than most anywhere in the USA," commented Jim.

Pete spoke up, "Long as we're spinning doleful yarns this morning, let me tell you a short story of a sad happening in my young life."

"We've talked about living around some mighty dangerous pieces of equipment on these old oil leases, and so as you could expect every so often some bad accident was bound to happen. This happening was to a dumb animal, but since it was my dog, I was deeply affected by it."

DEATH OF MY DOG

Throughout my boyhood a succession of dogs came and went. Of course, Old Shep was a mainstay and stayed for the longest period of time. But since he was the family dog, everybody owned him, and I wanted one of my very own, as did other siblings. Even with limited means, it seems we could always feed another doggy mouth, although it usually had to be satisfied with whatever food was available.

One brother had a dog of his own and had named her Cottonflower. She was a beautiful mid-sized snow-white female, smart, loving and affectionate. Shep usually just tolerated these interlopers and seemed to know he would outlast them all, which he did.

But back to Cottonflower … one time she came "into heat," and as we didn't want a litter of pups, she had to be isolated from potential lovers. Mother gave orders that she be locked in the outhouse during the nighttime hours for safekeeping.

On this particular night I had need of the outhouse, and slinging my overalls on I went down the hill for the interlude. Arriving there, I sleepily opened the door without thinking and received the shock of my life! No sooner had I opened the door than this white apparition shot out of the door onto me. I liked to died!

It could have been the first instance of a nine-year-old having a fatal heart attack. I was able to call her back to me, and she went back to her place of incarceration like a good doggy.

Several years later I owned a personal dog, which I had given the name of Kazan. I had read the book, "Kazan, the Wolf Dog" by James Oliver Curwood, and so gave my mutt this princely name. He was of an undetermined breed and definitely not wolf, but neither of us cared, we were good buddies. We were inseparable, and I loved him greatly.

Not having running water in the house, we had to take our water buckets and go to the water well the oil company had drilled for common use. Many of us living in the lease houses drank the water that smelled strongly of rotten eggs showing a high concentration of sulfur.

On this occasion I grabbed two water buckets, and with Kazan at my heels I headed down the lane about 100 yards to the water well. A rod line from the powerhouse located a quarter of a mile away powered the water well, and it slowly and rhythmically raised and lowered the pump jack to bring up the water.

On the down stroke the pump jack went all the way to the ground and then rose up a couple of feet on the upstroke. This left an interval of time and space between the up and down strokes when the area under the jack was open.

During the night a hapless possum had wandered under the jack, and not realizing its danger, the rodent was caught on the down stroke and squashed flat. Giving little thought to the dead possum I went on about my job of drawing my buckets of water.

Suddenly I glanced back at the animal and was horrified to see that Kazan, like any other dog, was interested in the smell of a dead animal. He went over to the pump jack, and while it was on the upstroke decided to investigate this interesting situation and give it a smell. It all took place within a heartbeat of time and I was frozen to the spot.

I screamed at him, but before he could obey the slowly moving pump jack ponderously lowered onto Kazan's head as he was intent on getting a better whiff of the animal. Needless to say, his head, being completely under the huge and unforgiving piece of machinery, he died instantly.

I ran to the house screaming, leaving the water buckets and poured out my grief to Mother. She was most sympathetic and had the older ones go with me to bring Kazan back to the house where we gave him a decent and proper burial … I even made a tombstone for him … a very traumatic experience for a young kid.

"What a freakish thing to happen," said Otto who had come in during the first part of the story.

"I think you'd agree with me," Doc sagely said. "As kids we really had to learn to understand life in all its realities and that death was just another one of the final things to come."

Jim spoke up, "I don't know if you'd want to classify this story as a good or bad memory. I'm sure, at the time it happened it was considered a bad thing, but in looking back it's one of those happenings you chuckle about. Time does have a way of softening some of the harsher things in life."

EARLY DAY DELINQUENTS

This story is about an older brother and concerns some shenanigans he and some of his friends pulled as teen-agers in Drumright. I believe you'll agree with me that it deserves telling since it shows that "the more things change, the more they become the same," especially as it relates to "ornery" boys in Drumright.

He was with the class of 1939 but didn't make it to graduation since he had joined the Army in 1936 at age 16.

From the earliest days, it had been the tradition or custom for each incoming freshman class at Drumright High School to paint their year of graduation on the water tower. This structure was located up by the sheriff's office, not far from Second Ward School.

Undoubtedly it was a custom that was frowned on by the establishment, parents and school officials. Superintendent Frank Hess had issued dire warnings and consequences to any participant. All these threats served to make it even more of an absolute necessity to get your class name splashed onto the side of the structure, but there was an extra "coup" scored if your class was the first and highest one to be listed.

It was a scary venture to scramble up to where the ladder could be reached and then climb on up to the catwalk that encircled the tower. It was no place for one with a "fear of heights" (whatever that phobia is). Climbing was hampered somewhat, for the "artists" had to carry up buckets of black paint along with brushes to smear on the paint. It then called for standing on the safety rail to reach as high as possible to be the top class on the side of the tower.

The daredevil brother felt it was only right that they should not just be listed on the tower, but should be the first ones in the school year represented. He looked for several friends to aid and abet and found eager cohorts in three stalwarts.

Picking a night in August with a bright moon, the group gathered the paint, brushes and met at the base of the water tower at a late hour to carry out the job. Climbing up to the ladder and going on up to the catwalk was a "piece of cake" to this bunch, for all four had cut their teeth climbing oil derricks.

However, as with most wrongdoers, they apparently made a few small, simple and damning mistakes. They didn't reckon on the amount of light from the moon and the neighbors who had heard their noisy ascent and notified the police.

Within a short time the group was pinpointed like bugs by the powerful searchlights on the police car of Chief Jack Ary and his deputy, Babe Carnahan, who ordered them down. Incidentally, Babe was a lawman who really put the fear in them. It hadn't been too long since he reportedly had shot and killed a prisoner.

The four boys were ordered to climb down immediately and to bring all their supplies and gear with them. It was a severely chastened bunch that took a lot of time in climbing down to step into the waiting "arms of the law."

The boys were taken to the police station and given a real scare of what could happen to them. Chief Ary then started trying to get in touch with their parents by phone. Only one of the four boys had a telephone at home, and the sheriff called the home. Luckily for the boys, this father was home and agreed to come to the sheriff's office. He came in to town, and after lots of conversation with the lawmen the boys were released into his custody.

There was no disciplinary action taken by the police except for some very stern admonitions as to what happens to "bad" boys and warnings against trying such a thing again. They got their 15 minutes of notoriety from the students in the high school, but some black marks from the school officials.

The Rest of the Story: I don't know if the Freshman Class of 1935 was ever represented on the water tower, but if it was, these four boys didn't take part.

Harold spoke up with a grin, "Believe it or not, I remember that happening. Those guys were treated like celebrities, but at the same time you couldn't be seen with them for being tainted by association."

I believe your brother quit school shortly after that little dust up and joined the Army at the tender age of 16," said Pete.

"Speaking of which, I'd like to add that the largest single event in our young lives was World War II," continued Pete. "We lived, breathed and ate this event for most of our formative years, and many of us eventually took part in the event itself in different degrees of service."

"Not living around here, I had a somewhat different experience," spoke up Clyde.

MEMORIES OF WORLD WAR II

We recently went to see the movie "Pearl Harbor." We had been sent tickets for Father's Day, so we went to a matinee showing … the first time we'd gone to a show in at least 20 years! … I wouldn't lie to you.

In my opinion, the story line was factually correct as to the events leading up to and including the actual attack. It had to have a love story to use as a vehicle to carry the entire movie along; otherwise it would have just been a documentary. Little bit far-fetched, but love usually is.

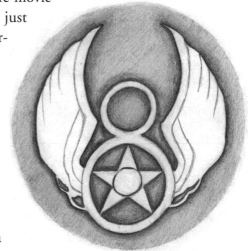

Many of you were old enough to have served in the some branch of the Armed Forces. I would also assume that a lot of you my age and younger made up the Home Front, and therein lies this tale.

As teen-agers growing up during the early 1940s, we had a

really difficult time fitting into the wartime society. We were too young to go to war, and yet we had a lot of living and growing up to do. Several have written commenting on scrap drives, Victory Gardens, Savings Bond Stamps and other efforts we used to defeat the "dastardly Japs."

We saved grease from cooking, observed "meatless Tuesday," peeled foil from cigarette packages, donated aluminum pots and pans and did without chocolate, sugar and many other food items.

Remember this little ditty? "Lucky Strike green has gone to war … yes, Lucky Strike green has gone to war." The cigarettes had been packaged in an ugly olive green package for years. They used the war to change the color to white. Also … remember Spike Jones and the song, "Heil … pfft, Heil … pfft, right in the fuhrer's face."

How about the guys using the Bugler machine to roll their cigarettes? My dad would take an evening and spend several hours rolling his supply of cigarettes. It was an ingenious little machine, for you could put the loose tobacco in one section, make sure there was a gummed cigarette paper in its proper place. With one deft movement the sucker turned out a professional cigarette.

Remember the rationing of tires for your car? How about the "Not Over 35 Club?" Many pledged that they wouldn't drive any faster than 35 mph to save rubber and gasoline.

On an out-of-town trip, try slowing your speed down to 35 miles per hour and driving at that speed for 10 miles or so, and you'll see what our dads had to endure for several years. We had a sticker in the lower left hand part of the front windshield that announced, "Thirty-Five MPH Club."

When my older brother went into the service in 1942, he left his 1936 Ford in my capable (?) hands. The tires were bald, and "boots" had to be inserted inside the casing to give a few more miles of wear out of them. If you had a really good tire "carcass," it was possible to have it re-treaded. You couldn't go top speed with a re-tread, but they beat nothing.

I remember loading the Ford with three or four buddies and heading out for the next town. We could always count on several flats. We got better than an Indy 500 pit crew at fixing a flat. Each one of us had his assigned duty, and we could have the old Ford back on the road in jig time.

The teen male had a strange place in wartime society. We were kids and yet were called on at times to do men's work. It seemed our relationship and hope for some "affairs de amore" was always clouded by the "other man." He was usually a handsome serviceman, always several years older. Dressed in his classy-looking uniforms, he made us look like war orphans. I remember the heartbreak I went through when my "main squeeze," Madeline, told me her heart belonged to a Navy man who she was waiting for. She married him.

How did that old wartime ditty go? "They're either too young or too old … they're either too hot or too cold"… or something like that … that was us.

It's no wonder so many of the young males would leave school and join the service as soon as they were old enough. I'm guessing, but I believe at least a dozen of my male classmates went missing during our senior year. I turned 18 in October of my senior year and made myself available for the draft immediately.

My closest buddies were all joining the Navy, but I knew that I got too seasick for that branch of the service. In January 1945 I was drafted out of high school, refusing a deferment, and was off to fight the war. Like all the rest of the guys, I was off to save the world for democracy or to fight the war to end all wars. What we didn't know was that the war was practically over, but few knew it. Germany surrendered in April and the Japanese in August.

In a burst of patriotic fervor the Superintendent of Schools said he would award me my high school diploma early … actually I was ornery as dirt and he wanted to make sure I didn't have to come back to finish high school.

At the war's end my folks had three blue star flags hanging in their window and one Gold star flag for their sons who were in the service. My older brother paid the ultimate price and the Gold Star belonged to him.

"I don't believe any of us were old enough to go enlist in any branch of the service the day Pearl Harbor was bombed, with the exception of Faye," said Harold. "We grew up and became old enough during the early 1940s, however, and I believe most every one of us served our country."

Harley spoke up to say, "That didn't keep us from being involved with all the love ballads that musicians were singing. Seems we matured earlier and had a serious sweet young thing on the string in high school. Remember some of those teary-eyed love songs you heard on the radio?"

MISTY-EYED LOVE BALLADS OF WWII

These memories could stretch out over several hours, but I'll try to hold them down to a decent time. If you share this with a younger person and they aren't familiar with a tune, you might take them to some friend who has an old 78-rpm platter of the song and perhaps a wind-up Victrola. They would get to hear them like we did.

Speaking of playing them together brings back memories of the juke boxes we all remember so well. You could play a song for a nickel, so with not much money you could play and dance all evening.

I think we should start off with a 1940 hit tune. This was about the time the government instituted the military draft, and those men who were called up were drafted to serve a one-year hitch. As the guys left to serve their year, the songwriters came up with "I'll Be Back in a Year, Little Darling." This is where fate jumped in with hob-nailed boots.

A few months later the Japs bombed Pearl Harbor and all bets were off. The one year's service ended up being " duration and six months," and for some guys this meant as much as five years away from home.

As more guys left their sweethearts waiting at home, the songwriters had a field day with romantic ballads to cheer and hold onto while you and your beloved were separated. Most every guy and gal had a special song to remember and hold onto with tender love along with many tears. It was "their" song to cherish.

The songs echoed the sentiments of the lovers, and who could forget "I'll Be Seeing You"? It told of all the commonplace scenes where the loved one could be seen.

Then there was "It's Been a Long, Long Time," telling of the long waits with only letters and V-mail correspondence to hold onto. The singer would croon "Kiss me once, and kiss me twice, and kiss me once again, it's been a long, long time."

Ah, yes, children ... we seniors were once young and filled with passionate love as the young always are. It was just a long time ago. We sang "My Dreams Are Getting Better," which said in part, "Well, whatta you know, she smiled at me in my dreams last night."

The list goes on and on ... "Lili Marlene"; "Till the End of Time"; "Symphony"; "No Can Do"; "Harbor Lights"; "I Dream of You" (more than you dream I do), "Deep Purple." On the lighter side we had songs such as "Don't Sit Under the Apple Tree" (with anyone else but me).

It seemed these songwriters could say the words you always wish you could have said when you were holding your beloved. My favorite was "I Can't Begin to Tell You."

As the war was winding down, we sang, "The White Cliffs of Dover," which told of the hope for the war's end and a brave new world when we all got back home.

This was the Big Band Era with bandleaders of note and huge orchestras to play the dreamy music for each of the tunes. All the ones mentioned, as well as most others, were dance tunes, and nothing could stir the emotions like holding your sweetheart tightly and slow dancing to the music listening to the band's vocalist crooning your special song.

During the long dreary days of fighting and monotonous waiting and watching, the love ballads of World War II were one of the greatest morale builders going for the troops on assignment scattered around the globe.

You could almost hear the long, drawn out sighs of love and contentment as the old guys' thoughts slipped back to a time when the green sap flowed in their veins and love was an emotion to be held and cherished.

"Next," continued Harold, " I'd like to spend some time on the 'fighting songs' of World War II of which there were many. They, too, were very important, not only to the soldiers, sailors, marines and air force men and women, but the civilian population needed the morale building boost as well."

FIGHTING SONGS OF WWII

The love ballads we sung were a very important ingredient in life's mixture to give us hope and courage in order to fight the five-year-long war against the Axis powers. The general population, or the Home Front, as they were called, also needed some rallying songs to listen to and sing along with as they worked long hours to ensure the extra production needed to supply the armies around the world.

I kept a scrapbook of newspaper items pasted from the *Tulsa Daily* paper and even tried writing a history of the war. I remember a young aviator who was pictured on the front page shortly after the attack on Pearl Harbor. He had shot down two Japanese planes, and underneath his picture was the caption: "Oklahoma – 2 … Japan – 0." We needed that.

Shortly afterwards a popular song came out called "Johnny Got A Zero." It told of an ornery kid in school who got zeros for grades, only now he was in the United States Air Corps and was shooting down Japanese Zero fighters. The song told of how proud we were of him for "getting a Zero."

Spike Jones and his City Slickers were well known for playing parodies on good long-haired classical music. However, for the occasion of producing a morale booster, they came up with a real "put-down" song on old Adolph Hitler. It was called "In the Fuhrer's Face," and the chorus would sing out lustily, "Heil, Phftt … Heil, Phftt … right in the Fuhrer's Face." We really spit in his mug.

As the war ground slowly on and losses mounted in the Air Corps while bombing Germany, the songwriters came up with a bittersweet song called "Coming in on a Wing and a Prayer." It told of a large bomber that had taken some bad hits but was still able to limp across the English Channel and get back to its home airfield due to some strong praying and a tough airplane.

Meanwhile on the Home Front as the work force became increasingly female, we had a little ditty called "Rosie, The Riveter," for these dear ladies practically won the home front war by pulling on long pants and doing what had been thought of as "man's work." Not so, we found out and the world hasn't been the same since.

Over in the Pacific the story went of an Army chaplain who helped load guns during a vital battle. This led to a song called, "Praise the Lord and Pass the Ammunition." True or not, it made a good fighting song and boosted morale.

I'll just name a few more, and you'll possibly remember them and others. How about "Goodbye, Mama, I'm Off to Yokohama?" "This is the G.I. Jive" for the dance crowd. The Home Front heard, "Milkman, Keep Those Bottles Quiet." (They actually delivered milk in glass quart bottles.)

Irving Berlin came up with a big musical called "This Is the Army" (Mr. Jones) that was filled with tunes to be sung and remembered. Then there was the little cutesy one called, "Bell Bottom Trousers, Coat of Navy Blue." (She loved a sailor boy, and he loved her, too.)

On the Country Western side there was "Filipino Baby" and another one called "There's a Star Spangled Banner Waving Somewhere."

We sang, "Let's Remember Pearl Harbor" with gusto as the answer to "Remember the Alamo" in another war. Then the Army Air Corps song,

"Off We Go, Into the Wild Blue Yonder" was sung by school male chorus groups. I was in the Boys Quartet, and we really belted it out. We got to sing "helluva roar" legally.

"Yeah," glumly noted Joe Bob, "our lives were pretty much controlled and shaped by that event."

With a break in his voice, Hank Blackwelder spoke, "I had two of my very best friends from Pleasant Hill School killed on the same day in the D-Day landings on June 6, 1944. They were a year or two older than I, but we grew up in the same neighborhood and spent many hours playing together. I still miss them and know they would have made a fine contribution had they got to live their lives to the fullest."

"An awful happening and one we never seem to be able to stay away from for more than a generation. Seems each new crop of kids sees a lot of adventure and fun in the old war stories they hear, but the reality is much different as we all know." Doc Roy delivered this little bit of philosophy.

Jim Kinnamon spoke up, "I can see we all gotta get on our horses and get on out of here, but I'd like to leave us in a little bit brighter mood by telling this story of how some of us earned money just before the war started. Does it ring any bells with any of you?"

ADULTS SELLING SCRAP IRON

Remember when someone told about kids collecting and selling junk to the old guy on East Broadway to pick up some small change to go to the show or otherwise jingle around in the pocket? It was penny-ante stuff compared to what some adult men sold to make some serious money.

In the latter stages of the 1930s war was looming ominously on the horizon and Japan was buying every pound of scrap iron it could in preparation for a war it knew it would be waging against the U.S. very soon. American businessmen were cooperating with them and were paying $20 a ton for iron and shipping it to Japan for a handsome profit.

No thought was given that very soon the iron would be returned to us in the form of shot, shell, tanks and bombs, for the country was still in the grips of the depression, and it didn't take very much iron to make a ton with a much needed payoff. Fortunately FDR clamped an embargo on the sale of iron to Japan, but not before millions of tons had been shipped.

The old oil leases proved to be a gold mine for the iron seekers. The oil companies had been most wasteful in leaving old machines, broken pieces of equipment and metals of all description just laying around for the taking. It didn't take long for the men to go around the countryside like a bunch of vultures gathering up anything salable. Soon the countryside was picked clean.

The plugged oil wells, abandoned equipment and even the cement-filled counterweights were broken apart with sledgehammers and the iron loaded up and hauled to the junkyards. Very soon it became harder to find a load of abandoned scrap iron just laying around, and before long some guys began looking to the company scrap heaps belonging to Tidal Refinery and other places who frowned on the taking of the material ... it was flat-out illegal.

My older brother, who was working for a dollar a day and was one of the junkers on his own time, reports that if you took a load of this variety to one particular junkyard the lady in charge would ask a question, "How warm is it?" This was interpreted as meaning, "Is it stolen?" but she wouldn't be that blunt.

If you said its temperature was fairly high, she would have you haul the load to the back of the junkyard and pile a lot of other chunks of iron on top of it. It would remain there, out of sight and hard to get to, until it was loaded up and taken to the railroad to be shipped. Some oil companies did make visits to the junkyards to see if some important piece of equipment might be found there

The polish rod" that the pump jack pushed up and down into the well was made of a solid brass alloy, weighed a goodly bit and was worth much more, so they were considered a prime find. One of the more difficult pieces of scrap to acquire was the old wire rope or cable. As the oil company finished with it, the cable was just left lying on the ground. After a season or two it would become buried in the dirt and hard to spot.

When the guys would find an end sticking up through the dirt, they would start pulling it up out of the ground. This was a backbreaking, difficult job, for it would wind off through the woods, tangled up with roots, and you really earned your pounds of iron with the cable. The old wire rope was usually rusted and had lots of "wickers" to tear into your hands. Gloves? Couldn't afford them.

You gotta remember that times were tough during this period. No one should even think of passing judgment on the activities that took place. Circumstances put a different slant on lots of actions ... many of these same guys went off to fight in World War II within a short time ... some didn't return ...

As was his usual farewell, Elmer left by saying, "Boys, it's been a little bit of heaven here this morning, but we'd better get on out of here before we get blown away with a tornado. I'll see you next week."

TENTH COFFEE
Food and Preparation

"Would you look at the heat waves bouncing off the car roofs out there,"
said Harley. "This is one hot day, I want you to know. Sure is a good day to be
in Marvin's nice air-conditioned restaurant. I almost stayed home and then
decided I needed to get out and about and revive the old brain cells."

"Yeah, I'll bet you could fry an egg on the sidewalk," replied Clyde Branson.
"I saw a news item on TV that down in Oklahoma City someone actually did
that very thing. I'm sure it was a TV publicity stunt, but it shows how hot it's
been."

"Faye, how have you been surviving this heat wave," Henry, better known
as Hank, asked the oldest member of the group.

Lafayette "Faye" Bucklin was truly a living, walking monument on the
streets of Drumright. He had arrived in town immediately after Wheeler No. 1
came in as the first gusher in the oil patch. In most discussions concerning early
day history or actual oil drilling, the men deferred to him as a final authority.

"Well," rumbled the gravely voice of Faye, "you just learn to take her as
she comes, boys. Now I'm not going to tell you how hot it used to be, for today
is about as hot as I want. I'm just glad I'm not out there rough necking on
some oil rig platform. I could do her as a young bronc, but my rough necking
days are over."

Desultory conversation went on as the men relaxed and enjoyed each other's
company. Most of them had switched to iced tea in deference to the heat and
humidity, and Ivey kept the cold tea coming with lots of ice cubes and sugar.

Phil spoke to the group, "We had us a watermelon last night, and it was
one mighty fine treat. I think it was a Black Diamond melon, although I
really don't know or care. I just want them to have lots of red, sweet meat. I
talked Helen into us making some preserves out of the rind. I told her I'd help
this afternoon.

"This was one of my favorite delicacies my folks used to make, and I had some mouth-watering dreams of preserves with hot biscuits. I don't know how you old boys fix them, but here's how we do it. I've had the recipe from my mother from many years ago and it still works."

WATERMELON RIND PRESERVES

All this hot summer weather that brings cookouts, picnics and other great food events calls to mind a delicacy from far back in the mists of time. It may be something that you still enjoy, but I only have it in my memory. I may want your recipe, if I can talk my wife into cooking them.

The other day I was finishing my lunch with a large slice of cold watermelon as dessert when the thought came to me, "What ever happened to watermelon rind preserves?" Now, I'm not talking about the "cheap immytations," as Lil' Abner used to say, but the mouth-watering, firm pieces of honest-to-goodness preserves that used to be made from scratch from a freshly eaten watermelon.

I knew we had a recipe for making them somewhere, for my mother had written down how to do it several years before she passed on. My wife went to her recipe file, and after some digging we found the original one she had written out for us.

It called for the selection of a melon that has reached just the right stage of ripeness, and this is, in itself, an art. Most experts use the middle finger thump as the best detector, while others swear by the condition of the "pig tail" on the end. Others will bend down and use the "smell method" of giving a sniff of the outside of the rind in several places. Most amateurs just take potluck and carry one to the checkout stand and take their chances.

Unfortunately, the grocery stores frown on the absolutely sure-fire method of plugging the melon with a large knife. A triangular cut is made and the sample pulled out, and with a visual and a taste test you can't go wrong … it's either good or it isn't.

Of course, in my humble opinion, the eating of a watermelon should only take place when the outdoor temperature is around the 100-degree mark. With modern transportation and marketing they can be bought most any time of the year. I just never could get excited about a watermelon from Peru, South America in the middle of winter … seems to be un-American … or something.

But back to the preserves … after the melon has been enjoyed by all

 and the seed spittin' contest has been held, there's usually a large pile of rinds for disposal. It becomes raw material for some very tasty eating and saves wear and tear on the garbage disposal.

It's necessary to cut the desired rinds into long strips about one inch wide. The outside green rind is pared off generously, leaving a thick portion of the white meat with just a tinge of the red melon clinging to the inner side for appearance sake. These strips are cut into one-inch cubes and placed in a large stew pan.

This next part of the process takes quite some time, for the cubes have to be boiled until they are tenderized. Now the proper consistency for the cubes is to be firm but not crunchy, at least for my taste. When you have them the way you want them, it's time to add the sugar mixture that has already been made.

This takes a lot of sugar, and when combined with water becomes the base for the final cooking. After draining off the excess water, the sugar water is poured over the melon cubes and put on a low fire. Somewhere along about now certain spices are added.

Once again, it's necessary to let this cook and blend the sweet mixture into the cooked cubes. As the translucent cubes take on a golden color, they have arrived at the peak of perfection and are removed from the fire and let cool.

After the cooling, the golden globes of goodness can be "canned" into pint jars and stored in the cellar for future eating. They go great as a side dish with the meal or can be eaten as companion to some hot biscuits and butter. Um-m-m — good !

Watermelon rind pickles can also be made, but for my taste they don't compare with preserves ... see you after supper ...

"I don't believe anyone makes them anymore," said Phil, "and that's really our loss. Man, the way you described how you go about making them makes me almost be able to taste them."

Hank spoke up and said, "Since my family came from a long line of German kinfolks, that wasn't one of our ethnic dishes. However, I've eaten them many a time, and they are just as good as Phil describes them.

"But now getting up close and personal with some good old German food, let me tell you about one of our family dishes that's been handed down from 'way back there. It was pretty much a tradition in our family. I can remember my grandma Blackwelder cooking this dish. In fact, it was usually what we ate on New Year's Day to bring us good luck."

SAUERKRAUT AND PIGS' KNUCKLES

With that lead-in I've probably got your mouth watering for a big old plateful of some real down-home, country eating. This is a traditional New Year's Day meal and is an older tradition then eating black-eyed peas. So, "Good Luck," fill your plate and dig in.

Sauerkraut was made in late summer, when the heads of cabbage were at their best. It was canned in quart jars and stored in the cellar to become the essence of heaven in taste. The pig knuckles came from the hog butchering that was just completed, and everyone knows these two delicacies go together like Pat and Mike …

It was probably made several different ways, but this is how I remember watching mother make it. Since we came from a long line of Germanic stock, sauerkraut was "in our genes."

When the cabbage heads were at their prime, they were picked and sliced in half. This let you check them out for cabbageworms and also to give it a good wash. In the meantime, the big kraut cutter was sharpened and cleaned to shred the cabbage finely. This was one dangerous booger, for it had a mean blade on it that could take off some meat if not careful.

The one doing the cutting would take a half head of cabbage with the core removed. The head was then pushed firmly back and forth over the cutter whose diagonal blade had been raised to the height needed for shredded cabbage. As the shredding was done, the head got smaller and your hand got closer and closer to that unforgiving blade. At this point you pushed the cabbage through the sharp blade with just the palm holding onto the cabbage for safety sake. A pusher could also be used.

The cutter had been laid across a large container, and when enough cabbage had been shredded it was time to make the kraut. We had several five-gallon stone crocks that were used for the curing.

The cabbage was salted, packed firmly into the five-gallon crocks, adding a minimum of water and some vinegar. Some of you may have had the kid with the smallest feet stomping the cabbage down, but we didn't allow that part. We knew where those feet had trod. Dad or Mother used their hands and a large wooden masher. It was packed firmly until the cabbage was about six inches from the top.

A cloth was placed on top of the cabbage, and a fitted board was turned upside down on the cloth. On top of the board would be placed a heavy weight. It needed to have a lot of constant pressure on it. That stuff got wild as it fermented and gases built up. During the curing process the kraut needed daily attention to remove the scum as it formed.

At room temperature it took about two weeks for the cabbage to become sauerkraut, and it was sampled often to see if it had enough bite to the taste. The smell was so good, and we could look forward to lots of good eating with wieners, mashed potatoes … and, yes, even some pig knuckles.

Another thing I just remembered was the heart or core of the cabbage head would be removed whole, and it was put into the stone jar of fermenting cabbage. When it was pronounced to be sauerkraut, the hearts could be fished out and eaten raw. They tasted like pickles.

For anyone curious about the nutritional good of sauerkraut, I went to my favorite search engine on the net, Google.com. The information said that raw cabbage is a great source for Vitamin C, but when made into kraut it loses about half its value. However, sauerkraut becomes a valuable source of Vitamin K, whatever that does for you. I'm not into health and nutrition, but always wanting to give you the big picture, I thought I'd throw that in. Vitamin K might be important … for something.

With pig knuckles it can become prime eating.

"I believe I'll pass on the pig knuckles, if it's all the same to you, Hank," Doc spoke up. *"I know how they are prized in that German community down in Fredericksburg, Texas, but I guess I don't care for all that gristle in them and also just can't get over seeing that dirty old pig pen where they walked around."*

"Aw, c'mon Doc," said Elmer, *"look at how filthy the old chicken is and what it eats. I don't see you laying off of any platters of fried chicken, now, do I?"*

"First thing you know, you guys are going to make me hungry enough to stay for dinner here today," said Joe Bob. *"I get kinda tired of doing my own cooking at home, and eating out is a real treat for me."*

"You guys remember how we used to get together with our girlfriends and make candy at home?" asked Harley. "When we could afford the sugar, we'd have us a real time dating our girls and stirring up some tasty candy for the sweet tooth."

MAKING TAFFY AND FUDGE

With Christmas creeping closer each day, it just might be possible to squeeze the budget a bit, buy some extra sugar and make some taffy and fudge. Now **that** was exciting news to hear. Some women were famous for their mouth-watering fudge while others were bragged upon for their peanut clusters, tasty taffy or divinity.

Since fudge called for nuts, as an optional choice we used black walnut meats, for we'd saved a bushel or two from the trees right after it frosted. Naturally, we had to compete with the squirrels for them, but in a good year there were plenty for all. With the husks cleaned off them, it was a small matter to crack a large bunch of them. We owned a large anvil, and with a claw hammer we'd crack up a gallon or two. It was a wise move to be most careful of the finger and thumb that held the nut. It was easy to lose a fingernail.

We didn't own fancy pickers, so we'd take a twelve-penny nail and pound the end of it flat on the anvil. And we truly did have a fun time sitting around picking out nutmeats as a family … and sneaking a large piece of nutmeat that just happened to fall onto the floor. Couldn't use a dirty piece, could we?

Meanwhile the chief candy maker would be putting all the ingredients together and cooking the fudge. This was the tricky part, and as it got close to being done it was necessary to get a small amount of cold water and drop in a small bit of the cooking fudge. If it made the proper ball dropped into the water, it was done.

All that was left in the process was to pour in the nuts and beat vigorously. This was the key part, knowing how long to beat the candy. I believe you stopped when the candy had lost its sheen and became dull. It was then ready to pour out and spread into a squared, buttered pan and leave until it had time to set up. Remember the clamor by the kids to be the one to scrape the pan. Cut into squares, this fudge was a creamy, luscious treat and had to be well hidden to have any left at Christmas time.

Taffy was candy that was more long-lasting than fudge. A batch would last a good while, for it was sucked on, making it a kid's favorite. On the down side it also could pull out a filling or loose tooth. Making taffy presented a great many thrilling prospects for the older boy and girl crowd due to the exciting possibilities a "taffy pull" offered.

After the mess of taffy was cooked the required amount of time, a small amount of it was taken and dropped into water until it formed a ball of a certain consistency. When the expert on taffy making said it was done, it was taken from the fire and beat vigorously for a goodly bit of time until it cooled. Now came the exciting part.

When the candy was cool enough to handle, it was "pulled." A mass about the size of your two fists was taken, and you and the object of your affection would stretch it out between you several times. This meant pulling it out, squashing it back together and pulling it out again. When the candy was brought back together, you took the opportunity to give your sweetie a kiss before pulling it back out. This was not in the recipe, just ingenuity and opportunism.

When it had been pulled enough, the candy was let cool in long ropes. It was then broken into convenient-sized pieces. You mean it doesn't sound romantic? … well, maybe you had to be there …

"Well," declared Otto, "I suppose we had to make do with a lot simpler stuff but, by golly, we had lots of clean fun while doing those simple things like that. Lots of good solid marriages were hatched in doing the homey type things rather than having to always be on the run in cars."

Food in various forms was discussed at length with each one extolling the virtues of his particular food. One in particular was poke salad, almost an ethnic dish for the guys who grew up in Oklahoma in the 1930s.

Hank Blackwelder then contributed his personal story of the gathering, preparing and cooking of poke salad.

POKE SALAD AND OTHER GREENS

Springtime in our neck of the woods brought us some mighty fine prime eating that supplemented the winter diets that normally graced our table at mealtimes. In the early springtime of the year we would go on walking expeditions to the woods to gather messes of edible stuff that nature provided.

We would go to the woods and down in the well-watered places and start looking. Mother could spot shoots of "poke" growing in abundance and would point them out to us. She had many years of experience searching it out and would quickly fill her paper sack with it. The plant was a purplish little shoot just coming out of the ground. It was best picked when young and tender and could be nipped off at the ground before it started leafing out.

Why it was called salad was always a mystery to me, for we didn't eat it raw as a salad, but rather boiled it in a pan of water until it was tender. It was best cooked in the black pot with a chunk of "fat-back" thrown in to give it flavor. It was supposedly chock-full of iron and other good stuff and with a pan of cornbread on the side made for a tasty meal.

I really don't know why I'm lying to good friends, for to tell the whole dog-gone truth ... I really didn't care one bit for the stuff. However, since there weren't a whole bunch of choices I ate it. I'd always have to drown it in vinegar to kill the taste ... and I loved the cornbread. Even as an adult my taste didn't change, for now that it's my choice, I won't touch the stuff ... won't eat mustard greens and barely tolerate spinach.

Along with the poke salad we also ate an assortment of other of nature's bounties. My parents, being old Arkansawyers, were in tune with nature. So we did the bit of eating lambs quarter, a plant called dock-weed and other stuff you were probably better off not knowing the names of. Frankly, when you threw them all into the old cook pot they all tasted the same anyway.

Some folks that we knew of also ate dandelion greens, but I don't remember eating them. Some even made dandelion wine, although that was a total mystery to me. At the present time my neighbor to the south, who doesn't spray for his dandelions, has enough of them to break the famine in Africa.

We did know of the little plant called sheep-shower. It was kinda like a four-leaf clover and had a sharp piquant taste. We loved eating the leaves and also the flower of the plant. We learned early on to examine the underside of the leaf, for there could be a deposit of tiny little yellow insect eggs attached to the leaf. We didn't allow as how we needed the protein to supplement our diet.

My older brothers took a shot of making sheep-shower wine. A great mass of the little leaves had to be gathered, washed kinda quickly and boiled in a pot. It would be necessary for them to acquire some of our precious sugar and maybe some yeast was added to the mixture. After boiling for a time, the entire mess was bottled in fruit jars. It was supposed to be strained when the final product was ready for drinking.

For some strange reason it was required that the fruit jar be buried in the ground. Naturally, the fermentation of the stuff required a lot longer time than the boys were willing to give. Like any good winemaker they felt the need to take a small taste quite frequently … starting with the second day … just to check the quality.

When the small amount that survived the sampling period was finally pronounced as ready, we would sit around sipping the rotgut. We postured and lied telling each other how swell it tasted when it was actually like drinking swill. An image just had to be projected by the male of the species. They wanted to maintain their macho image and not look like some wimp who had fallen off the turnip truck just that day.

Disclaimer: Since I wouldn't want this to be a recipe for kids nowadays I have left out the most important ingredient. I sure don't want to be accused of giving them wrong ideas or be a bad influence on the morals of our youth (wink-wink).

"Well, Hank, the truth finally comes out that you were actually an early day bootlegger," teased Jim. "I'm surprised that old Jack Ary or Babe Carnahan didn't thrown you in the clink."

"Nah," continued Hank, "you know we were an ornery bunch and we all had a go at that sheep-shower wine, either making it or at least drinking a gulp or two."

Like a bunch of professional sommeliers, the group discussed at length the various products used in wine-making. Some remembered watermelon wine being made using copious amounts of watermelon juice. It was also remembered as being a sort of a liquid dynamite in a bottle.

Dandelion wine was a better recognized commodity. Others told of making wine from the possum grape in the fall of the year. This was pronounced as being the smoothest and best-tasting of all the wines. Jim told the group that 1937 was supposedly a good year for possum grape wine. Naturally he was hooted at and called a disreputable vintner.

Phil Wiley, who had been rather quiet most of the morning, now spoke up, "Boys, when I see how hot it gets and the way we have to have our air conditioning it reminds me of when we were young and had never heard the word air conditioning. The Tower Theater was advertised as being 'water cooled,' but that was a ways from being cool.

The reason I mention it is that it would be on a day just like this one that my mom would be doing chores in a hot kitchen with the wood stove going full blast. This was the time for putting stuff away for the winter. It was time to get out the pressure cooker and do some canning.

THE DEADLY OLD PRESSURE COOKER

All of the people with green thumbs are keeping busy and enjoying all the "truck" from their gardens … weather has been cooperative, and so green beans, peas and other good eating has made the work worthwhile. Now, me, I'd rather cultivate friends with gardens than do one myself. A gardener always has too much and will usually share his abundance rather than see it go to waste.

Not the same story, though, when we depended on the garden to give us a wide variety of veggies during the hungry times. As for hoeing … hey, there wasn't a choice given to us.

Once the bounty started coming from the garden, we really ate high on the hog with English peas and little new potatoes in a cream sauce being a favorite. Okra came a little later, but was a prime side dish, fried or boiled. The good thing about okra is that once it starts producing it has to be cut off every other day or it gets too big. Also it continues producing until the first frost. I still love it. Wait, though, this tale is about how we took care of all the extra stuff, so I reckon I'd better get on with it.

From generations back women had always "canned" the garden stuff, and Mother was no exception … we had come into ownership or borrowed a huge, monstrosity of an aluminum pressure cooker. It was used to cook, pressurize and preserve beans, potatoes, beets, tomatoes and most other good things that would go to the cellar to get us through a long winter.

Problem was, these pressure cookers had a horrible reputation. We'd heard stories of the pressure building up, the sucker exploding like a bomb, wiping out the entire workforce in the kitchen … which was us!

Job number one was to get some Mason, Ball or Kerr fruit jars, wash and sterilize them like medical instruments in the operating room. They had be jars that had no cracks or nicks in the top of the jar so it would form a perfect seal while in the cooker. I remember us using zinc lids with a rubber ring and also jar caps with a flat lid with a built-in rubber seal.

When the stuff to be canned was ready, it was poured into the jars, the lids securely screwed on and then all placed carefully into the pressure cooker, not letting them touch each other. There were a bunch of screw-down hangers that were tightened, and the cooker was placed onto the stove and a steady, even fire kept going.

Before long the pressure in the cooker rose and the inside pressure of the cooker showed on a dial on top. I assume there were directions as to how much pressure was to be used, and we warily watched the hand creep up toward the red line. Remembering the explosion stories, I always like to have an excuse to go outside.

The handbook that came with the pressure cooker gave the length of time to pressurize most anything you chose to can, so there was actually little reason to have any fear.

When the cooker had been at pressure the required amount of time, it was removed from the fire and the pressure was let go down gradually to room temperature. This took quite a while as we readied the next batch to put into the cooker. Since it was summertime, the job was a really hot experience. The fire kept the kitchen like a boiler room, and no fans were owned to cool off. Just drink lots of water and use a fan to keep cool.

The luscious-looking jars of fruit and vegetables were allowed to cool to room temperature overnight and were then taken to the cellar and placed on the shelves. They were inspected at a later date, and if any bubbles had formed in the jar, the contents were pitched because of the danger of food poisoning. We didn't know the word botulism.

Many years later, as a young married couple, we were using a pressure pan to cook cracked wheat cereal for breakfast. It had a heavy, weighted cap over the vent that jiggled and let off steam pressure as the contents cooked. On one occasion the cooking wheat got into the escape vent and the pressure couldn't release. As too much pressure built up, the "soft plug" safety device on the lid blew out and spewed cooked cereal all over the ceiling and walls of the kitchen. What a mess … it stuck like glue.

So my worst fears of a cooker exploding finally came true.

"I vaguely remember hearing of a lady and her daughter who were burned fatally by a pressure cooker exploding up near Pemeta one time," said Cece. "So you see, it wasn't just your imagination. It actually could and did happen.

"All of you know I went to Pleasant Hill School and lived out on an oil lease east of town," continued Cece. "Well, we had a cow and a hog pen not too far from the house, and we kept an old sow and her spring litter of pigs.

"As the litter matured, Dad sold off some of them for cash money, and then we began to fatten the remainder so they would be ready for butchering when it got cold. We bought corn for them and fed them bran that had fermented, and in general we got the yearlings as fat as they could be. Little did they know the purpose and continued to eat to their hearts' content.

Finally the day arrived when it was considered cold enough for the meat to keep without refrigeration. This was a real holiday in the family and yet a day of intense, hard labor. We all had to work together like a well-oiled machine to butcher the hogs."

BUTCHERING HOGS

When the crispy, cool days of fall arrived, it was time to get with the job of preparing the winter supply of meat. This meant the exciting job of butchering one or more hogs to feed our large family. It demanded the cooperative effort of the entire family and was an event that took advance planning and much preparation. Dad had become proficient at the task and led his troops like a general going into battle.

In the summer it was determined which hogs would be the likely ones to be slaughtered. To ensure their suitable size and delectability, they were penned up separately for many weeks prior to the event. The selected porkers were fed a diet of corn and bran mash to increase weight and kept off acorns and other foods that would detract from the taste of the meat.

By the time October rolled around and frost was in the air, the chosen pigs were living plump and contented in their pen, little realizing their fate. I recall the breeds, Chester Whites, Hampshire and Durocs, and I'm sure others may be remembered.

Prior to **"The Day"** the slaughtering grounds were prepared. A 55-gallon metal drum was partially buried in the ground at a 45-degree angle. The purpose of the drum was the scalding tank for the hog. The black wash kettle was filled and a roaring fire built under it to bring the water to a brisk boil.

A strong, low platform about two feet tall and five feet long was erected. The purpose of this was to lay the carcass on in order to scrape the hair off. Adjacent to the scalding barrel and near the platform, a pulley was secured onto a stout limb of a tree and a rope attached through a pulley.

When all was ready, Dad would stroll to the hog pen and start talking quietly to the chosen hog. The pig might be fed a little slop in his trough and be grunting contentedly with all this attention. Dad, carrying a 10-pound sledge hammer, waited patiently, and when the right moment came he stunned the pig with a tremendous blow to its forehead.

The stunned animal would drop to its knees, and the next operation was critical. Dad would straddle the hog from the rear, reach around and sever the jugular vein with a mighty swipe of a very sharp butcher knife. The next few minutes were a blur of activities that had to be done in haste and yet done right. The animal had to be allowed to lay on the low platform long enough to "bleed out." This meant allowing all the blood out of its system so none would remain in the meat. This could cause spoilage.

While bleeding out, the tendons in the back legs of the hog were exposed, and into the tendons of the legs the hooks located at each end of a "single tree" were attached. This was a farm implement used for many purposes, and in this instance it was used to hold the hog's rear legs apart, and the rope from the pulley was attached to the single tree at its center. This enabled the strong guys to hoist the carcass up and into the barrel where the scalding water would have been poured.

The animal was "sloshed" up and down in the barrel of scalding water for a bit in order for the hair and bristle to loosen up. Scalding time was critical, for too long or too short was bad news.

Mr. Hog was then hoisted out of the barrel and swung back over to the low platform where the next task was to remove all the hair and bristle. All joined in grabbing hands full of hair, rapidly denuding the animal. Scrapers were used by the more able workers who completely cleaned the animal. When it was determined that all the hair was removed, water would be poured over the pig and a stiff bristle brush used to clean the animal completely.

The rope was heaved on and the carcass pulled up to a working height for the next operation, which was removing the "innards" of the hog, to complete the initial phase.

Cece then sipped on a glass of iced tea, wetting his whistle so he could continue with his story of hog butchering ...

MORE HOG BUTCHERING

With the carcass' legs spread wide with the single tree, Dad would then make the initial incision down the belly from crotch to head. Widening the cut, he would tie off the colon to eliminate any contamination and to ensure cleanliness in further work.

When the incision was totally finished, a stick would be inserted cross-wise in the ribcage to enable easy access in holding the sides apart in order to remove the entrails. This was done with care to ensure no accidental cuts to spoil the meat.

The innards were caught in a tub and taken off to one side. There, someone else would remove the liver and kidneys and other edible meats. After the excess fat was removed, which would be used at a later time, the entrails were carried off to be consumed by the dogs or buried. Even us "poor folks" drew the line at eating chitlins. The bladder might be saved, for it could be made into a halfway decent ball to play with ... honest we did, at least until it dried and cracked.

Next in order would be the removal of the head, which would be set aside and attended to by someone else in cutting it up into the usable parts ... we also didn't do snoots, ears, tails or pig's feet. We **did** have our standards! Much water would be used in sluicing down the inside of the hog to ensure cleanliness as the work progressed.

The carcass would then be allowed to "cool out" to make the meat cut up easier. Sometimes it was even left hanging overnight, in which event someone would have to stand guard to make sure no wild animals or the family dogs came around.

Next morning, Dad would take a saw and sharp ax and separate the carcass into halves at the backbone. This made the next operation, which was cutting the meat up into the various pieces, a more manageable job.

The halves would be laid on a higher table to make the job of cutting the hog up easier. Dad would take a freshly sharpened knife and cut out hams, ribs, bacon and various other cuts. While cutting out these pieces, he would trim them of excess fat and other meat, which would be saved for the making of the family staple, sausage. Some of the fat was set aside for the making of lye soap, which was a job for Mother at a later date.

We would always hope there would be some of the luscious tenderloin saved to have a feast on. This happened occasionally, but most of the time it was ground up and mixed with fatty meat and other less desirable pieces to make leaner sausage. We could always count on having fresh liver and/or kidneys for supper that night.

In due time the hams and bacon were trimmed and hung in the smokehouse to cure out and absorb the hickory smoke and ensure their keeping. The head would be trimmed of anything edible, and on occasions Mother would make "souse" or "head cheese," but it wasn't anyone's favorite.

At this point everything but the squeal would have been processed, and now came the making of the sausage. Anyone who has ever made sausage has his own recipe for the mixture of the various spices to make its distinctive flavor and taste. Just the exact measurements of sage, cumin, pepper and other favorite spices combined to make it a savory delicacy. All the pieces of meat would be ground in a hand-turned meat grinder and then mixed thoroughly with all the spices.

When the mixture was complete, the sausage would be formed into patties, fried partially done, placed in a ceramic crock in layer of grease and then stored in the cellar for future eating.

"Yeah, I know some people are turned off by hearing the basic facts of how we get fed," said the old retired vet, "Doc" Pringle. "They just have to realize that the food we eat doesn't come neatly packaged in plastic wrap and placed on the grocery store shelves. This food of ours can sometimes have a bloody trail leading to the guy who eats it."

"Let me tell you of something else that comes to the table with lots of hours of labor expended to get it there," said Harold Atkins. "We lived on this little old sharecropper farm, and my dad had one of the few sorghum mills in the county. We only lived on this farm for a couple of years, but I still remember vividly the making of sorghum molasses. It was an absolutely fascinating

experience for a little kid of about six years of age and I got to help … just a little bit."

MAKING SORGHUM MOLASSES

This wasn't a commonplace activity, and some of you may never have had the fun of taking part in it or even seeing it done. I'm talking about the old method of using a sorghum cane mill to help in making of a final product called molasses.

After the first hard frost in the fall the sugar cane would have reached its peak of perfection and was ready for harvesting. The older boys went to the cane field with 18-inch-long, sharp cane knives and cut each stalk down at ground level. It would then be gathered in bundles, tied together and stood up into a shock, first stripping off the leaves.

Soon after the horse-drawn wagon would be driven through the field, and the shocks of cane would be piled on the high-sided wagon and taken to the barnyard, and the making of the molasses would be ready to begin.

We had a sorghum mill, and my dad was a pretty fair country sorghum maker. He had lived near Jim Beavers, his father-in-law, some years earlier down near Okfuskee, Oklahoma. Grandpa Jim was the acknowledged "Sorghum Making King" of Okfuskee County, so Dad had been taught well by a master of his craft.

A sorghum mill has three large iron rollers in the center section, standing vertically and abutting each other. This made it so when the stalks of juice filled cane were fed into the rollers it would be squashed flat, squeezing out all the juices which were funneled into wooden barrels below.

These rollers were turned by a system of gears with the power being furnished by a horse harnessed to a 20-foot-long gin-pole. The animal patiently walked in a circle round the mill, slowly turning the gears that turned the rollers. Kinda like a one-horsepower machine. As a little guy I sometimes got to ride the horse … what fun …

The juices were poured into a long cooking pan about 12 feet long and six inches deep. To cook the juices into sorghum, it was necessary to have controlled wood fires burning under the pans. It couldn't get too hot or it would scorch the juice, and if too cold it would mess up the entire mixture.

The cooking trough was divided into compartments, and after the cooking in one compartment a wooden gate was opened to let the juices flow on into the next compartment for further cooking.

Each "Cooker Dad," as the guy in charge was called, had his own recipe for producing the final product, and the length of time the juices were cooked in each compartment depended on his feel for the process. Sulfur was added to the juices at some point, and the cooking juices had to be skimmed often to rid the syrup of the foam, which formed as it cooked.

This foam was quite tasty and also really sticky, so we kept it pretty well licked up until we got sick of it. What we didn't lick up was fed to the hogs, who loved it.

When the Cooker Dad felt the syrup was the proper consistency, color and taste, it would be drained out of the last cooking pan into gallon buckets. His reputation depended on a batch that was neither too thin nor thick. Above all, it couldn't have a burned taste from overcooking. A professional sorghum maker made most of his decisions by intuition and feeling.

Several farmers in the area would bring their cane to our mill to have my dad make their molasses. His pay consisted of taking a small portion of the syrup for his expertise and labor. It was always a festive time when neighbors came with their cane and kids.

The cane that had the justices squeezed out was piled on the ground and would later become fodder for the animals on the farm. Since the work was done during the warm Indian summer days of fall, there was always a large swarm of honeybees around the cane pile sucking up the juices from the pile. This led to some painful bee stings when we would contest them for the cane that had yet to be put into the mill.

Who remembers striping off the outer layer of a cane stalk and chomping on the inner goodness of pulp? … chew up a mouthful and then spit out the husks. Teachers frowned on the activity, and many's the licking given for getting caught chewing it in school.

"Yeah, when I was a kid going to school at Fairview," reported Harold, "I remember the boys who lived way east always carried a lot of those cane stalk sections."

"This was usually right after the break we took from school to pick cotton," continued Harold …

"You gotta be kidding," said Clyde. "You mean you actually got dismissed from school to pick cotton?"

"You bet your last dollar, we did," said Harold. "When cotton is ready, you got to get in and get it out of the field ASAP, and this meant all available hands would be necessary to get it done. One good hard fall rain could ruin the entire crop of cotton. School was dismissed for about two weeks right at peak time."

"But back to the cane sticks," reiterated Harold … "These boys would make some dandy trades for the sweet stuff. You just had to eat it during recess and at noon hour. You didn't provoke authority by taking it into the classroom, for there was nowhere to spit the pulp, and you sure didn't dare to swallow it"

"Talking about the fall of the year, did any of your folks ever make any of that dish of green beans and field corn called succotash," queried Hank? "My folks were big on it, and Mom always canned up lots and lots of jars of it. It went well with bread and butter pickles or some piccalilli or chow-chow, whichever you called it."

"Oh, yes," chorused several of the guys. "It was supposedly an ethnic Indian dish, but I don't know if they ever ate it or not, I know us old pale-faces sure did."

DISHING UP HOMINY AND SUCCOTASH

According to historical lore, the Indians taught the Colonists how to make hominy from dried field corn and succotash from green corn and different kind of beans. If the truth be known and the Indians would have had any idea that these rascally palefaces were bent on stealing all their land, they might not have been so generous.

Since there was little or no refrigeration the old-timers had to have some way of saving the fruits and veggies for a long hard winter. Most usually this meant that lots of the produce was dried. It would be stored away and used when the cold winds blew. All that had to be done was add water to the dried produce and it was an edible. At a later date much of it was canned and stored in the storm cellar.

From the dried preservation of corn the early day people learned to make a food that many of you may remember eating. It is called hominy and made from dried field corn. It was a long process and called for some know-how.

We made hominy while living on Section 14 northeast of Drumright. We were living on a 60-acre sharecropper farm and raised a little field corn along with some bottomland cotton, a few hogs and other livestock. When the corn had matured in the late fall, it was pulled, shucked and hung in the barn until time to use it. Some was used to feed the livestock and the better ears set aside to make hominy. It was usually made from yellow corn, although white corn could be used.

Once again the trusty standby, the useful black wash pot was a vital part of the process. It was filled with water and a fire built under it. It was necessary that lye be mixed into the water where the shelled corn was boiled. This was so when the corn was cooked for a certain period of time the outer husk of the corn which was not eaten would come off.

These old-timers knew that if you didn't have any lye you could produce the same thing with oak wood ashes. The cold, dry ashes were sifted through screen wire and then mixed with water. This produced a caustic solution like lye. I really don't have a clue how this is possible, but it really was done.

The corn was boiled over a hot fire for a long period of time until the grains were tender. When the husks would come off, the individual grains the corn were poured out into cool water in tubs and rinsed. It was important to get all the lye water off, so several rinsings were necessary. As this rinsing was being done, the husks also came off so that all that was left was the finished product of tender boiled hominy.

To be perfectly honest, I never thought the stuff had much taste unless you slathered it with butter, and then it was passably eatable. 'Course you are all familiar with another product of corn. This would be the grits that are usually found on restaurant menus the further south you go. My wife, from Iowa, learned to like them … if she could sprinkle some sugar on them and add milk … kinda like a hot breakfast cereal.

As most of you know, the word succotash is an old Algonquin Indian word which, when translated, means, "We know this stuff isn't any good, but we oughta be able to palm it off on these dumb palefaces." I'm kidding … it isn't so bad.

"Succotash is a mighty fine meal with any or all of those condiments you mentioned," opined Joe Bob. "I believe we preferred white field corn to yellow in making succotash, but in hominy we preferred the yellow variety because it just looks more appetizing.

I'm fixing to tell you of something else my mother made for the table that hasn't been equaled to this day. That's cottage cheese. I don't why the dairy processors can't come up with a recipe that will come a little closer to the taste we used to have in it. The big old curds today have no taste at all.

THE BEST COTTAGE CHEESE — EVER

Yeah, I know what you're thinking … how can anyone get excited about this stuff? It doesn't do anything … just lays there on a bed of lettuce with maybe a few sliced peaches on top hoping to add a little color to the meal. What **you're** thinking of is that wimpy stuff you buy at the supermarket, and what I'm talking about is that lip-smacking, honest-to-goodness taste delight that used to be made at home.

The store-bought stuff, with its tasteless blobs of rubbery curds and watery whey, is so bad that I'm not surprised that the Muffit kid and the spider **both** ran away … can't say that I blame them. On that subject, whatta you reckon a tuffit was, anyway?

But getting back to the cottage cheese … as with most of the old-time recipes there are about as many variations of it as there were cooks. I'll remember with you the way my folks made it and leave it there.

You started with skimmed milk, which would qualify for low fat today. It was let set until it clabbered or turned to heavy curd. At that point the curds were poured into a cast iron pot and brought to a high heat, but not to the boiling stage. This kinda served to homogenize the milk. It was then let cool down to room temperature, and now some active buttermilk was added to the mixture and let stand.

This was to introduce some fermentation to the process or some such thing. These old-timers didn't understand the whys of all the things they did … they just did them because … that was just the way it had been taught to them.

After it had been heated to the desired temperature for the amount of time needed, the mixture was once again removed from the fire. The curds were poured into a stone crock and covered with a cloth. It was let cool to room temperature and set overnight so the fermentation process would get active.

The next morning the curds were ladled out of the stone crock into cloth bags, about three-fourths full. I remember them as being salt or sugar sacks. In the earlier day they were both bought in 10-pound cloth bags that came in handy for many jobs. The sack was then fastened securely at the top, and you had a bag of curds.

Now comes the part I remember most vividly. My mother would then take the sack or sacks of curds in the cloth bags out to the clothesline and tie them securely to the wire line. The sacks of curds were then left hanging to have all the whey drain and drip out of the mixture. I have no idea how long they were left to drain, but while they were draining the younger kids had the job of keeping the flies off the sacks. When it was judged to have all the whey drained from it, the mixture was brought into the kitchen and emptied into clean bowls.

The cottage cheese had a sharp, piquant taste, and the finished product had a mealy texture. Since it had fermented somewhat in the hot sun during the draining process, there was a distinctive taste to it. It was also moist only and not the consistency of the store-bought product today.

If anyone did want it to be more moist, all that had to be done was add a little milk to the cottage cheese, but the moist, mealy variety is the one that I remember with fond memories of having a great taste. Some folks liked to sprinkle it liberally with black pepper. It was especially good with baked potatoes … makes me hungry …

"Durned if we didn't get off on nothing but food today," said old Faye. "Are you guys trying to starve me to death? You knew I'm on a diet to reclaim my girlish figure, didn't you?"

"You old buzzard," snapped Jim, "You could work on it for 16 years and never even come close to your old figure, girlish or boyish. You might as well

accept what you see in the mirror for that's what you're stuck with."

"Whoa, now, Jimmy Boy," said Faye. "I reckon you could give me a lesson or two in shedding some pounds. When you say something to me about my wanting to lose weight, it's kinda like the pot calling the kettle black."

"You know I was kidding, Faye," replied Jim. "I've enjoyed putting on every extra pound I carry around. One of the ways they get added is by eating deep-fried fruit pies ... let me tell you."

A STACK OF FRIED PIES

Step right up to one of the most delicious desserts that ever graced a table. Remember how they used to be made? The cook would fry them in a cast iron skillet, and they would be laid on a platter, two pies to a layer. Shoot, they would be stacked a foot high — but they sure wouldn't last long. They disappeared like the proverbial "stack of hotcakes."

Fried pies were made from a variety of dried fruits. You could choose from apricot, peach and apple, which were the fruits of choice I remember best. I think my all-time favorite pies were made from dried apricots. They had a tart bite to them and yet were deliciously sweet. Peaches were a close second, with apple coming in last. Back in the days when we didn't know any better, we ate lots of foods that were fried in pure lard.

We didn't realize we were taking part in such an unhealthy diet, for these pies were deep fried until they reached a beautiful, crispy golden brown. When you bit into a golden delight, the crust crunched and the warm fruit would squish out around the bite and maybe down onto your chin ... Nirvana!

Since we lived a rather self-subsisting life, we had to dry our own fruit for it was dearly expensive at the grocery store. Apples, peaches or apricots were picked or bought from an orchard and prepared at home. They would be cleaned, peeled and sliced thinly to make them ready for the drying process.

When the fruit slices were all ready, they were taken to the washhouse for drying. Clean dishtowels were spread on the tin roof and the fruit slices distributed evenly in one layer. This was done in the bright, hot sun, and the fruit would be left outside during the daylight hours and taken in at night. It dried hour after hour for several days until most all the moisture was sucked right out of it.

This made for a small health problem, for as the fruit dried it was an enticement to flies. I'll give you one guess who was responsible for keeping the flies off the drying fruit. We younger kids worked cheaply … how about nothing …. and, oh, but it got boring fanning the flies off the drying fruit. It was possible to sample some of the drying fruit occasionally.

After the fruit was sufficiently dried, it was stored away until the special occasion came about when fried pies would be made. The dough used was the same kind used to make biscuits. It was rolled out fairly thin and then cut into a round shape. The fruit would be cooked in water and then was ladled onto the dough shape. It was then folded over and pinched shut and was ready for the Dutch oven or cast iron skillet of lard.

With a family of six hungry kids, a huge stack of pies could disappear in short order. If, in the unlikely event any were left over, there was nothing better than leftover fried pies washed down with a cold glass of milk.

Years later my wife tried making them using the dough of canned biscuits and using dried apricots that came in a cellophane bag from the store. It was a good try but seems to have missed something in the making. Maybe it was because she wouldn't use lard to fry them in. She refused and used some kind of vegetable oil we had on the shelf. The effort was appreciated, anyway.

I was invited over to a lady's home recently to sample her mother's fried pies. She was an Okie from a 'way back and solved the deep grease or lard way of cooking the pies. She made them as usual, but when it came time to cook them, she put them on a flat cookie sheet and baked them in the oven. They were equally as good.

"Like the old saying goes," philosophized Jim, " 'you can't go home.' The same thing is true of recapturing the smell, feel and taste of the old-time fruit pies … it just can't be done, so maybe that other saying is appropriate, 'Don't cry because it's gone; smile because it happened.'

"I really feel that's one of the reasons we like to come here every week and dig up old bones and chew around on them. I think most of us have few regrets for what happened and have lots of things to smile about for what did happen. That's why it's so great to sit with a bunch of friends who shared in pretty much the same things we all did and tell stories."

"Since it's about time to leave for lunch, I'd like to close today out by a story of how we lived close to nature in many ways," spoke up Phil. "We've talked about eating poke and other things, but that only scratched the surface of the bounty old Mother Nature had for us."

SHARING NATURE'S GOODIES

Along about the time school started, we started thinking about Thanksgiving and Christmas coming soon and the extra special, scrumptious meals to be eaten. We seemed to look forward to it more for our normal fare was pretty simple … lots of beans and 'taters.

Mother would gather up the kids, and we would head to the woods to do some "nutting" to get some of the bounty to spice up the cakes and pies. Dead ripe persimmons were mashed up and used to make some very tasty persimmon bread … kinda like pumpkin bread. We always knew where the best groves of trees were and soon had a good supply of them. 'Course a good old 'simmon fight always took place. Ever been hit with an overripe one that splatters good?

If there were pawpaws in the area, I never knew it. I saw my first pawpaws to my knowledge along the Caney River when we moved to Kansas. Now, there is a deadly missile when it's overripe. They tasted similar to a banana but were way too sweet. They weren't favored.

Earlier in the season we always knew where to find some tart-tasting sand hill plums that cooked up into a great jelly and/or jam. This was canned in pint jars and stored in the storm cellar to be smeared onto hot biscuits and lightbread.

In our walks through the woods we would stop off at a stand of red haws and eat some … remember red haws? They had a tarty taste and had a huge seed in them and didn't have much meat, but we still liked them. All manners of birds loved them. Then along the creek bank we came to a bunch of black haws that were also pretty much all seed. Birds and squirrels loved both kinds, and we didn't collect any for cooking … just to munch on.

Also along the creek bank we would find large clusters of purple possum grapes hanging on their vines. These made great eating and talk about sour … wow. They would really make you pucker up your kisser. Later the older boys would go back and gather a large supply of them and would make up some possum grape wine. In a teetotaling family it wasn't encouraged, but it was done anyway …

That wine kinda fell into the same category as dandelion wine and would never make it in fine restaurants. You had to mash and boil the grapes, mix them with some yeast and sugar, bottle it up and leave it to age. I believe three days was considered the proper aging time.

Possum grape vines also furnished us with some smoking material, for we would take a dead vine, break it into six-inch lengths. On the sly, we would then light up our stogie and have a smoke. Prince Albert pipe tobacco's motto was, "Does not bite the tongue" ....

This couldn't be said of our possum grape vines. It didn't bite the tongue ... it chewed on it. Your tongue would go completely numb after a few drags .... but, man, were we macho! You also didn't inhale the smoke for it would set your lungs on fire...

Possum grape vines also furnished us with some great swings. Finding a sturdy vine that came to the ground, we would cut it off about head high. Making sure it was attached well up in the top branches of the tree, we would be able to get a run and swing 'way out over the creek bank on the vine. The braver ones would swing out and drop off into the water, if it were summertime.

When we came to a hickory nut tree, it was time to take our gunny-sack and pick up the largest nuts to take home and crack. I remember very few walnut trees around. We would avoid the small nut that was a relative of the hickory nut called pignuts for their meat was bitter ... did pigs eat them?

We would then crack a large amount of nuts and spend some evenings picking out nutmeats to be used in baking ... occasionally swiping and eating some.

Some great times were had out in the woods just doing the simple things. I kinda miss it ... but aren't we glad it happened ...

The guys all arose slowly to their feet and went to pay their bill for the morning iced tea. Marvin was glad to just have them in the café so it would look like he was getting a lot of business.

Several voices were heard, "See you guys next week, same time, same station."

ELEVENTH COFFEE
Play and Entertainment

As predictable as sweat on a hot summer's day, the crowd of coffee drinkers began to gather. It was a balmy Tuesday morning in late October and time for the weekly gathering of the older gents. As the nine o'clock hour approached, they could be seen coming from several directions.

Predictability was not the way most of them had lived their working lives, but since retirement they looked forward to the camaraderie of the group. Some would even admit it kinda broke the monotony of their lives.

All but Faye Bucklin were still young enough to be physically active and kept busy at various hobbies, doing lawn work, gardening or doing as they pleased. If doing nothing pleased them, then that's what they did. Several still had mates who provided companionship, and all of them had extended families to rely on, although none lived in town.

Cece Damore and Harold Atkins were devoted fishermen, having had recreational homes on Beaver Lake in Arkansas since their retirement. They found few places around Drumright to do serious fishing, but contented themselves with local farm ponds catching crappie.

Jim Kinnamon was a serious wood worker and had a complete wood shop in his backyard. He had built his kids and grandkids all the furniture they could use and was still hammering away.

Otto Irving, Pete Ledbetter and Elmer Butterfield were the dedicated gardeners and could be found discussing something concerning vegetables and how to raise them. With garden season winding down, they were already looking forward to next season. The rest of the gang spent lots of time cultivating them, for they furnished them with fresh tomatoes, okra and all other truck that they raised.

Doc Pringle was the financial wizard and spent hours on his computer or telephone on money matters. All looked to him for advice in investing money and how to best stretch their pensions and other income.

Hank Blackwelder dabbled in raising quarter horse, and at his place could usually be found Joe Bob Smith, the old ranch hand. They enjoyed each other's company and made a most unusual looking pair with Bob standing way over 6' tall and Hank stretching to make 5'10". They were normally attired in cowboy clothes from hats to boots and could be depended on to be carrying on a conversation about horse-related subjects many times.

When all had settled in and relaxed, Ivey came around with the hot java and set a pot on each end of the table where all could reach it to just help themselves.

"What world problems are you guys going to solve this morning," she asked. "I want to see if it's worth my time to hang around the table."

"Hey, there's always something to be gained around this bunch," stated Harley. "Seeing old Hank and Joe Bob swaggering in like two desperadoes makes me think of how we used to make ourselves guns to play with," he continued. Some of those rubber band guns we made were almost deadly weapons, for those rubbers bands could carry a wallop. I can remember when we fought our wars there would be as many as six or eight on a side, and lots of bullets would be flying."

"Well," said Clyde, "are you going to tell us about it or keep it to yourself, Harley?"

"I thought you'd never ask," retorted Harley.

GAMES KIDS PLAYED

When we tired of listening to Orphan Annie, the Lone Ranger or other radio adventure shows, we would head outside and entertain ourselves with games and other amusements that were available or what we thought up. Store-bought items were rather scarce around our house, so we were left to our own devices and creativity to make our own.

I'm sure many of you played with the same type of home-made items. One of the most favored was the rubber-band gun. All-out war was declared when a bunch of us, armed to the teeth, met for a showdown. It made the gunfight at the OK Corral in Tombstone look like a Sunday School picnic.

The guns were sawed from one-inch boards and ranged in length from a short six-inch pistol to three-foot long rifles. Inner tube rubber, cut in circlets and stretched the length of the gun barrel, provided excellent

210

ammunition, and when fired close up to the victim could raise a welt. The yellow inner tube was considered the most elastic.

When you had cut a good supply of your ammunition, it was strung around your waist on your belt, or if you were not wearing one, then a rope was tied around your waist and the rubber bands were strung on them.

Guns were usually given exotic and lethal names such as "Widowmaker," "Sureshot" and "Lightning" to increase their deadliness, in our imagination. With a clothespin attached to the handle for the first shot and five notches loaded on the barrel, it made a formidable six-shooter. Rifles were deadly with many notches and a string to pull all the "bullets" out at one time, or you could pull slowly for single shot or slow fire.

When arguments would break out as to whether you hit the other guy, we would take fat, ripe pokeberries and glob juice on the rubber band. When you scored a hit, there was no doubt, for there would be a large purple splat all over the victim. There could be no further argument.

Home-made stilts occupied a lot of our time, and we vied in seeing who could make and use the tallest pair. I had an older brother who made a pair so tall he had to get up on the front porch to get on them. Of course, he had to be the biggest, fastest or toughest in everything we did.

Agility was a must, for some nasty falls could take place when we had fights on them to see who would be the last one standing. Races were run, and climbing over an obstacle course was a challenge for the fastest time.

An indoor sport during the winter months or in inclement weather was making spool cars. Initially, a large wooden spool was needed, so we robbed Mother's sewing machine drawers often, as well as begging from the neighbors.

We would then cut a circle of soap the size of the spool's end and make a hole in the center of the soap. A quarter-inch-wide rubber band would be strung through the soap and spool. Holding the rubber band was a nail at one end and a matchstick at the other.

When completed, the rubber band was wound a bunch of times and then set on the floor or table. As the rubber band unwound, the spool car would take off across the surface. Notches were sometimes cut into the rim of the spool so it would be a climbing car rather than a racer. We would try to have one of each kind with its appropriate name.

Races would be held for speed and climbing obstacles for pulling power and endurance produced many hours of amusement for us. If the rubber band was wound too many times, it would break and it would be "back to the pit-stop" for repairs.

An outdoor activity that provided hours of entertainment was one called rollin' casin's. Car tires were known as casings in the earlier days, and all red-blooded boys and some girls had a used tire or casin' to roll ... really ... I'm sure it doesn't sound like much, but many miles were traveled rolling the casin' along ahead of you. Couch potatoes just didn't exist in our neighborhood. Each guy had a name for his casin', and it was "parked" outside the door at night to await the owner the next playtime. You didn't mess with another guy's casin.'

I can remember an expression used by the guys. On a bright moonlit night someone would say, "Man, it's light enough to roll casin's."

My older brothers thought it would be funny one time, so they had me scrunch up inside one of the large casin' and then rolled it down a hill. When it hit the bottom, I was so dizzy with vertigo I couldn't walk. I was not a candidate to become a space cadet.

For a time the men/boys at the table sat in silent reflection. The many activities that were recalled spun tales of individual memories in each head, and smiles of remembrances played on the faces of many. Once again they were transported back many decades and were reliving the lives of 10- to 12-year-old boys.

"Oh, my goodness, but didn't we have a bunch of things we did?" spoke up Jim.

"That tale brought back more memories than you can shake a stick at. Wasn't it grand what we did, especially during the long lazy days of summer when school was out?"

Phil replied, "Yeah, and in addition we really wore out some Saturdays and Sundays after chores and church were taken care of. We didn't waste a minute's time for there was always a new activity."

"Say, guys," spoke up Ivey Jones, who had been standing nearby and now took a seat at the table. "Some of you may remember a young kid by the name of Jack Stephenson who lived here many years ago. He's a distant relative of mine, and last time I saw him he was telling me a neat story that I'd like to share with you. It concerns an airplane ride and Bob Wills. That ought to catch your interest."

"Well, with a 'come-on' like that who wouldn't want to hear it?" chorused several of the guys.

FIRST AIRPLANE RIDE

Well, like I said, the story is a contribution from a cousin of mine named Jack Stephenson, who told it as a memorable event in his young life. Jack lives in Bartlesville, Oklahoma, but lived and went to school in Drumright at the time of the story.

By 1937 aviation had progressed beyond its infancy into young adolescence. Lindberg's flight was history, and airplanes were a common, if not curious, sight at county fairs and other public gatherings. Barnstorming, daredevil pilots would perform aerobatic maneuvers and other stunts. Wing walking on bi-planes was an awesome sight, as well as parachute jumps.

It was considered bad luck to watch an airplane fly out of sight on the horizon. Not sure if the bad luck was for the plane or the watcher. Flying was in such an early stage that we would still watch with curiosity as the beacon at the Stroud airport swept the sky.

Amelia Earhart, Jackie Cochran, Wiley Post, Clyde Cessna and many other notables were setting records on a regular basis for speed and endurance. The continent was being spanned by commercial flights regularly, and Pan Am was flying to Europe and the Orient on a timetable.

All these events stirred the imagination of many boys and girls who had been bitten by the flying bug and not the least of these was young Jack Stephenson. This is close to how he told his story to me.

It was back in 1937, and he's never flown in an airplane but wants to in the worst way. Jack said he had built several model airplanes, but model airplane building was "small potatoes" compared to actually flying. He wanted the actual experience he had dreamed about for several years.

To the rescue came none other than Bob Wills ... this is the same old Bob who was the very popular Western swing bandleader of the group called the Texas Playboys. His popularity had become so widespread and the band was playing for dances in so many far-flung places that he had bought an airplane for transportation.

The Texas Playboys performed in many small towns all over the state of Oklahoma. In Drumright he would play for dances at the Legion Hut and in Oilton at the KKK Lodge. No town was too small for them as long as a crowd could be guaranteed ... and it usually was.

Bob owned a Ford Tri-Motor airplane, which enabled him to fill engagements, as well as doing publicity promotions. Never one to pass up a dollar, Bob Wills made the following offer: For only 50 cents and a Playboy Bread wrapper, a ticket to ride on the old three-engine Gooney Bird could be had … this was an opportunity young Jack couldn't pass up.

When his schedule brought Bob Wills to the Drumright area in the Gooney Bird, Jack was prepared. A landing strip had been acquired southwest of the Drumright-Stroud "Y" intersection. He hopped on his bike, with the bread wrapper and 50 cents in hand, and rode out to the designated place … to find about half of Cushing and Drumright already there!

After waiting impatiently for what seemed forever, his turn finally came. A friend from Edison School was with him on this memorable occasion, and Jack says a decision had to be made. You could choose to fly over either Drumright or Cushing. He chose Cushing for it meant a longer flight.

There were not enough seats to accommodate the number of tickets sold to go on each flight, so my friend and I had to stand … along with an aisle full of other "standers." The number of people aboard probably far exceeded the reasonable capacity of the plane.

There was never a more heavily loaded plane than this one that successfully got off the ground, made a safe flight and landed without mishap. This highly dangerous practice and others of its kind undoubtedly gave strong voice to the formation of the F.A.A. to regulate such activities.

"With my "white-knuckle" attitude about flying on a big commercial jet, I could get the total fantods just listening to that tale," reported Elmer Butterfield. "I don't believe I knew Jack, but if he grew to manhood, which he did, then his guardian angels were watching out for him."

"I'd believe anything said about old Bob Wills and his desire to make money. That rascal would go anywhere and play at the drop of a hat if he could gather a crowd," said Faye. "I can remember him and his band coming to the Legion Hut and playing for the adults here in town"

"Yeah," Pete said, "us younger kids used to sneak up and peek in the doors and windows and watch all the adult activity, and this included fights out back in the alley. I heard my parents tell how Dr. Starr had to stay open late on the night of the dances and keep his nurse on duty for all the injured guys that were dragged to him with knots on their heads and bruises and contusions everywhere."

"Not to change the subject, which I am," said Clyde, "but I gotta leave you guys here in a few minutes to go for a haircut. I called for an appointment and it's coming up soon."

"Well, it wasn't like that at my house when I was growin' up," said Hank Blackwelder. "When my mother opened her shop up for us boys, there was one chair and no waiting. It didn't take long for her to cut a head of hair."

HOME STYLE HAIRCUTS

I went to the barbershop recently and got trimmed up by a lady barber, and she did a mighty fine job. I'd been going to "Good Old Rick" who prides himself on being the "fastest barber east of the Pecos." He said, if pressed, he could do a head of hair in three minutes and I don't doubt it … they look it.

Reason for this story is this; I didn't go to a regular barbershop and sit in an adjustable chair until I was 14 years old. This memorable event happened after we had left Drumright, so I'd never had a Drumright haircut by a "for real" barber.

With five boys in the family and shallow financial pockets, my mother took on the chore of cutting the five heads of hair. Occasionally Dad would perform the job, but it was a rarity since he worked away from home. He did a much better job, but, oh, he was so infernal slow.

It was a sad day when the announcement was made that it was "haircut day." The day to cut hair was chosen by looking at the length of our hair, so there was no debating. This normally meant when we looked like children reared by wolves and had just been brought out to civilization.

It meant getting a #3 washtub and turning it upside down out in the backyard, if it was warm. A chair was put on top of the tub, which raised you to a proper height, and the first victim mounted to his fate, much like Marie Antoinette and the guillotine.

Early on, in the learning stages, Mother's only tools were a pair of scissors and a comb. Later, as her competencies improved and money was available, she bought a pair of hand-operated clippers. Using them, you squeezed back and forth and they cut a smooth furrow … sometimes. If you didn't squeeze and push at the same time, these clippers tended to pull out about as much hair as they cut off.

This led to some inevitable bawling and squalling by the younger ones, and hair mixed with tears makes for an unholy mess. Bawling led to more pulling which led to more crying, etc. and etc. … You had to have a spare cloth to wipe your nose, which tended to drip when the bawling took place. This could always be counted on at some time before the end of the chore.

With five heads of hair to cut, the first rule was speed. Unfortunately, speed ruled out excellence in the quality and looks of the haircut, and the old joke about being able to screw your cap on afterwards was no joke. Except we didn't wear caps. Contrary to old stories, however, I knew of **no** family who used a crock to place over a kid's head to use as a guide … just an old urban legend …

Not much attention was paid to the evenness of sideburns. She would stand in front of you, take a quick look at the sideburns, and as long as the hair lasted she could … and would continue to try to even them up. If she ran out of hair on one side … well, that's just where she left them. After an hour or so the itching would be gone…

We therefore had to remember Mother's bit of advice about her handiwork, which was, "The only difference between a bad haircut and a good haircut is about two weeks." And you know something? By golly, she was right … in spite of the nicks and other small mistakes, come Wednesday, week following, we looked okay. It didn't matter so much anyway, for most all your friends used the same family of barbers, so we'd kinda cast a look, turn our heads and grin.

"I sure remember having to 'wear' some of those haircuts," nodded Phil. "I also remember making fun of one kid whose mother was an even worse barber than mine was. He really did look like he had had a bowl set on his head and his mom just cut around it. He got upset when I teased him and told him he looked like Moe of the Three Stooges. I believe it resulted in a bout of fisticuffs after school."

"Who do you reckon won that little tussle?" asked Elmer. "I remember you as being more of a 'lover boy' than a fighter."

"Well," said Phil," I could lie to you and show you some scars from that or some other small battles I was in, but I won't. I'd rather tell you a memory of some old animals we used to play with. Most every summer we all had us one of these fearsome looking critters as a pet or maybe one of each."

MOUNTAIN BOOMERS AND HORNED TOADS

Anyone seen either of these two critters around the countryside any more? Do any young kids walk around in the summertime with a horned toad tied to a string, wonder and marvel at the little mini-dinosaur? I remember both of them as being in good supply when I was a kid.

They were both hot weather animals and were surely cold-blooded reptiles. We made pets out of the horny toads, but not the mountain boomers. We'd been told the boomers were deadly poison and so avoided them or even tried to kill them to our shame.

Take the horned toad … they were small little rascals that would just about fit in the palm of your hand. They'd scurry and try to escape you but were quite easily caught. They were uncommonly ugly with rough scaly hide with horns ringing their necks and spikes down their backs. We had all kinds of stories about them, most all just a pack of lies or legends passed from kid to kid. You gotta admit we had vivid imaginations.

The horned toad supposedly could flatten itself out totally flat so a car could run over it and do it no harm. Another story was that, when provoked, it could squirt blood from its eyes. I've no idea why no one ever tried proving or disproving this story, but no one did. Another story sworn to was that one was put in the cornerstone of a public building, and a hundred years later when the building was demolished the horny toad was alive and well. Wonder why no one wondered why one was put in there in the first place?

Another gospel truth told was when the mother's young were threatened she would open her mouth and all the little boogers would leap into her stomach until the danger was past.

Mountain boomers were a more fearsome-looking critter, and we admired them from a distance. They were about 15 to 18 inches long counting the tail and quite distinctive in color. They were many-hued, and the colors ran all the way from yellows to blues, greens and shades

in between. They were really quite beautiful, but sadly for them they had the bad rap of being poison, so lots were killed by kids chunking rocks at them.

They could be found on old abandoned wellheads, along the railroad tracks and anywhere else where it was extremely hot and arid. If one were cornered, it would open a fearsome mouth full of teeth and hiss at the intruder in a show of force to scare them off. They were **not** poisonous and only did good stuff by eating lots of insects and small rodents.

One time, several years ago, when striper fishing at Lake Texoma State Park, we visited a small display of wildlife in the Park Rangers building. I saw my first mountain boomer and horned toad in probably 60 years. I made sure my two grandkids got to see them. The Ranger told us the mountain boomer and the horned lizard or toad were endangered species. I really can't imagine what predator would destroy them, but Mama Nature does strange things and does them in her own way.

Another critter I've enjoyed from Oklahoma is the large, hairy tarantula. They are basically harmless but may make you hurt yourself avoiding them. As principal of an environmental school, we brought a couple back from a campout. The kindergarten kids were letting them crawl up their arm and dared me to do it. I felt I had to do it in order to save face ... but, man, I could have died!

"With a face like yours, you might have been better off not saving it," smarted off Jim Kinnamon.

"All right for you, Kinnamon," retorted Phil. *"Just when I was prepared to buy your coffee for you this morning. You've done gone and fouled your nest but good. I was just about to say that the face of one of those mountain boomers reminds me a lot of your mug, when you interrupted me."*

"Now, now," soothed Otto. *"You guys know you gotta leave your sweet talk for private discussions. This is a public gathering and we must remain peaceful like."*

"Aw, Phil knows I love him or wouldn't be making those disparaging remarks about him," replied Jim. "I'll be looking for an insult from him at a later date. He'll get even."

"Do you guys remember all the fighting and arguing we used to do when we would play games?" queried Harold?

"Yeah," said Clyde, "if you were anything like we were when I was growing up, you spent a lot of valuable time on who was it, or who was cheating, and so on as we played at these indoor games or the outside ones."

Harold went on, "Seems we had a lot more time for board games and other games around the kitchen table. Maybe it was because there wasn't television to watch. Nothing wrong with selective TV watching, but we did have a lot of family fun playing games together."

"Of course, having a large family helped a lot," said Joe Bob. "There was just me as a kid, and my parents were totally work-a-holics and never had time for something foolish like playing games. I really believe I missed out a lot on it as a kid. I know I enjoyed going over to friends' houses whose families played games."

"Well, you all have heard of the old saw, 'the family that plays together, stays together,' and our bunch were strong advocates of that philosophy," spoke up Harold. "Our place was well known in the neighborhood as a fun place to be during the course of an evening, for something was most always going on."

BOARD AND TABLE GAMES

Not long ago I bought a box of Pick Up Sticks in an antique store and paid what was probably 10 times what they cost new to buy them. They rang memory bells of many hours of playing games and arguing and wrangling with brothers, a sister and friends around our kitchen table. They were in mint condition and even had the value of each different colored stick printed on the box.

Ours was a "gamey" family who enjoyed all sorts of fun around the table. Fact be known, our family was a gathering place for lots of kids who knew that we played games where many of their families didn't allow them for many reasons. Mother was the instigator most times, for Dad couldn't care less. He'd be off somewhere tinkering with something, not wanting to get involved in that "tom-foolery," as he called it.

In addition to Pick Up Sticks, we played dominoes a lot and also many games learned from Mother that were old ones from her childhood.

One was a "counting out" game, played not for any prize, but just to be the winner. Each of us put our extended fingers in toward a center spot on the table. One, who was the counter, recited this verse touching a different finger, going around the circle of fingers.

"William Trimble Toe, three geese in a row.

One flew east, one flew west, one flew over the coo-coo's nest.

O - U - T spells out of here, you old dirty dish rag YOU.

The last finger touched had to be turned under and the game won until there was one last winning finger left.

You may have played it using a slightly different verse. That's the beauty of these homespun verses. People in different parts of the country had heard and used different versions of the same game. Nobody was right or wrong … just different.

We loved to hear the old nonsense verses from Mother and learned some by heart. One we memorized was called "Old Aunt Mariah" that went like this:

"Old Aunt Mariah jumped in the fire,

Fire was so hot she jumped in the pot;

Pot was so black she jumped in the crack;

Crack was so high she jumped in the sky;

Sky was so blue she jumped in the slough;

Slough was so deep she jumped in the creek;

Creek was so shallow she jumped in the tallow;

Tallow was so soft she jumped in the loft;

Loft was so rotten she jumped in the cotton;

Cotton was so white, she stayed all night."

You can easily see why they were called nonsense verses, but it was fun committing them to memory as we sat around the fire. We'd try to see just how fast we could say Old Aunt Mariah and had contests to see who could say it the fastest.

Even old Dad taught us one that was kinda rough, but we loved it … naturally. It was called "Club Fist." He came from Germanic ancestry, and the game came over with an ancestor, four generations back.

The first player sits with his left fist on the table with his thumb extended up. The next player grasps the first one's thumb and extends his thumb in the air. The third guy would take the extended thumb and extends his thumb ... so forth until the players had a tower of fists on the table. It was so rough that normally only boys would play it.

Now the mayhem began ... the guy whose fist was on the bottom asks the top guy, "What'cha got there?" He answers, "Club Fist." The guy who is designated "it" says, "Knock it off or take it off?" The top guy has the choice of saying, "take it off" and just releasing the thumb he was holding, and the game goes on peacefully, OR ... he can say, **"knock it off."**

If he chooses to use the option to "Knock it off," It becomes a battle of the "machos" while the guy who is "it" whales away at the guy on the top's fist. This is where the mayhem comes in, and sometimes Mother had to come in and lay down some calmer ground rules. When **she** said, "Knock it off"... **Boom,** she was the instant winner.

Well, assume the game continues peacefully and the fists are finally reduced down to the last two ... the guy whose fist is on the bottom is "it." He and the other player now go through this routine.

The bottom guy starts the next phase of the game by asking questions, and the second guy has to answer them all while the group sits in a circle around them.

The first question is, "What'cha got there?"

Answer by second guy, "Bread and Cheese."....

Q. "Where's my share?"　　A. "The rat ate it."
Q. "Where's the rat?"　　A. "The cat killed it."
Q. "Where's the cat?"　　A. "The dog got it."
Q. "Where's the dog?"　　A. "In the woods."
Q. "Where's the woods?"　　A. "Fire burned them."
Q. "Where's the fire?"　　A. "Water quenched it."
Q. "Where's the water?"　　A. "Ox drank it."
Q. "Where's the ox?"　　A. "Butcher killed him."
Q. "Where's the butcher?"　A. "Rope hung him."
Q. "Where's the rope?"　　A. "Mice gnawed it."
Q. "Where's the mice?"

"Out behind the church house cracking hickory nuts with a little glass hammer, and the first one to smile and show his teeth gets a little red box with five nails in it."

As you may have guessed, the red box is a slap in the face, and the five nails are his fingernails.

At this point, everyone in the circle sat very still with their lips firmly together and thinking sad thoughts so they wouldn't grin and show their teeth, for the guy would slap you up side the head if you did. Eventually someone would do something silly, and someone's face would split open with a grin ... very noisy ... here comes Mother again ...

After this noisy interlude, she sometimes insisted on us playing a game of her choice, which was called "The Old Woman and the Crippled Boy." Here's the way it went. The kid was handicapped and couldn't move around. One of us was chosen to be the crippled boy. This person would let his eyes rove around the room and pick out an object someplace in the room. It was up to the group to ask questions of this person to determine what had been chosen.

It was a lot like Twenty Questions or Animal, Vegetable or Mineral, but she had learned it by the old name and that's what we grew up calling it.

She tried to con us into playing a game called "Quaker." In that game everyone just sits quietly like Quakers at a meeting without moving or saying anything for as long as you can. We were too smart to fall for that one.

Some of our games were scientific experiments. Did you know you could make a needle float on top of water-filled glass on its "surface skin?"

We bought a wooden Chinese checkers game called "Hop Ching" which I still have in my possession. At some time we all signed our names on the back of it. A neighbor girl's name is on there, too. She was a beautiful Indian girl and a classmate of mine who had a couple of us in love with her.

"Sounds like you guys had lots of fun," said Ivey, getting up from her chair and going back to work. "Lots of fun and loud and noisy, too, huh?"

"We also had a lot of outdoor games we played where the amount of noise made didn't bother," said Cece. "How about some of these wide open games? All you needed was a gang of kids, a bright moonlit night and the game was on."

"Yeah, I can remember us playing outside, even up to 10 o'clock some-times," said Doc. "We'd be so hot and sweaty from running each other down in the dark, and it's a pure wonder that we didn't kill ourselves running into a tree or some such obstacle. Once again, the guardian angels were with us. I imagine they even had some fun, too."

PUNCH THE ICEBOX AND OTHER GAMES

Long, warm summer evenings were wonderful times to be a kid. Our mother was a kid at heart and would usually join us in the games. All our friends knew this, so it was a normal happening that the children in the neighborhood would congregate at our place, for we also had a large family. It was a popular hangout.

Mother was a talented storyteller and could hold a group of kids enrapt with her spooky tales of the Ozarks, haunted houses, real live ghosts and the like. She was a natural raconteur and made up for the lack of any knowledge about a subject by a bright and vivid imagination.

Punch the Icebox was a form of Hide and Go Seek with a twist. To determine who would be "it," one individual would face away from the group, leaning against a tree with eyes closed.

The following chant was mandatory:

"Now, I draw this magic circle, dot it, erase the dot and dot it again."

The second dot was made by one of the group that the one with eyes closed had to guess. If the guess was right, the "dotter" was "it." Lot of cheatin' went on, too.

Another favorite that required a larger group was a game we called "Pop Goes the Weasel" "London Bridge." My wife said in Iowa they called it "London Bridge"… but what did they know?

Here was our version. Two captains face each other with upraised arms clasping hands forming an arch we called a "bridge." The rest of the gang would walk slowly under the bridge singing;

> "Needle's eye, the best of ply, the thread that runs so truly.
> Many a beau have I let go because I wanted you-ly.
> Y-o-u, no one but you,
> Mama taught me how to sew and how to thread the needle.
> But every time I take a stitch, **POP** goes the weasel."

The kid under the upraised arms at the "Pop" was caught and subjected to some tall bribery by the captains. She was asked if she would rather have some ice cream and cake or all the chocolate candy she wanted. The choice would be made, and she went behind the captain who gave her that choice. We were a hungry bunch and always used food in the bribery.

After all were chosen, it would be a human tug of war with each side grabbing the one in front of them around the waist and on signal starts pulling, trying to get the opposing side over a line. It was a great opportunity to give a big hug to your best gal if she was the one in front of you.

If enough kids were there, we would play Squirrel in the Tree, which is the same as Three Deep. A large circle of players was formed with couples standing one behind the other. One guy would chase another around the circle of players and try to tag him. The one being chased could stop in front of a couple, and immediately the one behind became part of the chase.

Last Couple Out was a wild game with everyone in a large circle holding hands. A chosen couple would run around the outside of the circle. When ready, they would hit the held hands of two people who then had to get out of the circle, run the opposite direction and try to get back to the empty space before the first couple did. This caused some bad collisions at times ... all this makes me tired just telling about it.

Party games included Wink-um, which gave you an opportunity to wink at girls without taking heat. In a circle of chairs the girls would be seated with a boy standing behind. One guy would be without a Sheila, and he could wink at any girl in the circle, and if she got away without the guy swatting her on the head, she would fill that empty chair. If you wanted to get a special girl, you just half-heartedly tried to tap your girl deliberately, letting her get away ... those not being able to wink were obliged to blink ... very demeaning ...

On the school playground we had a rowdy game called "Blackman." On our large playground a few guys would stand out in the middle. All others on both sides were supposed to run across the open space to the other side. The ones in the middle tried to catch them and pat them on the back three times. These guys then became part of the ones to catch the next runners until all were captured.

I've spent many recess periods rassling a guy around trying to turn him over to pat him on the back ... we got filthy dirty in the process.

Always a favorite was a game called "Capture the Flag." It was a nighttime game, especially fun to be played when there was a full moon. Only problem was it needed to have a large number playing to make it interesting.

Each side had a "flag" which was a piece of cloth two foot or so square. This flag was tied to a low branch of a tree or onto a bush or shrub about 50 yards apart. The winning side was the one who could successfully "capture" (grab) the opponents' flag and run it back across the centerline without being touched.

Played in semi-darkness, you could always count on bumps and bruises, scratches and lacerations as the players dodged among the trees and bushes and slithered in the grass to get close enough to the enemy's flag to steal it.

Okay, we thought we were having fun ...

"Yeah, there was nothing like those long summer evenings for all kinds of fun and games," said Hank Blackwelder. "Living on an oil lease meant there were usually lots of other kids running loose, so we never lacked for someone to play with."

"I can guarantee you that we didn't take nightly showers either," confessed Jim. "Just a wash-up and that was it. We just didn't have the water or the facilities to do all that bathing and stuff, and I can't see that it ever killed anybody. And I don't reckon we offended anybody with unwashed bodies. Shoot, too many of us smelled the same way."

"All the stuff we did wasn't of the violent nature," mused Elmer. "Remember how we sometimes would get us a older quilt and spread out a pallet in the grass and wait for the night to get dusky dark and then go to full dark?

"This was the time reserved for the fun activity of chasing and catching lightning bugs or the fancy name, fireflies," he continued. "A lot of them were sacrificed for our enjoyment, but I don't reckon we diminished the population by a single lightning bug. They are still around today, just as thick."

LIGHTNING BUGS AND SKEETERS

There's a big thrill in spotting your first lightning bug in the spring, for you know a warm summer is at hand. We'd go out in the backyard, spread a pallet on the ground and lay there watching night come in on us.

We'd watch the stars come out and make the obligatory wish, "Starlight, star bright, first star I see tonight. Wish I may, wish I might, have the wish I wish tonight." Wonder how close I ever came to getting one come true in those dear, dead days of long ago?

When it got full dark it was time to catch some lightning bugs. On a nice humid evening we'd wait a bit and ..."There! See, there's one." We'd head for the blinking light where we last saw it. A bit later another light and we'd be hot on his trail.

We kept this up until we could see him go to grass or sometimes even capture him on the fly. We'd have a Mason fruit jar with a lid and we'd chunk him in the jar and go for more. Why did we want them? Well, shoot, everyone knows the answer to that.

When we had a goodly number we'd go sit on the pallet and take them out and perform the most gruesome act you could imagine … you know what we did, don't you? Yep, we took that poor little innocent bug, crushed him and smeared his lit-up tail onto our foreheads, onto our cheeks, chin and even around our fingers to make fiery-looking rings. Man, did we look cool!

When you take an honest look at what we were doing, it's actually pretty yucky. We were smearing pure-dee bug guts onto our faces and hands. There's no two ways about it. The glow wouldn't last very long, and we'd head out for some more facial make-up.

I know some of you are a curious bunch and are wondering how the little critter makes light. I'm going to make it really simple for you. The tail contains both lucerferin and luciferase. The luciferase is an enzyme, and when it hits the lucerfiren it changes chemically and produces light. Whenever an electron drops an energy level in a molecule, it gives off a photon of light … now, you guys understood that perfectly? Sure is a good thing I wrote that all down so I could read it off to you …

To be totally honest, we were interrupting a mating rite by the little guys. The male of the species sails around over the grass turning his light on and off. Down in the grass is a lonely female. The poor female of every species always has to wait. When the lady lightning bug sees a series of lights she likes, she flashes him back and he comes zooming down into the grass panting with his little tongue hanging out for a torrid get-acquainted session.

If she made a mistake and his sequence of lights was wrong, she eats him on the spot … truly. You don't fool with Mother Nature. If the light sequence is right, she takes him as a mate and shows him a good time. I can see some really good things we could learn from lightning bugs. We could lower our divorce rate considerably if we'd follow their mating rites. 'Course it would be tough on those males with the wrong light sequence, or whatever.

Lightning bugs were as much a part of summer as watermelon and a freezer of ice cream.

"I don't think kids have the fun of spreading a pallet in the grass in the yard like we used to," spoke up Harold. "I suppose they are afraid they might get some chigger bites or West Nile Virus laying in the grass, and I suppose there is the possibility they would."

"I wonder if we just scratched and thought nothing of it," broke in Harley. "They didn't usually start itching until the next day, then you just put a dab of coal oil on the bite and that would take care of the chigger bites."

"Say," continued Harley, "on the subject of insects like the chigger, let me tell you of some fun I used to have with some bugs and such."

TUMBLE BUGS AND BULL FROGS

This tale has its inspiration from a literary short story written by Mark Twain. Maybe some of you have read or heard of it. It was one of my early favorites, a classic called "The Celebrated Jumping Frog of Calaveras County."

The gist of the story is a contest of whose bullfrog can jump the furthest. In Mark Twain's story the favorite frog was a shoo-in to win many pokes of gold in this little gold rush town in California back in 1849 or so. I can't remember which mining camp it took place in. Could have been Angel's Camp, Poker Flats, Cut and Shoot or Hangtown, I'm just not sure.

As with all things to do with gambling, some low characters raised the odds on that frog to win and then proceeded to get him on the sly and poured him full of buckshot. When the pistol shot signaled the frogs to jump, the poor old bullfrog was anchored to the ground with a double handful of buckshot. It's still a great read and worth another look for a chuckle.

Seems we got a lot of our pleasures out of the little creatures of the earth, and the lowly tumblebug was one of them. Call him dung beetle, scarab beetle, tumblebug or plain old doodle bug, and by any name he was a colorful and interesting bug. The ancient Egyptians called it the scarab beetle, and it supposedly possessed mystical powers.

We would find them on a hot summer's day busily trundling along the ground pushing a symmetrical ball of dung along ahead of them headed for home. The ones around Drumright were a beautiful burnished gold, green and blue and had beautiful markings on their back.

Since those early days I've learned the purpose of the little ball of manure. It was the egg case for hatching out more little tumble-bugs. The mama or daddy bug patiently hauled and heaved the ball to the entrance to its home and plunked it down the hole. The eggs were rolled up in the ball, and as they hatched there was instant McDung for the larva. Keep your ears open and you hear lots of good information here.

Long as we're being literary, you may remember reading another neat adventure story by Edgar Allen Poe called "The Gold Bug." Shoot, the bug by that name was no more than a lowly tumble bug, but was empowered with the ability to smell out the monstrous chest of treasure they were able to unearth. The servant in the story was deathly afraid of what he called the "Gool Bug."

As with the spiders, wasps and bumblebees, we used these lowly insects for different types of games. I hadn't been introduced to the "Gold Bug" as a story, so had no idea of getting rich with one of the rascals. Instead we would use several of them and have a contest kinda like the Jumping Frog.

Drawing a large circle in the dirt, two or more of us with a tumblebug would place them in the exact center of the circle. With no urging, bribing or otherwise influencing our particular bug, we would have a contest to see whose bug would crawl out of the circle first. It was permissible to pound the ground and yell all we wanted, but it was strictly taboo to touch, push or otherwise propel your bug. They were the most patient little insects and would slowly meander their way to the outer edge of the circle

Amazingly, we could continue this activity for several hours, for one race would never do. We'd have to challenge to a two out of three or even more.

After we tired of the game, we'd take the bugs out to the chicken pen and toss them in to the old roosters. How fleeting glory can be!

Doc Pringle broke in at this point saying, "Harley, Harley, only you and your ornery brothers could ever think up an activity like that, and to think that after it provided you with all that enjoyment you let a rooster gulp him down. That's a mighty poor way to express gratitude, don't you think?"

Harley replied, "Just goes to show you that a poor old tumble bug has a rough row to hoe. You got to admit, Doc, any bug that spent his life working with dung can't expect much more out of life, can you?"

"On that bright note," Doc pontificated, "I believe it's time to declare this week's session of entertainment and enlightenment closed, and I believe I'm going to go home and get myself some lunch, if I haven't lost my appetite."

TWELFTH COFFEE
Adult Activities

Tuesday morning's sun shone brightly down on the "City of Hills" as another day yawned to awaken the town. Monday had come, been conquered, and now Tuesday was bidding to be a wonderful day to continue the race to earn a living at whatever endeavor might present itself.

The Boomtown Café was booming with early morning breakfast eaters and also with the ones who ate their meals at home and dropped in to have a cup of coffee and catch up on the latest news and gossip. This crowd was made up of the merchants from up and down the hills mingling with those who had jobs scattered throughout the oil patch.

The café provided sack lunches for the guys who needed them to take along to the sites in the oil patch where they would be putting in an honest day's toil away from eating facilities. In many cases it was deemed a big-hearted policy on the part of the guys so their wives wouldn't have to put up a lunch ...

Marvin Cutler, owner and cashier of the place, was ably assisted by a couple of waitresses and a cook he had hired recently. Ivey Jones was the older and more seasoned waitress. However, anyone having the temerity to call her a seasoned person of any stripe had better be ready to take the consequences, for Ivey considered herself just an "experienced lady of quality." Helping her out as an apprentice waitress was a much younger Martha Bell Pines.

This most attractive young lady was working to supplement her income in paying expenses to attend the local vocational technical school where she was enrolled in a pre-nursing curriculum. Most everyone eating at the Boomtown Cafe had made a pet of her and spoiled her rotten.

As the morning wore on and the working crowd diminished, their places were taken by the "Retired Gentlemen's Group," as they sometimes called themselves rather than "The Old Toots Club." Using that name was blasphemy, as they would tell you.

Their usual table by the front picture was fairly well occupied, and the low hum of conversation from those present was comforting to hear. Marvin had joined the group this morning, and the group leaned in to see what his stake in the conversation might be.

Marvin cleared his throat and said, "I've been listening in on you old boys and your weekly discussion for a long time. I thought this morning I would like to join in and add a little memory of mine to the discussion."

Harley Sprague spoke up, saying, "Well, Marv, we're honored to have you, but your memories fall several years from being the normal age ours do. We're all older'n mud and you are just a young pup."

Ignoring the gentle, verbal jab, Marvin went on. "This story is about an informal social event that took place daily out on the lease where I grew up east of town," Marvin continued. "It had to do with nothing more exciting than the daily mail delivery."

R.F.D. SOCIAL HOUR

There was an interesting social happening the housewives engaged in on a daily basis living out in the country on a Rural Free Delivery mail route. Just like today, everyone along the rural road had a metal mailbox out by the road with their name and box number painted on it. The number on the box corresponded to the number of houses there were on the route.

While living out east of town on the Magnolia Lease, we had about a dozen boxes out on the gravel road that ran from Drumright to Sapulpa. They were out on the road about a hundred yards in front of the house, a box for each one living in the lease community.

For a time we were Route 1, Box 8, but additional homes between us and town had moved us up to Route 1, Box 14. While I'm at it, I would add also that mailboxes were vandalized back then just the way they are today, so little has changed with the young ones. How does that go? The more things change, the more they remain the same ...

The daily arrival of the mailman was an occasion that made for a relaxing break in the housewives' daily routine. He could be bringing baby chickens, an order from Monkey Ward's or just a letter from Aunt Susan. Anyway, it was an occasion that became a kind of social ritual for the housewives in the community.

If you had outgoing mail and didn't have a stamp, you could clamp

three cents to the envelope with a spring-loaded clothespin, and the mail-man would take the money, lick a stamp and put it on the letter for you.

In warm sunny days it was customary for the ladies to gather by the mailbox well in advance of the mailman's arrival. They would spend this time waiting, talking, exchanging gossip and in general just socializing. Everyone knew most all the particulars about each one and the kids all played together, so it was a close-knit group. In those days few women worked outside the home at a paying job.

However, there was an undercurrent of unrest stirring among the women as they waited, for there was "coup" to count just like the Indians of yore counted collecting scalps. How so? Well, the purpose of the coming of the mailman was to bring mail … okay? Then it was important that each of the ladies have a goodly number of pieces of mail delivered to the family mailbox.

The number or bulk of the daily delivery gave status to the one on the receiving end. A package was a big plus … first class mail was especially nice for it could be opened, read right there and shared. Even junk mail could be faked to look like important stuff. But horrors! Nothing lowered your status more than scoring a dry hole on a given day. The winner could walk smugly back to her home looking with disdain on the one who had struck out as she slunk her way home hoping for a better tomorrow.

Now my mother was a most resourceful person. She was highly competitive and most protective of her image. She didn't like coming up empty handed at the mailbox social and devised a scheme that most usually insured that she would get several pieces of mail.

She would leaf through magazines and newspapers and find applications to send requesting all manner of things. She would fill them out and send them in to the various addresses. Made no difference what it was for as long as it was something free. Doing this was about like listening to every telemarketer and getting on their mailing list.

I'll give you one guess whose name she put on it as the one to receive this type of mail … **me.** When the mailman delivered the bunch of letters, she would get them and say, "Now, what has that young scamp sent for this time?" She didn't want to be the one to get that kind of junk mail, so I became the fall guy. She counted a lot of coup being the winning mail getter this way … and I aided and abetted her … unknowingly …

My dear devious mother …

"Yeah, I reckon that was one sneaky way to get mail," said Hank. "I surely do remember my mother, along with the neighbors congregating up by the mail box. I didn't realize it was a contest at all. It's amazing how much goes right over a young kid's head who has other things to think about."

The group of men spent the next few minutes talking about the amount of junk mail that was received as compared to the amount received at the present. Marvin had gravitated back to his usual place at the cash register, making small talk with a couple of customers who had wandered in for coffee and conversation, not of this group.

"Hey fellahs," spoke up Elmer Butterfield. "If we're talking about social activities that took place, I'd like to relate one about an activity we did for fun as well as make some hard cash when we lived back in the hill country. I remember I must have been around 12 years of age before they would let me go along on one of the exciting possum hunts."

Immediately there was a buzz of conversation around the table from many of the guys and much nodding and shaking of their heads. This was a topic that really rang a bell, and they all listened as Elmer began talking to make sure he got it right.

LET'S GO POSSUM HUNTIN'

Hey, boys, whistle up Old Blue, roust old Rounder from under the porch and uh, let's take along the old "potlicker," Sadie and her yearling

pups … it's time to go possum huntin', and the young'uns have gotta learn sometime.

In the olden days by late October or early November of the year the weather would have been cold long enough for the fur on the animals to have taken on its winter thickness and would be in prime condition to be sold. Good pelts meant some cash money in the pocket, and law knows that was hard to come by. A prime possum pelt would bring a quarter and a raccoon as much as two dollars.

Competition among the older guys in the area around Section 14 was pretty stiff, and on many nights the hills would ring and echo back with the sound of hounds baying in the frosty air as they followed the trail of a wily possum or raccoon. There were still ripe 'simmons hanging from some of the stunted trees and, man, didn't old Brer Possum love them. You bet.

The activity was as much a sport as it was a way to earn money. Serious hunting took place at night, preferably with a full or near full moon. Since most people couldn't afford a flashlight, a coal oil lantern was usually the source of light in the hunt. It didn't give off much more light than a firefly, but it was the best we had. The big guys at the head of the group carried the lantern, leaving the younger ones to stumble and stagger along at the back of the pack.

When the dogs picked up the scent of an animal, they were turned loose to track and run him down. In a good chase, several miles would be covered over the countryside or down to the creek bottom where Mr. Possum or Mr. Coon would make his final stand. This was usually in the uppermost limbs of a tree where the possum or coon would sit surveying the baying dogs and eager hunters.

One of the smallest of the boys would be boosted into the tree. This would be one of the daredevil little kids wanting to earn his spurs and prove his manhood. Scrambling up the tree, he got as close to the animal as he dared.

The tree climber shook the limb vigorously, and eventually the 'possum or 'coon would lose its grip and tumble to the ground. The animal no more than hit the ground when the dogs pounced on it. The raccoon was capable of putting up a fearsome fight and often did some damage to some dogs. After all, it was fighting for its life.

The 'possum on the other hand would do his usual act. He would play 'possum, that is, he would just curl up and play dead.

They could and did bite an unwary kid, so some care had to be taken. Gunnysacks were brought out and the possum placed in one for easy transport. The animal wasn't shot or otherwise harmed, for a full, undamaged pelt was needed for top money.

The next day the animals captured would be dispatched and skinned carefully. The pelt was then fitted, with the hair side in, over a board shaped like a miniature ironing board to hold its shape. The excess fat on the skin was scraped off. The hides were hung on the south side of the barn to cure out in the sun.

When enough hides were collected, they were taken to whoever was paying the most money for the skins. There was usually several competing hardware, feed stores and the like.

A good friend who lives in California reports that younger kids like him would go out in the daytime where the dogs would lead them to a hollow tree or stump where possums lived. They would take along a steel hook and bring them up from their hiding place and take them home.

There the possum would be killed, scalded and the hair removed like a hog. His grandmother would then make a delicious meal by baking Mr. Possum in a pan surrounded by sweet potatoes. It made mighty fine eating for us people with lesser means.

If hearing about all these good things to eat made you hungry, let's eat out tonight. There's no telling what Marvin's cook might be able to stir up.

"Umm, umm," salivated Pete. "That's enough to make you come back for seconds and then thirds, huh? That's one little delicacy I've never tried, and if it's all the same to you I believe I'll leave it that way. Say, Marv, how do you reckon that would go over here at the Boomtown?"

Everyone at the table heard his loud grunt of denial and took that as a definite no that they would not be served up any of the delicious possum.

"What I'd like to relate to you guys," said Jim, "is an adult activity that is a universal pastime still practiced in many backyards and alleys all around this

town, as well as anywhere you might happen to find a group of the male species and their automobiles.

"I don't remember which one it was, but one of you old boys mentioned some time back about a love affair with the automobile, and this is just a good example of how that love was shared among relatives and friends. Even though I wasn't a real car fanatic, I enjoyed bonding with the males of the family."

PLAYING HOODS UP

This story is about a "boys only" activity. To qualify as one of the good old boys, you had to own some type of an internal combustion engine vehicle, namely a car. The game got its start way back when the old "flivvers" had hoods that raised up from the side of the engine and flopped back over the opposite hood. The social activity evolved over the decades and can still be observed even unto this day, and is best played under a generous shade tree.

It's kinda like the biblical verse says, "Whenever there are two or more of you gathered together," for that's when the activity heats up. The rules state that one guy puts the hood to his car up. He can either start the engine immediately, or they can gather around the cold power plant and look at all the doo-dads and thing-a-ma-jigs that make up his car engine.

Oh, I forgot to mention … for best results in playing, all the cars should be aimed in together … all pointed at each other, nose to nose … so it

looks like a pioneer encampment on guard against the pesky Redman. This saves time in walking around to different cars.

The guy whose engine is being examined gets the floor first, and the others listen politely as the owner extols the virtues of his car. They would then make appropriate comments when called for. All knew their turn would come later, for that's how it worked, and **they'll** be the center of attention and their car will be spotlighted. The rules are rigid, and another car can't be brought into the discussion at this point. Later on, the merits of different vehicles can be discussed … but only politely.

The activity wouldn't be complete unless the engines were started and many comments made as to how "she is running." Seems it's always been of the female gender, for I don't remember anyone ever saying how "he is running." H-m-m-m, that's odd. It was okay to have a couple of engines running, but never the entire group. You were listening to a specific one … any more would have made too much noise. So, for an hour or so the continuous "vroom, vroom" would be heard coming from the observation arena.

Usually there was a "boss hog" in the group whose comments carried a little more weight. He might be the oldest person or one others would defer and listen to. My dad was the world's greatest shade tree mechanic, so he was usually the authority in our group.

As the game wound down, the group might walk around and check the other finer points of the car, other than the engine. They might even give the tires a 32-pound test kick and comment on tread wear, toe-in and alignment. One of the best compliments was if you were asked to take some of them on a test run out on the highway.

As an adult with four brothers and a brother-in-law, we most **always** had a game of "Hoods Up" at a holiday when all would gather in the backyard of the family home. Since I've always looked at a car as just something to get me there and back, I was pretty much an onlooker at the game.

I didn't know or give a hoot what all those "thingies" were under the hood. However, I would make a supreme effort to look wise and say, "Yep, I've got one of those too … right down there."

I **did** get my '48 Plymouth in the circle and tried to look wise, but fooled absolutely no one. My contribution to the total exercise? … I gave it the name, "Playing Hoods Up."

"I never heard it called by the name "Hoods Up," but it's surely a unique and descriptive name, for that's exactly what we did and still do," remarked Harold.

Several others of the group made remarks along that same line, but thought it sounded just like something Jim might make up.

"Well," said Pete, "it's a perfect name for something you could dive into and come out as greasy as you wanted to be. I will say that the older cars were a lot simpler to work on, and nowadays you gotta be an expert to do most anything on one."

Pete continued, "You know they are all computerized now, and usually the agency garages are the only ones who can afford to own the specialized equipment needed."

The old retired farmer, Hank, spoke up, "Yeah, but that doesn't mean I can't miss the camaraderie of a bunch of old boys and their cars, for I surely do."

"Out on the farm, however," Hank continued, "we had an activity I'd like to tell you a story about a piece of work that doesn't exist anymore. That would be the washdays when it was done outside and was an all-day chore. It started with the filling with water of the black cast iron wash kettle the night before."

WASHDAY BLUES

Recently there was an interesting piece making the rounds on the e-mail circuit. Some with computers may have seen have seen the list of instruction from a grandmother to a bride in Kentucky in back in 1912 on how to "warsh" clothes. It set me to remembering, so I'll tell you how it **really** was in Drumright on Devil's Run in the early 1930s. I'm talking about the washboard, black wash pot and all those other pre-modern conveniences.

Washday was approached like a military campaign with Mother as commander-in-chief. All the kids old enough had their assigned jobs. The day began the night before with a supply of wood cut and a fire laid around the black wash pot.

Early on washday the wash pot was filled and a fire lighted and kept blazing high. You had to be sure to put the wash bench and tubs upwind from the fire so you wouldn't get smoked out. While this was going on, the clothes were separated. The greasy ones from Dad's oilfield work were soaked with coal oil to release the grease.

With the wash pot boiling furiously, a cake of homemade lye soap was shaved into the water, and the white clothes were dumped in and pushed down with the punching stick After a short time the clothes were taken to the tub with the washboard and any stubborn places scrubbed out.

Sometime along here it was necessary to wipe the galvanized No. 9 wire clotheslines off so they wouldn't make any stains on the clothes when hung up. The clotheslines were often strung between convenient trees. If pipe was available, two heavy-duty T's were welded together and cemented into the ground, and four wire lines could be attached to the arms of the T. These were fancier and also could hold more washed clothes.

The women who washed clothes by hand had a rough row to hoe. Their hands were roughened and red from using the strong lye soap, and broken, short nails came from using the washboard. With no clothes wringer the women had powerful arm muscles from hand-wringing the pieces. It took a woman with a lot of strength and character to do the daily chores back then …

There were normally about three rinse tubs of water used. After the wash boarding the clothes were put into first rinse, soused up and down and then wrung out and put into the second rinse. Same process, then into the final rinse and the wrung-out clothes were put into the clothes basket to be hung up. Bushel-sized peach baskets were used by us.

Heavy overalls were a real trial to wring out, and two kids would usually grab onto separate ends and do a sorta twist to squeeze out as much as we could. We tried to do anything to make some fun of a hard chore. All of the rinse water for the above rinsing had to be carried from the well. This was drawn up by rope in a tin cylinder and the water released into a bucket … about one cylinder full per bucket.

It probably was a pretty sight to see all the clean clothes hung up on the lines with bright colored alongside sheets and tea towels. I'm sure we didn't appreciate the beauty. for we'd rather be off someplace messing around. A good breeze always made for faster drying time … and, my, didn't the odor of freshly laundered clothes smell good.

I've never forgotten the ditty we used in remembering how to hang the different clothes on the line. It went something like this, "Shirt tails up and britches down." That way you knew how to hang them. Seems there was more to the ditty, but I don't remember how it went.

Finally, as the times got better the folks were able to buy a square tub, gasoline-powered Maytag washing machine along with a power ringer. It

sure was a boon to the women and even came with rinse tubs on a stand. The power ringer was a scary item, for we just knew if you got your hand in it it would squash you up clean to the shoulder. In truth, it had a safety release on it.

Tough times for tough people … they were **not** the good old days. How about a trivia question? Do any of you guys remember in what town the Maytag washer was manufactured? I'll give you a hint … it was in Iowa.

"Well," spoke up Cece, "it so happens I can be the winner of the cigar by answering that one. It's Newton, Iowa, isn't it? I don't know how I remembered that, but us kids used to read where so many things were made on products that one just stuck in my memory box."

"That entire story was just about the way my mom did it out on the ranch," spoke up Joe Bob. "She didn't have to be concerned about greasy clothes as my dad was only around horses. I'd imagine the horsy smell was kinda hard to get rid of, too. I can still see my mom bent over that old washboard doing the rub-a-dub-dub. Don't you know that was brutal work?"

"I don't remember who it was that recently told us about digging a storm cellar," said Clyde from down at the end of the table. "It might have been Elmer, but anyway, what I wanted to relate was how we relied on the old cellar or 'cave' or whatever you called it when the storm clouds roiled up in the southwest."

HEAD FOR THE STORM CELLAR

Tornadoes are without question one of the most terrifying events that can occur to anyone living in the Midwest. Due to the devastation and havoc they create and the destruction they leave behind, the terrifying storms are widely feared for good cause. Having a storm cellar, or access to one, was an absolute necessity. In the early days before television and other weather warning devices, tornadoes would strike with little or no warning.

Since my dad worked away from home a lot, my mother was left to be sole caretaker of her brood. Although she was never in an actual tornado, she had an unreasonable fear of them and would go absolutely "postal" when black clouds turned greenish and came boiling out of the southwest. Unfortunately, her unreasonable fear of them made such an impression on me that for many years I, too, was terrified of storms.

Now, going to a storm cellar with a storm approaching was actually the lesser of two evils. Cellars were an environmental paradise for all kinds of creepy, crawly things that loved the cool, dark sanctuary they called home. In addition to spiders, uncounted bugs and centipedes could be found, and an occasional black snake, with all critters living contentedly together. Although the blacksnake was a harmless variety, we considered all snakes dangerous, thanks to that sucker in the Garden of Eden. He gave the entire snakedom a bad name.

My mother believed in "an ounce of prevention" and didn't wait until the storm was upon us. At the first sign of a dark cloud, she would marshal the kids, close up the house, grab a coal oil lamp and head for the cellar. We all knew the drill, and each quickly grabbed a piece of survival gear. These consisted of a fly swatter for the crawlies, a rug, quilts, some food and water and Mother's rocking chair.

The oldest one would swing the heavy cellar door open and hold it while the rest trooped down the step into the dank, damp surroundings. When all were down the short flight of steps, he would go down a step, muscle the door closed, hopefully without being squashed by the door as it banged shut.

When all the kids were down and situated, the first task was to claim the cellar as our own by knocking down spider webs, killing or shooing the other critters away. The snakes had slithered away to their hidey-holes at our approach. We did all this housekeeping by the feeble light cast by the coal oil lamp setting on a shelf. It wasn't much, but it managed to move all the boogy-men safely back into the shadows.

To pass the time as we waited out the storm, Mother took charge. She was a gifted storyteller, and we would usually clamor for stories about the "olden days." She would reach back into her repertoire of endless memories and enthrall us with tales of her childhood.

We grew angry hearing about her mother's "wicked step-mother," of her school days back in Arkansas, but most of all we loved the ghost stories she could spin about the haunted hills and spooky hollers of the Ozarks. The cellar made a perfect story setting for ghost and goblins, and we shivered with delighted fear in the dim, flickering light of the kerosene lamp.

As I grew older, I realized that what she lacked in remembering specific details in the stories, Mother made up and enhanced with her own very vivid and colorful imagination. She didn't tell any falsehoods, but rather embellished and gave more detail to the facts that she did know. I believe the fancy word for a gifted story teller is a raconteur, and my mother fit the description perfectly.

When the "thunder-bumpers" and the rain drumming on the cellar door had quieted down, she would climb the steps and take a wary look around. If the house was still standing and if she thought it was safe, we gathered our gear and made our way back outside and into the house. Another crisis had passed and we had been saved for another day.

"Boy, I'll never forget that musty cellar smell if I live to be a hundred and ten," spoke up Pete. "Our family spent many a watchful hour down there, too. All you had to do was see the damage a tornado could actually do and you didn't mind it at all."

"One of those twisters would sure make a believer out of you, and yet we had some people who absolutely refused to go into a hole in the ground, as they called it," this from old Faye. "They called it a 'fraidy hole' as I recollect."

Cece spoke up for the first time in a long time, "Boys, I just love to sit back and listen to your stories and only wish I had started taping them weeks ago. Speaking of the house rocking and rolling with a tornado brings back a much happier memory that I'd like to share with you."

"For one entire winter," continued Cece, "when we lived out on the Magnolia lease we had a most talented musical group that played in our home almost on a weekly basis. I'd give some big bucks to have a recording of some of those sessions."

SWANG YORE PARDNER AND DO-SI-DO

Actually you wouldn't have seen much dancing being done, but could you ever hear the rafters ring with the sounds of a fiddle, banjo, guitar, piano and bass fiddle? The old lease house would really shake, rattle and roll with the music. There just wasn't enough room to dance. Neighbors would congregate in the yard and on the front porch while a wonderful evening would be spent playin' and singin'.

The musicians were young teenagers who lived in the neighborhood and went to Pleasant Hill School. Preston (Peck) Harrall on bass or fiddle; brother, Roger (Rod) Harrall on guitar; Clyde Fultz on the piano, and my dad on fiddle occasionally. He wasn't as talented as the young boys, but he sure made up for any lack of it with his experience. Actually, the Harrall boys were talented on several instruments and would switch off as the occasion called for it.

The music sessions just kinda evolved over a period of time. The Harrall boys lived across the hollow from us. Clyde was a family friend of both the Harralls and us, and so all just gravitated to our house. Dad had been an old-time Arkansas fiddle player from his youth on and loved to play old fiddle breakdowns and sing. Somehow Mother had saved her butter and egg money and bought a much used upright piano, so the living room made a natural center place for all kinds of music.

She had some inherited talent and aptitude for music, as did a younger brother. She hired a lady to come to give him lessons and would lurk about to pick up what she could learn at the same time.

Peck, Rod and Clyde would come driving up bringing their instruments, and the evening would start off innocently with just some simple pickin' and strummin', and as they warmed up the serious stuff would begin. Clyde was a maestro on the piano, and he could play individual songs as well as serve as "second" to the other musicians. They really produced a great sound with fairly complete instrumentation.

I still see Clyde, sweating up a storm, sitting on the piano bench and literally bouncing up and down with the rhythm of the music. He really got with it. Money couldn't buy what a recording of that bunch would be worth. How I would love to hear it!

My sister, Frances, was at a teen-age hormonal stage and had a crush something awful on Rod Harrall. He was a little older but that made him all the more desirable to her, for he was a handsome dude. One night when they had finished playing some number and during the lull in the noise, Frances spoke up brightly and said, "Rod, do you know "You're the Only Star in My Blue Heaven"?

It got real quiet and she heard what she had said and the double meaning it carried and literally melted in embarrassment. Of course, there was a song with that title, but the way it came out and knowing her feelings for him, she left the room in a roar of laughter and wouldn't come back all evening.

No one ever complained about the noise from the jam sessions, and most neighbors would stay until the musicians ran out of steam and went home.

Bill, a younger brother, told me some time ago the youngest brother; James, was also talented in art. After graduating from the Kansas City Art Institute, he became a capable artist. Following an accident which left him a quadriplegic, he developed a style using a brush in his mouth and completed a host of paintings that sold well.

My mother's old piano also served as a form of entertainment with another type of music. The singing of hymns was a popular pastime, and different people would gather in our home to sing "Farther Along," "In the Garden" and other old-time favorites, and a different sound would carry out into the warm summer evenings. While Mother wasn't an accomplished player, there was a young lady in the neighborhood who was most talented.

On one occasion, this girl, who was quite heavy, was seated at the piano bench, occupying most of it, playing and singing "Love Lifted Me." My younger brother, about eight years old, and I were in the background listening. He pulled me over to one side and whispered, saying, "Love would have to be really strong to lift her."

"Now, that's cruel," said Doc with a twinkle in his eye. "I can just see that happening with a couple of characters like you two were. But what do you ever reckon happened to that bunch of musicians? Seemed to me they were ready to take their act to Nashville and get on the Grand Opry stage."

"Naw," retorted Harold, "it was just a passing phase in their lives. The younger ones had a war to go fight, and that kinda took precedence over making good music, but boy, they were a bunch of good musicians. I know. I heard them several times."

"Say, Ivey," spoke up Harley, "these coffee cups have sprung a leak and sure enough need to be refilled, if you've got the time. Meantime, I'd like to spin a tale about how we managed to drive our old flivvers when we got in high school and even beyond."

"You know me," Ivey called back. "I'll be there in a jiff with a fresh pot of both regular and decaf. I might even work up a smile for you while you tell your lie ... er ... I mean story, Mr. Sprague."

FREE GASOLINE! YOU MEAN IT?

The story may sound like an advertising gimmick for some enterprising oil company, but I won't spoof you. We actually were able to get free gasoline when I was a kid, but not from a pump and it had no brand name. The process was possibly a light shade of gray as far as legality was concerned, but everyone looked the other way. After all, the price at the pump was sometimes as much as 15 cents a gallon and that was outrageous.

In the oil fields there were hundreds of producing wells "doing their thing" 24 hours a day; seven days a week. The crude oil would be brought to the surface with the pump jack, and the oil would then be sent by a smaller pipeline to a storage tank at some distant point. Now some of these wells were pumping a superior grade of crude, and therein lays this story.

Hopefully, no petroleum engineer is lurking anywhere close, for my version is coming from a background that has not one drop of oil in it. A professional, scientific explanation is welcome if any of you old retired oilmen care to give one, when I finish.

But ... back to the story ... in the process of the oil coming to the surface there was a petroleum by-product in the crude apparently caused by the distillation of water and a clear, liquid oil product. This clear liquid was highly volatile and extremely high in octane and was unwanted in the crude. In some manner it was drawn out of the crude and off into a holding tank in the vicinity of the oil well for disposal. Was it called "casing head" gasoline?

This unwanted clear liquid, along with a large quantity of saltwater, was allowed to "drip" into a large underground tank where it would be released into a nearby creek or low spot that fed into a creek. The Environmental Protective Agency was many decades in the future.

The saltwater and gas product collected mostly in cold weather for some reason, due to distillation. That was the time when the young guys with cars and skinny pocketbooks would sneak down to the holding tank and get a great supply of gasoline. Since the process was a drip method, the gasoline was called "drip gas."

The process was called "blowing drips," for when the valve was turned on the water and high test gasoline came roaring out under a lot of pressure, they were literally "blown."

You had to time your trip to the drip to miss the pumper who had the job of going to each well and emptying these holding tanks into the waste area. The oil companies wanted you to buy their gasoline at the pump, not get it free from the drip site. Usually the pumper, an understanding guy, would look the other way, or his own kid might be in the group getting the gasoline.

The water, being heavier, blew out of the discharge pipe first and then came the beautiful "white lightning" or high-test gas. Even then it was sometimes mixed with water and/or dirt, so it was necessary to strain the drip gas before using it. The best strainer was an old felt hat that had very fine mesh and would strain out impurities. With no hat available, ladies silk hose or underwear was acceptable.

Since the clear white gasoline had the volatility of aviation gasoline, it was unsafe to use it in the engine of your car "straight." Therefore, it was diluted with coal oil or some "store-bought" gas.

My older brother would take us two younger ones along on these very early morning excursions to help carry the gasoline back. He was in competition with a young neighbor to see who could get to the well first. If we had been bested on a particular morning, my older brother would insist that we still walk by the neighbor's house carrying our five-gallon buckets as if they were full so not to look like he had come in second that morning.

Now, that's quite an act, to carry two empty five-gallon buckets pretending they are full of liquid. But teen-age boys had their image to uphold.

For some time the talk broke down into individuals talking with their neighbor, and a general amount of confusion ensued. No one seemed to want to be the authority on how and where drip gas came from. It was agreed that it certainly was a super high-test fuel and not to be used as a straight product.

Elmer did speak up on one point. "Boys," he said, "why do you reckon the drips only produced during the winter time? Do you suppose it has to do with the condensation process," he said, answering his own question.

Cecil opined that there really and truly wasn't a petroleum engineer in the crowd, and to tell the honest to gosh truth they just plain didn't know the answer.

Cece went on to say, "Since I wasn't always a high school science teacher, let me tell you of a fun happening out in the rural part of the state where I worked before being hired to teach at the high school here."

"Well, Cece," said Jim Kinnamon, "just let 'er rip and let's hear your story."

"This little activity had a dual purpose in the small rural districts," explained Cece. "First off, it was a fine social happening in the neighborhood, and second it was a money maker to be used to buy supplies for the school. It was either a box supper or a pie supper, depending on what the sponsors wanted to call it."

BOX SUPPERS

You could count on an evening of fun and excitement when a church or a school planned to sponsor a box supper or maybe a pie supper. These social activities were popular as a money-making project. The box supper was usually followed by a dance or perhaps just some "play party" games. It was, for sure, an adult-only affair. The event and the date was announced several weeks in advance of the occasion so the ladies would have plenty of time to find and decorate a suitable box to hold the eats.

The container had to be something like a shoebox or larger to hold enough food to feed the old boy who would be shelling out money for a meal. The women vied with each other to see who could come up with the fanciest decorated box. They took lots of pains with ribbons, crepe paper, buttons, dolls and any other creative things they could think up to bring out a creation to o-o-h and a-a-h over.

Since it was a fund-raising event, there usually would be a contest held for the prettiest decorated box with the men voting, with so much money being paid for the box of their choice. This voting was done after the boxes were brought, but before the men saw who brought in what box. In some instances some ladies would drop a very broad hint as to what her box looked like … just in case …

After the box judging was done, it was time to get serious, for it was past suppertime and these old boys were hungry after a hard day's work. Every community had some guy with some experience at auctioneering or someone who was a "wanna-be," and he was called upon to do the honors and auction off these boxes of delicious food to the highest bidder. He didn't have to be good … just willing.

I failed to mention that a full several course dinner lay beneath the lids of these boxes, and the odor of fried chicken permeated the air drowning out the toilet water of the ladies. No fast food could be found, but whipped potatoes and gravy, green beans and hearty food such as that made up the box's contents.

Many times there would be two or more guys who wanted to spend the evening eating with sweet Sally Jo, and this caused some interesting events. They had to know (or think they knew) which box was hers. After that the bidding would start. The price continued to mount higher and higher until finally the guy with the deepest pockets would win out and get to swagger up and pick up the box. If he'd guessed right, he'd claim Sally Jo as a dining partner, and off they would go with the food. If he'd guessed wrong, as a gentleman, he couldn't show it.

Sometimes some ornery guy would purposefully run the bids up just to watch the other guy sweat as he got down to his last bit of change. Of course, it was all in fun, and the idea was that no one was the loser and the church or the school was the winner with the money it took in.

Now if you're talking about a pie supper, it went off just about the same way, with the exception that you ate supper before you came and what was for sale was just a pie. You knew as you bid what kind of pie it was, so you could wait on your favorite, unless too many other guys had also waited. In that case the bidding was on and the price of pies became astronomical.

My students had a box supper when I taught them back in the '60s, and it went over great. I'm not so sure how it might sell with the cool kids of the 2000s.

"It's been years since I went to my last one of those," said Phil. "Remember how old Charley Hightower would always volunteer to be the auctioneer? He wasn't bad at it until he had a nip or two, and then he'd get his ' twongue all tisted up.' It got to be hilarious at times."

"You sure could get your fill of food," retorted Otto. "Those little ladies made sure you did with an entire fried chicken or a whole slab of ribs in her box. As a matter of fact, that's where I first decided to settle on Hester as the woman in my life. It was an adult box supper sponsored by her church group. I found out she sure could cook."

Several of the men gave each other a nudge with their elbow and a sideways grin and wink at Otto's mention of his beloved Hester. While Otto was an accepted member of the group. they were all acquainted with the oversized and overbearing wife of his and gave thanks each night for their good fortune.

Pete, who had gone to the bathroom. came back to the table and showed the guys a bottle he had picked up from the shelf on the way back to the table. It was an empty antique bottle of what had contained Watkins Liniment. He held it high for all to see, knowing it would bring a deluge of comments.

He wasn't disappointed as Harold spoke up and said, "For pete's Sake, Pete, where did you find that relic?"

Pete answered, "Back there by the men's restroom old Marvin has a shelf loaded with old antique bottles, and this one caught my eye. This brand name product made for a nice interlude in our lives when the Watkins man came calling."

THE WATKINS MAN

The Avon Lady who comes calling on today's household had several rivals many decades ago as I was growing up. Who might remember the Rawleigh man and the Jewel Tea man? The one I remember the best and most fondly was the cheerful old Watkins man. I'd bet a dollar to a dog biscuit he had a real name, but if it was ever used I don't remember it. He was just called "The Watkins Man."

In the pioneer days of our country we had men who carried their wares in a pack on their back and walked the populated areas selling all different kinds of things for the home. Potions and lotions and things for the health and well-being, plus needles and pins for m'lady were always popular items. These guys also served as the news media, for they carried the information and gossip from one settlement to another

By the modern days of the 1930s these guys had cars that had been converted and were equipped to carry an entire store in the back of their vehicle. Early on, our Watkins man had a little Ford Model A coupe with storage bins where the rumble seat was. Later on, he had a small truck chassis with a built-up cab on behind where he had much more room for his wares.

The coming of the Watkins Man was an event for everyone. I'm sure their prices were low, for they were selling in a most depressed economic time. They filled a large need for the housewife and her family who had limited mobility. These were the days of one-car families, and the breadwinner might have a more important use for the family wheels.

The J.R. Watkins Company was from Winona, Minnesota. Now, never having been out of Creek County (that's a fib ... for we went to Cushing occasionally) — anyway, Winona, Minnesota sounded like an exotic place.

The company must have had a contract with whoever made Black Jack Chewing Gum, for I remember standing around with one bare foot rubbing the other leg and just waiting for him to say, "Would you youngsters care for some chewing gum?" I'm sure if we'd known it, we'd have said, "Do Russians eat borsht?"

Naw, we wouldn't have been that impertinent, but we took the gum and went off to chew it and turn our teeth and gums all black for a time ... u-m-m ... that licorice taste was wonderful. My wife also remembers being given Black Jack Chewing Gum as a kid up in Iowa, so it must have been in their orientation.

Anyone who has ever gone into an antique store and browsed for awhile will know how expensive Jewel T dishware is, and that was a bonus if you shopped with them. As time passes, it just gets more pricey.

All three companies sold a fine line of flavorings, and other extracts and from Watkins we additionally bought first aid materials. Watkins liniment was great as a cold medicine. It would be mixed with very hot water and some sugar and then used as a drink for sore throat and cold. My wife says they used it for stomachache.

Another Watkins product we used was a carbolated ointment in a red striped can. It had a fearsome odor, but it was a cure-all for many ailments. I think it had a mixture of carbolic acid and salve. We kept one can in the barn to use on the old milk cow. If she came in with one of the spigots on her udder cut or otherwise injured, the ointment would be smeared on the affected member until it healed.

We own a half-filled tin found in an antique store ... still use it ...

"I've sat here so long this morning, I'm gonna have to find me a can of that stuff to rub on my posterior," reported Hank. "This has been a fun time to listen to and has certainly enlightened anyone who is of the ignorant persuasion. However, like all good things it must come to a close, and if you'll bear with me I'll tell a short tale to hang a close on this line for today. Okay?

"Bear with me while I relate a tale of some more adult activities that took place when we were young and the juices were flowing freely.

"This has to do with a serious event and was a solemn occasion, and I'll treat it as such. It's about the old-time prayer meetings. In some ways it seems that people were more interested in this type of activity back in the 19 and 30s. Maybe it was just because they didn't have so many places to go, and so they treasured going to simple things like prayer meetings."

OLD-TIME PRAYER MEETING

Before I get into this memory, let me repeat and assure you that there is no disrespect intended in any way. I'm making no jokes at all or poking any fun at any of these good people. Several of them had a positive influence on me as a youngster and it carried over into adulthood. Now, with all those disclaimers, reckon I can milk anything out of this subject?

Our little group of "RLDS Saints" was rather insignificant in number and met in a small white church house just east of the Ball Tank down under the hill from the lease houses. The small gathering included some families from Drumright, some from Oilton and as far away as Jennings. Several families came that lived on leases scattered all over the oil patch.

I was always proud of the fact that Inez Slover, a teacher at Third Ward, was a member. This sisterly relationship cut you exactly no slack with her when we were at school. She was quick to use a ruler on your knuckles, as a brother of mine found out.

He loved motorcycles, and one time he had his school scissors opened up full width. This made a contraption that looked somewhat like a two-wheeled vehicle, especially if you're a young man with a high-powered imagination. Old Will was deeply engrossed in a make-belief adventurous journey across the country on his desktop. Ms. Slover came down on him with the "wrath of God to come."

Well, on Wednesday evening, as good staunch members of the little flock, you were expected to attend prayer meeting at the little white church. Most of the time we did, when we had transportation.

When the people gathered, the first order of business was to take care of the kids so the adults wouldn't be interrupted. Several of the adult couples had a big flock of kids, and the younger ones, birth to five or so, were bedded down in the back of the church on pallets.

As the prayer meeting began, there was usually a hymn, an invocation followed with a few words by the one in charge setting the theme for the evening. Short prayers by anyone who felt so moved would usually follow this.. Everyone remained standing and, as you were moved to say a few words, you did so. Seems every week the same old brother would launch into a prayer that was endless. It sure made a long stand and a lot of hunkering over the pew ahead of you.

After a song came the testimonies from anyone who felt like talking that night. I'll always remember most testimonies started out, "Well, I'm glad to be out tonight," and then they would go on. Many times they would end their testimonies by saying, "And you pray for me and I'll pray for you." As a smart-alecky kid, I always wondered why they didn't just pray for themselves and cut out the middleman.

A few of the members always got emotional when they were telling their stories. It was usually the same ones, and I'm afraid when I got older some more guys and me got kinda sacrilegious betting on who cried first.

Meanwhile, back in the popcorn section a few visits had to be made to put a damper on the noise that usually happened. The babies and little ones would be falling asleep. I remember one time I was sent out to the car. Being half asleep, I crawled into the back seat of the wrong car. It must have been just a couple, for they got completely home before discovering me!

In our car my mother always said we had so many kids they didn't even miss me until they were going to bed. Any way, the people who had me drove to our house and traded me off. Not sure what they got in trade.

"I don't imagine our parents worried so much about us being kidnapped back in those days," said Pete as he and the others got up to leave. "Any kidnapper would know our folks would have no money to ransom us. My dad might have given the kidnapper 15 cents to have them keep us. "

"I'd like to ring down the curtain on this week's kaffe latch with a story about old-time radio," Doc said. "Anybody need to leave? Seeing no one bolting for the door, I'll begin."

OLD-TIME RADIO

"Don't you dare touch that radio dial." Remember when the announcer would give us that dire warning. We knocked each other down trying to be the first one to get to the radio and touch the dial.

I'd like to talk a bit about the subject because I learned since I've mentioned it a bit in the past that there is an entire group of people who are practically a cult who are so into Old-Time Radio. They have chapters in larger cities; collect dues and all that good stuff. They also collect anything and everything relating to old-time radio. There are more websites on the subject on the Internet than you ever want to read. We're not gonna go there.

Remember some of the old-time announcers that used to hawk the products that brought us our favorite radio program? Who remembers a guy named Hy Averback? I remember him, for it was an ongoing argument among the kids in our house. One brother thought they were saying Hy Apperback and got really angry when we argued about it. Hy was on as an announcer for several shows.

How about Harlow Wilcox? Bet you heard him dozens of times. He was the guy who hawked the products for the Fibber McGee & Molly show for years. Johnson's Glo Coat was the sponsor for the program.

Speaking of products, does anyone remember one called Bab-o? I sure didn't, but my wife does and says it was something like Old Dutch Cleanser or Ajax. Remember "Ipana for the Smile of Beauty and Sal Hepatica for the Smile of Health." Ipana was a tooth paste and Sal Hepatica was maybe for colds ... or a laxative ... not sure ...

We had to be at 79 Wistful Vista every Tuesday night. This was the address of Fibber & Molly and the stories usually played out in their home each week. Remember the closet and what happened every time they opened the door? It was an old worn-out gag, but we still laughed every time it happened. Reckon we were kinda simple? Naw ...

I found there really is a Wistful Vista in California. Don't laugh 'cause there's a Gene Autry, Oklahoma.

Actually, the announcers were about as much a part of these old radio shows as the stars themselves. We knew their voices and names about as well as we did the main characters. Remember a guy named Harry Von Zell? He advertised for lots of different shows and went on to make movies with the Three Stooges at one time.

More on sponsoring products ... Bob Hope was brought to us by Pepsodent toothpaste. Remember the commercial about poor Miriam who had yellow teeth? Well, the dear girl started using Pepsodent and the song went, "Dear Miriam, sweet Miriam, now she's using irium." Seems irium was a secret, magic ingredient found in Pepsodent, and that's all it took to make her teeth gleam.

I wonder if all these whitening products that are on the market are just a take-off on Irium? Miriam would really have enjoyed having to just put paper strips on her teeth at night rather than having to brush with the stuff.

I wonder if anyone else remembers an announcer by the name of George D. Hay. He was called the "Solemn Old Judge," and he did the honors for the Saturday night show broadcast from WSM in Nashville, Tennessee. I'm talking about everybody's favorite, "The Grand Ole Opry." Well, maybe most everybody ... well, some of you?

I could write several columns on the nostalgia of the Grand Ole Opry, but I won't. I might lose too many of the readership of this little exercise. I would like to end this story with the closing words the Solemn Old Judge used each week to end the show.

"That's all for now, friends, because the tall pines pine and the paw paws pause and the bumblebees bumble all around. The grasshopper hops and the eavesdropper drops while gently the old cow slips away."

Yeah, it doesn't make sense, but it was a gentler time.

"I'll see you gents around town and here at Marvin's again next week," Doc concluded. "Just remember not to do anything illegal or anything that I wouldn't do unless you got a lawyer handy."

THIRTEENTH COFFEE
Travel and the Automobile

All at the table had been poured their choice of coffee, everyone had been howdy-ied, and another enjoyable hour or so of fellowship was ready to begin. The table by the front window was their spot of choice, for it afforded them a look up and down Broadway. This provided an opportunity to keep tabs on what went on in town. They weren't nosey, just curious.

The table was full on this particular morning, and the men were chatting each other up as if they hadn't seen each other for some time, when in reality it had only been a week since the last get-together.

Pete and Clyde were deep in a discussion at their end of the table, and several just sat and listened to their line of talk. They were discussing a TV program they had seen sometime during the past week.

"No," said Clyde, "I don't think the guy deserved getting the woman at the end. He was a bum and had shown it during the entire show."

"Well," Pete replied in a conciliatory voice, "I would agree with you, but that's not the way Hollywood likes to end them, so the bum gets the woman."

"Sounds like you two were involved in watching some pretty heavy drama," retorted Cece. "Must have been some torrid love affair, huh?"

"Ah-h," Pete snorted, "we both just happened to watch the same channel and were rehashing what we saw when we both know it's just a make-believe show to waste an hour of your time on Monday night."

"Well," said Jim Kinnamon, "speaking of love affairs, I can tell you of one that's been going on in our society for a long time and we've all come to just accept it."

Several of the guys leaned forward, cupping their ear to hear what they thought was going to be a bit of local juicy gossip.

A LOVE STORY

It's the honest truth, fellows, there has been an ongoing love affair in our midst for the past 100 years or so, and most of us have been a willing partner in the activity. Now, this isn't going to be a steamy story, so you can sit back in your chairs and relax.

I'll make sure I talk loud enough to reach the other end of the table. See, I'm talking about the love affair that exists between men and women and their automobile. It used to be that it was strictly a "guy" thing, but now the bug in varying degrees has bitten individuals of both genders. Proof of this is in the large number of young ladies driving huge SUV's with a load of kids.

I'm sure it all started when bragging rights were claimed for the best horse or team of horses and who had the fanciest rig. So it was an easy transfer to the "flivvers" when they replaced horseflesh. Contrary to what you may think, I do **not** relate to the horse and buggy days, or to the Stanley Steamer. I came along with the Model T's and later.

The name "hoopie" was a common generic nickname for cars in general, especially an older one. Actual names of the various models of Fords, T's, B's and A's, followed by the Ford V-8. People of lesser means drove them, as well as the Chevrolet, Dodges and Buicks. I'm sure that you will all recall the names of some of these lesser known cars. Some of them were the Hupmobiles, Whippets, Willis-Overlands, Reo-Wolverines, Lafayettes, Hudsons/Terraplanes, and the Jones 6, made in Wichita.

Of course, the dream cars and the ones that were drooled over were the expensive ones such as the Cord, Cadillac, Packard, Graham Paige, Pierce-Arrow and the Lincoln Zephyr. According to my good friend, Ralph, the Lincoln Zephyr was the car of choice driven by the Green Hornet in the weekly serial at the movie house.

These big old boats were also the cars of choice for the mafia and other gangsters of the "bloody Thirties." Some of these infamous outlaws were Al Capone, Bonnie and Clyde, Pretty Boy Floyd, "Legs" Diamond and Machine Gun Kelly. Again there are many more cars and outlaws you may remember.

Early day design of the automobile was simply a continuation of the horseless carriage design. Cars were built as a simple square, boxy body on a set of wheels. These designs changed rather quickly and resulted in a much more streamlined profile that developed less wind resistance. Speed became more and more a motivating factor in car design.

Remember how the new models were anticipated? They would be hyped like the second coming, and sometimes the new model would grace the showroom floor covered from bumper to bumper with a concealing cloth. The unveiling was a special event that took place with lots of fanfare. It was the time of revolutionary changes, and the companies vied to see who could make the most improvements.

It was an example of American technology and ingenuity at its best. Car companies knew they had a love affair on their hands, and everyone expected to see changes and improvements in the object of their affection. Some changes were lasting, while others changes were tried, found wanting and then were quickly discarded.

Fierce loyalties developed among car owners, and many heated arguments were held and sometimes blows were exchanged over the relative merits of a Ford versus a Chevy. These were the two most frequently argued about for they were ones most people owned.

The 1928 Star we owned was most fancy … had elegant cut-glass vases located on the back window posts where fresh-cut flowers could be placed. It also had pull-down black window blinds for the back and side windows … o-o-o la, la … and we think darkly tinted windows are improper now.

It also had a heat-gauge thermometer located as a hood ornament up front. When the car overheated, you could just look to see how high the red stuff was and judge accordingly. Our gauge had been broken, and Dad had removed the glass, and in the space had put in a baby picture of my mother and me. What a distraction!

How many remember riding in the rumble seat of one of these cars? This was the extra seat that folded up in back of a coupe to give added seating. It required some physical ability to climb up and in, so it was

usually reserved for the younger set. It made for a cozy little nest in which to up close and personal with your lady friend.

When your trip took you over dirt roads, the ones riding in the rumble seat ate lots of dirt as the car rocketed down the road. Also riding in the back in the wintertime meant bundling up like Eskimos. Again, young lovers enjoyed it for the opportunity to snuggle and "spoon." Now, what in the world was spooning? I was too young to be a participant but had heard of the activity.

"Yeah, I'll just bet you were, you old Casanova," teased Doc. "I can well remember how shy and retiring you were when you were younger. You were a pure caution around the young ladies."

"Now, please, Doc," Jim bristled and frowned at the disparaging remark. "I'm not through with my story, for the love affair continues on. Please give me your undivided attention, if you please, for the rest of you, ignore the interruption on my right."

A CONTINUING LOVE AFFAIR

In the dear, dead days of long ago it was quite an adventure to sally forth (wonder why Sally? ... why not Mary) in the family car. Like the philosopher said, "The journey itself made reaching the destination worthwhile." However, I think he would have amended his statement just a bit if he had ever driven on some of the back country roads in Creek County. If your trip meant getting off the few miles of narrow concrete ribbons, then you could be assured of either mud or dust and sometimes both … at the same time …

How many times have you taken old Highway 33 north on Harley, on past the Ball Tank, veered right at the Oilton Y and driven on to Tulsa to pay a visit to Mohawk Park?

With turn indicators far in the future, all turns and stops had to be signaled with the left arm sticking out the window, Of course, you remember those hand and arm signals … froze your fingers in the winter, huh? Heaters were primitive and wafted equal parts of warmth and carbon monoxide into the car.

One early innovation tried was called "freewheeling." By pulling out on a lever on the dashboard you put the transmission in neutral, and on a downhill slope you barreled downhill on your momentum. The plus side of the invention was an effort to save gasoline. When you were coasting, the engine was only idling and a possible savings on gasoline could take place. After all, it cost 15 cents a gallon.

Freewheeling didn't last long, for the driver had less control over his car when the freewheeling lever was pulled out. The car engine wasn't being used as braking power, and it proved to be dangerous.

Some early day models were advertised as being able to keep going on three wheels. A dear friend relates that on a trip his dad gave out a yelp. There, ahead of them rolling down the center of the road, was the left front wheel. Easing off onto the shoulder, they jacked up the axle. Hunting in the tall grass near the Cimmaron River, they located the wheel, put it back on … tightened the nuts **very** tight and drove on.

Before the invention of the starter, it was necessary to crank "Old Betsy" to get her going. This was also true even if you had a starter but had other electrical problems … like a dead battery. Cranking was supposed to be done with a strong yank on the up-stroke only, for otherwise the engine could kick back resulting in a broken arm. I've seen big old bruisers who could actually spin the crank in complete circles until the engine fired.

Cold weather brought a whole 'nuther dimension to starting the flivver. If you had electricity, a light bulb was nestled somewhere in the innards to deliver some warmth. Otherwise, a tea kettle of hot water poured over strategic places would usually be successful.

The most common piece of bad luck in driving was the flat tire. This happened quite frequently and was kinda taken in stride. There was a practiced drill in the repair. Pull the car over, scotch or block a wheel to keep it from rolling backward or forward before getting the tools. Jacks were uncomplicated, and it was easy to find the axle for the cars were high enough off the ground so even a big guy could crawl under to place the jack.

The tough part came in getting the tire off the rim, which usually resulted in some skinned knuckles and the loss of some religion, blessing the process. After finding the leak, the Camel Patching Kit came out. The kit contained a big piece of patching rubber, and a liberal-sized patch was cut

The top of the patching kit had an abraded surface that was used to roughen up the area around the puncture, the better to hold the patch. A small tube of a compound we called monkey blood was squeezed liberally onto the area where the patch was to be stuck, scraped off and let dry. The patch was applied to the tube and crimped down really hard to make it stick.

After getting the tube back in the tire and on the rim, it then took many up and down strokes on the manual pump to get the tire pumped up. Lacking an air gauge, any guy worth his salt could judge the proper inflation by giving the inflated tire an educated kick with his foot. It was re-mounted on the hub, the lug nuts tightened, and you were on your way.

"Jim, you gotta have a dry whistle after that long spiel," said Pete. "I really did enjoy your telling the story like that. Why, you're just a born raconteur, aren't you?"

Jim came back with, "Ledbetter, you'd better watch what names you call me. I don't have my dictionary with me and that, raccoon … thing you called me … whatever it was had better be something good."

This brought a gale of laughter from the group, and a gaggle of confusion existed around the table for several minutes.

This even brought Marvin back to the table, where he asked if there was any need for him to call for the bouncer or maybe one of Drumright's "finest."

Hank finally brought some order to the group and said, "We seem to be talking about cars and going places this morning. In that vein of thought, I'd like to tell about a trip we used to take that was a pure-dee delight to us kids."

GOING TO GRANDMA'S

These were exciting words to hear from Mother and Dad as we were growing up.

Actually, we called them Papa and Ma, and they were my maternal

grandparents who lived on a small one-horse cotton farm near Okfuskee, trying to eke out a living. The farm was about a mile north of the big city of Okfuskee (population 65 in 1930s). Okfuskee is fairly close to Nuyauka where the high school was located. Aw, you know where it is.

From our house to their farm was all of approximately 45 miles and, let me tell you, that wasn't a trip to be taken lightly. That was a fair distance to travel. When the decision to make the trip was made, usually several weeks in advance, there was lots of planning and preparation to be done.

Letters had to be exchanged with Ma and Papa to make sure it was okay to come for a short visit. With the size of our brood, it **had** to be a short visit. Someone had to be found who would milk our old cow for a couple of days. The chickens had to be fed and watered and the family dogs tended to.

Dad would pull the old car under a shade tree and tune it up and get it ready to go. He was a "shade tree" mechanic par excellence. He soon had the car running like the proverbial sewing machine.

When the great day finally arrived, which seemed to take forever, we all piled into the old square-bodied Hupmobile, and with the car packed full of kids and gear we were ready to go. It was prudent to get up early and leave just after dawn cracked, for it was a long trip and you never knew when a flat tire would happen or the engine quit on you, in spite of the tune-up. Dad traveled well equipped with a fully stocked toolbox.

We normally headed east out of Drumright to the small hamlet of Happy Corner. At this point the way headed south. Dad was a past master at short cuts, and I don't have a clue as to his route. He took us through byways, farmers' pastures, 'cross gullies until we finally we arrived at Bristow.

The last part of the trip was an exciting one. Going down some main dirt road we came to an elevated section that ran seemingly for miles. This section was made of heavy planking nailed to stringers attached to massive piling sunk into the muddy water below. The road ran over water and swampy land full of what we knew was filled with water moccasins and maybe even alligators.

We just called it the "Deep Fork Bottom," and I learned many years later that it truly was the Deep Fork of the Canadian River, and it's so named on maps.

We thought it was great fun for, as you know from driving over wooden bridges the noisy, rumbling sound a car makes, there is always the possibility of one of the planks breaking. We waited with suspended breath for something bad to happen, but it never did. Cars traveling on this section drove at a safe and sedate 20 miles per hour, and you passed by one another with great care.

At long last we made the final twists and turns and came to Okfuskee. It had a "filling station" on one corner. A filling station is the same thing as a service station in later days. We called it like we saw it. We filled up at it, so it was a filling station. On another corner was located a general store and that's about all I remember of the town. Dad usually filled the gas tank here, and sometimes we got to have a candy bar in honor of making a successful trip.

We drove the short distance to the farm where Ma and Papa would be waiting for us on the front porch along with my Aunt Sis. She was the youngest of the bunch and the only one still home. Papa had sired ten kids, and they had named the tenth and last one Decomus, but we called her Aunt Sis.

Ma must have been a romantic, a scholar or a realist for naming the last one Decomus … isn't that Latin or Greek for ten? Should have called her Caboose. I had another aunt who married a guy, the oldest boy in his family, whose parents had named him Alpha. Learned people in those days.

"Hear, hear, Hank, well done," said several of the group.

"If you made that trip today, you could be down there in less than an hour, couldn't you?" asked Cece. "Travel was a real adventure, for the highways as we know them just didn't exist for several more decades."

"Yeah," replied Hank, "but somehow the one-hour trip just wouldn't compare to the three-hour ones we used to take to make it. The excitement just isn't there. And, of course, my grandparents have been gone for many, many years."

Otto spoke up, "Say, fellows, we used to take a trip that was maybe even a bit shorter that the one to Okfuskee. This was all the way to the big city of Tulsa to see our ancestors in the zoo up there."

GOING TO MOHAWK PARK

These words, spoken by Mother and Dad, were also sheer magic when I was a little guy. They provided many days of excitement and anticipation of wild animals, picnic food and even some sweet stuff, maybe. Those words rated right up there with "Let's go to Grandma's" as bribery material to get all kinds of work done around the house and garden.

Now, I haven't been back to Mohawk Park since our kids grew up and left home. I'd bet it has been improved and enlarged to where it's a prime tourist attraction in Tulsa. You just don't go to zoos as much if you aren't a kid or have kids of your own. Back when we were kids, the park I'm talking about was the mostest bodacious wild animal park imaginable.

To us it rated right up there with the African veldt and an Amazon jungle. The park was located somewhere in the north end of the big metropolis of Tulsa. It, too, was not a trip you took lightly and on the spur of the moment. It was at least a 45-mile drive and required some planning.

On some fine day, we would all pile into our big and roomy family car, the faithful Hupmobile or Studebaker, and head north up Harley. This was Highway 33, and it wound past Fourth Ward School, Wayside Inn, Manuel Station and on up the hill turning east to go around the Ball Tank.

Staying on the narrow concrete ribbon of highway, we passed the metropolis of Crow and hung a right at the Oilton Y. We stared in awe as we drove past the legendary "Bloody Bucket," an infamous honky-tonk located near Silver City where untold murders had taken place … we told each other.

Old Highway 33 followed a picturesque route as it wound along the bluffs of the Arkansas River through Mannford and Keystone. This was before the Keystone Dam was built, and somewhere along here there must have been a bridge across the river. Does anyone remember?

Also Either Keystone or Mannford or both had been located right next to the river and was moved up to higher ground to keep from being flooded. The government paid to move the towns higher, including moving their cemeteries. I vaguely remember the going wages were pretty high for the ones hired to move the bodies. It was supposedly a dangerous job, disease wise.

We came in to Tulsa by way of Sand Springs and then to the heart of downtown. Dad always warned us of the danger of "sunburning our tonsils" gaping up at the tall skyscrapers. It **was** a pretty awesome sight for us small town country bumpkins.

We wound our way to the north side of town and finally came to Mohawk Park. We were hungry as bears and as grouchy as lions, so the first order of business was to eat whatever Mother had scrounged for our picnic lunch. The park had beautiful facilities, and we had our choice of spots in the tree-studded acreage.

I remember the park as having a pretty good assortment of wild animals, and we took our time in moseying around to all the cages and dens to see what we could see. Of course, our favorite was always Monkey Island, and we spent a long time watching the antics of various apes and monkeys. We'd always find a strong resemblance of some of the animals to someone we knew, and we'd get a lot of laughs out of the shenanigans they would pull.

Along toward the shank of the afternoon Dad would announce that we had better get on the road for he didn't like to drive after dark. Old car headlights just didn't light up the road to give a really safe drive, so we always tried to be home by dark.

It would be a tired-out bunch of youngsters who made it home, got the chores done and fell into bed early ...

"Yeah, Tulsa town was a huge metropolis back when we were kids," spoke up Hank. "We thought we were really world travelers when we made a trip up there, and it was all of about 45 miles."

"Well," said Jim, "how about the shorter drives we took in the family car for no other reason than just to be together and see some sights we were familiar with, as well as going to some new and different ones. I still even do this with my grandkids when I go visit."

SUNDAY AFTERNOON DRIVES

Occasionally after we had gone to Sunday School and had eaten our dinner, we looked forward to a slow afternoon before going back for Sunday evening services. On some Red Letter occasions there might not be evening services, and the kids greeted this reprieve from more church with a sigh of relief. Our parents would mention that maybe we'd like to take a Sunday afternoon drive, a remark that was met with enthusiasm and shouts of glee from the younger set.

I don't suppose the suggestion for a Sunday afternoon drive today would produce the same amount of bounding gusto. The little darlings would probably look at you blankly and say, "Whatta you mean, a drive, Dad?" … "Where to?" or "Why?" or "When will we be getting back?" … "I gotta call Suzie Q" … or some such.

We thought an aimless drive with no time frame or destination in mind was a fun thing to do, but then we weren't saturated with cell phones, Game Boys and all that other truck I can't even name, to occupy our minds. After all…what did we know?

If I sound "geezer-ish," I really don't mean to … I have no quarrel with the present day kids. They are absolutely no different from any generation you might want to look at in the past. They're just living in a different set of circumstances.

The decision was made, and we loaded up the car with whatever ones were free to go. The teenaged ones usually had other plans and begged off. After short arguments about who got the window side, Dad started the car and moved down the lane to connect to the main road. At this point the decision to turn left or right determined the direction we'd go on that day.

One popular drive for us was to go into Drumright, continuing on west over into Payne County, past the Euchee Creek Bridge. Somewhere along here we'd turn north and go up to the Salisbury berry farm, the family who raised so many berries. If it were berry picking time, we'd get us a box of berries to eat along the way.

We'd drive by the notorious Turkey Track Ranch and Dad would tell us again of its history. Now I could be wrong due to the long passage of time, but it seems we were able to cross the Cimarron River on a rickety wooden bridge someplace around Markum School. Correct me if I'm off the mark.

Getting back on the other side of the river, we would sometimes go to Texas Park to play on the equipment. It wasn't far from there to make the short drive into Oilton where we would drive in unannounced for a visit with a special family of church members. In the olden days you didn't always have to be invited or let people know you were coming. You also didn't expect to be fed like we tend to do now.

The Bunch kids were about our ages and were church friends. We'd just seen them this morning, but this was a different setting and more fun. Our combined families made up a large number, so lots of outdoor games were enjoyed.

Getting along toward the shank of the afternoon, Dad would announce that we had better be getting on our way back home. Chores had to be done, and since tomorrow was a school day we knew we'd better wash good behind our ears so we'd be ready for inspection by Mother.

It was a most satisfying end to a wonderful Sunday afternoon drive. Can't do it now, for the roads are too crowded and gasoline is too high priced.

Author's Note: I'm aware that the following is a modern day story, but for no other reason in particular I'm going to include this "Tale" that has become such a fond memory in our household. It was a lot of fun for us, and simply because, "I like the story," I'm running it. Hope it brings a smile or a chuckle to you. Looking back on the events, it was a fun time.

CALIFORNIA VIA AMTRAK

In October a couple of years ago, my wife and I arrived home from a 12-day trip from visiting a couple of our kids. We normally fly, but this time we decided on a new adventure and made reservations on the Amtrak train, a first-time experience. This let us get off in Albuquerque to visit our son and wife, then continue on to California to visit our daughter, husband and grandson.

The schedule called for us to board our train 20 miles from home, the nearest loading point on Amtrak, at 3:08 a.m. (that's early morning). We stayed up late to get things arranged and make sure all our clothes were in order and our pills were packed. At 1:00 a.m. we called an 800 number to see if the train was on schedule and were told that it was running four hours late!

We decided to go to bed and try to get at least a little sleep. It was not to happen ... we tossed fitfully for a couple of hours and then, fearful we would oversleep and miss the train, got up. We left home early so we could stop and eat some early breakfast, then go on to the depot.

At the depot I unloaded the bags on the platform and went to park the car in the long-term lot. My wife went to the baggage area to check several bags, and the attendant, not your smiling person seen on Amtrak ads, said gruffly, "Just carry them around here." She was flabbergasted, for they were much too heavy for her to pick up and carry. She finally managed to slide, tug and push them to the check-in counter. This rude encounter was the first of many incidents that characterized the trip.

When she told me the baggage man story, we gave each other a bleary, sleepy smile and assured ourselves that this was just one guy and we weren't going to let it mar our trip. Much too late, I concluded it was at this point I should have started writing down names and ID badges. After another 30-minute wait, we went out to the platform to await the train, which was coming in from Chicago at full speed.

The train roared in to town at a high rate of speed as if it planned to make up the four hours it was late. It squealed to a stop far back up the track, leaving us a two-block hike to board our coach, me loaded down with carry- on luggage.

Not a soul met us at the door to tell us what to do or where to go. It is our first experience on riding the Amtrak, and so here I am, loaded down like a pack mule, with carry-on luggage over both shoulders and a bag in each hand boarding a pitch dark train with no help. We staggered down an aisle and found an unoccupied seat, but before we could sit down, a spectral, disembodied voice said, "All the seats in this car are taken. Try upstairs."

The train was back in motion by this time. so all the next activities had to be done with the lurching and swaying that goes with railroad cars. The engineer appeared to be hell-bent on making up his lost time at our expense.

We found the stairs. and I had to turn sideways to squeeze me and the luggage up the narrow, winding steps to the upper level. Still no one met us with directions. so we stumbled down the aisle. and by this time we were steaming. At the last seat in the car a sign over the seat said, "Crew Seat." We took it!

I got the carry-on luggage stowed away. and we sat down and reclined the seats to settle in with a look and attitude of "move me at your peril!" An attendant finally came by and apologized profusely for our inconvenience. She said, "You looked familiar. I thought you had ridden with us before." This flimsy excuse did little to heal the wound, but once again we vowed we were having fun and wouldn't be grumpy old travelers. Should've taken another name.

We stayed in these seats attempting to get some sleep as we rumbled across western Kansas and eastern Colorado. I had always pictured the Amtrak trains as flashing down the track at 70 and 80 miles per hour. Wrong … we learned that Amtrak doesn't own the tracks it runs on, but instead they are the property of the freight lines. This meant that most trains had the right-of-way over us, and many times we had to slow, pull into a siding while a mile-long freight went by. At one point in the early morning light, I swore that I saw a handcar with two guys pumping madly up and down go by while we were on a siding. However, my wife concluded I was only hallucinating.

After changing crews in La Junta, Colorado, we sped (yeah, you bet) our way on down to Raton Pass, still four hours behind time. It was full daylight by this time, and we watched some colorful desert-like scenery go by where we had traveled before by car. The railroad does take a somewhat different route than a car, so there were a few things different.

We went to breakfast and soon found one large saving grace to all the negatives we had encountered on the trip. The quality and service of the meals was superior. Getting to the dining car, however, was an adventure in itself with the train lurching and swaying its way down the ribbon of steel.

We walked through the dining cars, grabbing first onto one table and then another as we wobbled our way down the aisle to our table. We just smiled sweetly and murmured apologies to the passengers seated at the tables we grabbed onto to keep from falling on our faces.

It wasn't only the breakfast menu that was outstanding. All meals were superb and the service impeccable. We supposed this was to salve our wounds for all the misdeeds back in the coach car.

Our son was to meet us at Albuquerque, and as we approached town, we envisioned going out with them to enjoy a tasty, sociable meal. It wasn't to be … 30 miles out of town we slowed to another halt and sat … and sat … and sat.

We were sitting on the railroad trestle high above I-25. We sat for 45 minutes while the evening sky went from the gloaming to full dark. An official-sounding voice came on the public address system after an hour's wait to make an announcement.

It was the conductor who said, "Sorry for the delay, ladies and gentlemen but we think we may have hit a pedestrian."

My first thought was that if we had truly hit somebody they had to be a totally handicapped person or else he was the slowest guy west of the Pecos.

The law requires that the train cannot proceed until the problem is resolved, so we continued to sit and listen to rumors. I felt like saying, "Hey, if you truly think you hit somebody, why not go check the front end of the train, there might be evidence." But I didn't say it.

As we waited, the road below us filled with emergency vehicles and police cars. The rumor was that some hunters had been out on the long trestle when they spotted the train bearing down on them and ran to the nearest end and either fell off or rolled off.

The law, according to rumor, also requires in the event of an incident that all crew members be tested for drugs, so this entailed more waiting. Another crew change was to take place in Albuquerque, so the new crew was brought out and took the place of the old one.

We visited in Albuquerque for three days and checked the local paper daily but never saw a news item on what had happened, so we'll all just have to keep on wondering who, if anybody, got smacked.

Finally, six hours late, we got into town and again were let off two blocks from the depot. I brayed loudly, shouldered the luggage and trudged toward the station Our son met us, and we waited on our baggage that had been checked to be unloaded. Naturally, when it was delivered one bag was missing.

Our son went to the baggage car to look for the missing bag. He was told to get onto the train and search for the missing bag. He found it at the last minute and just managed to bail out of the car as the Amtrak roared out for Flagstaff. ... it was a near thing. I shoulda got the name of that baggage guy.

We spent a great three days in Albuquerque during the Balloon Festival and even went up in a hot air balloon which is a whole 'nuther story. It was fun. Also took the humongous tramcar to the top of 10,600-foot Sandia Peak.

After our visit it was with much trepidation that we once again consigned our bodies to Amtrak for the trip to Los Angles. We had sleeper car reservations this leg of the trip, and it was late so we went early to bed. By the way ... sleeper car is the world's greatest oxymoron.

The sleeping compartments are about the size of three telephone booths laid horizontally on top of each other. Two seats face each other and slide forward, and this becomes the lower berth. The upper berth is folded into the wall near the ceiling, and the clearance between your nose and the ceiling is about six inches.

I had lost the flip of the coin and had to take the upper berth. Naw, I'm fibbing for I volunteered. Getting up in that sucker was a feat that would have been a challenge to a finely tuned athlete. To a stiff old senior it was like climbing Mount Everest with a piano on your back and no Sherpa guide.

Once bedded down, I found there was a canvas strap rigging that had to be hooked around you and into the side of the car. It didn't take a rocket scientist to figure out that this was to keep you in the berth during the swinging and swaying while you were attempting to sleep.

It did pose another problem ... some of you may have the same problem I've developed ... during the night I'm sometimes given a call of nature which can't be ignored. Normally this causes no problem, but strapped into a narrow bunk at the top of a swaying train it becomes a Herculean task ... but not to be talked out of ... can't be done. You say, "Naw, I don't have to," but the bladder says, "Oh, yes, you do." You can start a waterless diet at 3:00 in the afternoon, and the renal system doesn't care ... it still wins out.

We awoke in sunny California and pulled in to the station at Los Angeles only one and one-half hours late. Our car attendant said he would take our bags off and show us where to catch the next train up the California coast to our destination. Apparently we didn't tip him big enough, for after carrying off just two of our four bags he pulled a vanishing act. Amtrak policy say tipping is not necessary ... haw! That's another name I should have gotten.

The Amtrak train, the "Coastal Starlight," runs a route that is eye popping along the beautiful coast of California with the ocean in full view for many miles. This leg of the trip went off very well, although it was interminable with the long stops on the sidings. Since we were back on a coach, we had to sleep any way we could by reclining the seat and getting a crick in the neck.

Arriving at Davis at 11:30 p.m., two hours late, we were met by the kids. Spent an uneventful six days relaxing and enjoying family, and then on the fateful day we surrendered our bodies and consigned our souls to Amtrak once again for the return trip home.

In order to get back to the Southwest Chief which was to take us home, we had to take commuter busses and connecting trains from Sacramento, south several hundred miles to San Bernardino. We spent the day running through train depots and bus stations, but finally boarded the Chief to return home. By now we were so numbed with fatigue and felt and probably looked like two zombies. and if there were any glitches they weren't noticed.

After our final boarding we rode the train for 38 interminable hours, arriving at our home depot at 5:00 in the morning. I knew better than to ask the nerd at the baggage counter to load the bags for me ... I just piled them into the car trunk, and we were home in another 30 minutes.

This may be one of those experiences you look back on and laugh, but for many months after our return any smile I started to make turned into a grimace. I have these words of advice for anyone who is thinking of taking Amtrak:

"FLY THE FRIENDLY SKIES."

Post Script:

We arrived home on Friday morning … Saturday morning the news out of California told of an earthquake of 7.0 magnitude hitting southern California and knocking Amtrak's Southwest Chief off the track just east of San Bernardino. We missed it by one day. Shows clean living really does pay off.

FOURTEENTH COFFEE
Just Stuff

"Hey, Phil," came an enthusiastic chorus of voices. "Happy Birthday to you and may the Bird of Paradise land on your head. How does it feel to be another year older and not a dime richer?"

With a come-on greeting like that, Phil wisely chose to remain silent on the subject and to wait and see what might develop.

Marvin, café owner, had stopped by the bakery and bought one small cupcake covered with thick pink icing, and it sat on the table in front of Phil Wiley with a lone flickering candle on it.

With the coffee group gathered, the guys ventured out on a ragged rendition of "Happy Birthday" in several different keys.

When the raucous noise died away, Faye leaned over to Phil and in his gravely voice rasped, "We couldn't find a pan big enough to bake a cake in to show your age, Phil. We decided instead of lighting enough candles to show your age, we'd just go out to your house and set your lawn on fire."

"Well, fellers," said Phil, making no attempt to suppress a huge grin, "I'm deeply touched by your good will and generosity and know your hearts are in the right place."

Talk continued around the table for some time, for it wasn't every day the gang got to celebrate a birthday.

As the conversation eventually wound down, Harold spoke up. "Say, fellahs, remember recently when we were talking about taking turns talking? Well, what would you say if we tried that deal this morning? What if we just go around the table, and if the guy has a story, then tell it. If he doesn't have a story, then just pass it on to the next guy down the line."

Pete Ledbetter spoke up to say, "I don't want us to get too formal, for I enjoy just having pop-corn talking, but I'm not against doing it once. To show my cooperation I'll just kick things off with a tale about our family in its woodcutting days. Have you ever heard of these wood cutting aids?"

MAULS, GLUTS AND AXE HANDLES

This subject may be new for Clyde and maybe even some others … it's supposed to stir some interest as to how in the world a story could develop with that kind of a come-on. Frankly, I'll be a little bit surprised, myself …

There really is a connection with these words, but you might have to be either an older person or at least someone who burned wood and cut their own, for these would be tools of the trade. You'll remember lots of us lived a self-subsisting life in the days of yore, and so many, including my dad, made lots of their own tools due to a shallow, skinny pocketbook.

The wooden maul used in splitting wood was called by a derogatory name, which is not appropriate … so we'll just call it a wood maul. It was used with a glut to split logs into sections, and when hammering wood on wood both tools would last longer.

Dad would find a likely hickory tree about six or eight inches in diameter. Hickory was best because it was a really close-grained and hard wood. The tree would be sawed off about five feet above the ground, leaving the lower section as a stump that became the maul. Next order of business was to saw a circular cut all the way around the upright tree about 12 inches above the ground, but not all the way through (this is the hardest part to visualize).

He would then take his sharpened axe and start hewing the surplus wood from the upper part of the standing tree. ending where the lower circular cut was made (I may lose some of you here). He was making the handle for his big maul. He hewed it down, leaving a handle two inches or so in diameter and about four feet long, still attached at the bottom end. The purpose of leaving the tree standing was to have a solid work piece to hew on.

When the handle was to his satisfaction. he had a skinny handle sticking up attached to the base of the tree. Now, all to be done was saw the tree off just above ground level and, voila, he had a mighty cudgel to pound with.

Making the glut was a simple job. Using a double-bitted axe, he would find a hickory limb about four inches in diameter and about 15 inches long. With the axe he would hew one end of the limb into a wedge shape, with the other end squared off. Actually, the glut was just a wooden wedge to bust the wood apart, using the wooden maul to pound with.

Using our few iron wedges and sledge hammer, a long log would be split open and then the gluts would go into the small splits, and with the maul the log would be laid open in jig time. These long sections then became fence posts or were sawed up for firewood. The gluts would get all boogered up being pounded, but they were easy to make and wood supply was plentiful.

If an axe handle was broken by one of the boys, a normal happening, Dad made a new one from a hickory limb. Using the old one for a pattern, he would hew it into shape with another axe, a hatchet and his pocketknife. The final smoothing of the axe handle was done with a piece of broken glass.

The wood for these handles had to be cured rather than use the green wood. The tricky part was shaping the handle so it would go up into the axe head tightly. With the handle snugly fitted into the axe head, a metal wedge was driven into the axe handle to totally secure the head onto the handle. It could be embarrassing to have the head fly off while chopping … and a whole bunch dangerous.

Remember the old saying about using wood for heat? It heated you up five or six different ways. You got warm sawing the wood, loading and unloading the wood, and finally when you burned it. Truer words were never spoken. Using a chain saw, I helped our son earn spending money during his high school years sawing wood and selling it. In the olden days it would bring $2 a rick … he got $60 …

Elmer spoke up, "Pete, I'd say you did a masterful job of describing those tools, and no, I wasn't familiar with all of them. Iron wedges and sledge hammers, yes, but those other things, no. I know what a glutton is, but never heard of a glut."

Clyde questioned, "What is the difference between a rick of wood and a cord of wood. Are they the same?"

"Oh, no," Elmer replied. "A rick of wood is four feet high by eight feet long and two feet wide. A cord is twice that much. They can vary a bit in width, but in general the cuts are 24 inches wide."

Since no further remarks were forthcoming, Jim spoke up to say he had thought of a story to tell the group and leaned back to begin his tale.

EARLY DAY SOAPS

The Adventures of Judy and Jane, Ma Perkins, Stella Dallas and Pepper Young's Family. Now … I'll give you one guess as to where this story is headed … you got it! These are just a few of the heart-rending, cliff-hanging daily tales of human woe and misery that kept many people glued to the radio back in the 1930s.

Who remembers Stella Dallas wailing for "Lolly"? Lolly was actually Laurel, her daughter, who had a special talent for getting herself in some terrible messes. Stella was always there to save her from a fate worse than death. Then there was Judy and Jane. They were a perky pair of working girls whose story line revolved around their troubles in their day-to-day work life and their love lives.

I didn't care to listen to "One Man's Family." It was the story of a very upscale family called the Barbers. The old couple and head of the family were called "Fatha Ba-ba" and "Mutha Baba." I thought they were a really wimpy pair. Their life style was poles apart from anything we knew and we couldn't relate to them.

I remember Ma Perkins as being a very nosy individual who was always prying into other people's business and trying to run their lives.

The radio soaps were a universe away from today's steamy afternoon, sometimes X-rated dramas. When just listening to the soaps and their story line, you had to be much more creative-minded and use your imagination. The dramas were all oral and made use of your auditory senses, which meant the listener got to produce the mental images of the characters, the scenery and the action taking place.

These mental images could actually lead to some disillusionment at times. I was totally in love with both Judy and Jane. and I'll never forgot my disappointment when I found what they looked like in real life. I had them pictured as beautiful young ladies with my terrible adolescent crush on both of them. Imagine my shock when I found out they were two middle-age women who must have been at least 45 years old.

Do you remember that "Mountain Grown" Folger's Coffee brought us the Adventures of Judy and Jane? Who did Lustre Crème shampoo advertise for? Or Palmolive, the "soap of beautiful women." I'll never forget my surprise when I heard "Claire de Lune" in later years to learn it was classical music. I connected it with a soap opera.

The cast members gathered around a microphone in the studio and presented the stories live with the required emotion and feelings. Sometimes the same person would read the lines for more than one character. At the same time there was a talented sound effects person who had to be ready to become a squeaking door, lonesome train whistle or barking dog, whatever the story line called for.

You could listen to the soaps and go on with your work of doing the washing, shelling beans, mending socks or whatever. There was no problem of missing out like with the television soaps if you step away from the TV or if someone gets in the way of the screen.

I'm sure the TV cast members are much more talented than the old radio people were. They are also much more beautiful and hunky. Of course, we didn't have all the sensational weekly magazines to give us the inside stories on the personal lives of the actors. If you remember, all we had, other than the daily paper, was the *Grit*. Does that name ring a bell? The *Grit* was a newsy paper sold from door to door.

Harley said, "You made a good point when you said several of those smarmy romance stories still contaminate the airwaves, for my dear wife, Joyce, is addicted to several of them. Only this time they are on the television rather than listening to the radio. She tried to interest me in watching, but I told her I'd rather go have a root canal."

"Here, I thought you were going to continue on about the Grit newspaper," rumbled old Faye Bucklin. "I sure never saw any of that stuff, for I was too busy working on the oil rigs."

Otto spoke up, "Yeah, Faye, but you must have done some things for fun. A man can't work seven days a week all his life."

With a twinkle in his eye Faye rejoined, "As a matter of fact, we did kinda loosen up once in a while. I'll tell you what we used to do that made us too loose at times. This'll be my contribution for the week."

HY'AR COME THE REVENOOERS

Back in the early days and probably since the settlement of Oklahoma there has always been a sturdy bunch of old boys who made their living at "runnin' a still." Quality white lightnin', squirrel whiskey and sometimes just plain old "rot-gut" was produced to satisfy the never-ending need by some people for their strong likker ...

I know some interesting stories on this slightly illegal enterprise. One old ex-moonshiner even gave me a most detailed set of instructions on how to do the entire process. I'm going to share some of it with you, but better not go into too much detail. Winters get really cold down at the McAllister Pen ...

There was lots of wild country around Drumright, especially up around the Cimarron River and some places were so remote you had to walk to get there. Up many of the "hollers" could be found the family stills that produced a mean bunch of refreshment. It wasn't advertised, but most everyone knew who produced what and even the quality of the corn likker. I'm sure there were price wars, but the old boy told me they got five dollars a gallon for prime stuff … cash on the barrelhead and you come pick it up.

Old Joe told me a bunch of stuff, and when I asked him about moonshinin', he said, "Sure, Daddy made it and all us boys helped out on it." It always helped to have a friend in the sheriff's office in order to know when a raid could be expected. He reported that one time they had five oak barrels of the stuff aging out in the draw somewhere.

The friend from the law office came out and told them a raid was planned for the next day and to be prepared. Well, old Dad got all the boys started to work and spent all night burying all five of the barrels. Can you imagine the back-breaking work it would take to dig holes big enough to bury a 40-gallon oak barrel and then have to lug the full container to the pit and lower it in? He said they made it and camouflaged the site to where it was missed. I'll bet the price went up a bit.

Another time they weren't quick enough and the lawman tipped the barrels over, took an axe and stove in the wooden tops, spilling the stuff out on the ground. He claims that after the law left, they sopped up what they could and re-jugged it after straining some of the dirt out of it.

Most every moonshiner had his own recipe for producing the most high-grade stuff, but it essentially started out the same way. You got a 40-gallon wooden barrel, put a cup or so of gasoline in the bottom of it with the top out. You back off and toss a lighted match into the barrel. It catches fire with a loud explosion. After burning off the gasoline, the barrel is turned upside down to snuff out the flame. The container is now clean and has a charcoal lining suitable for sour mash.

Next is added a 100-pound sack of sugar, 75 pounds of ground corn and fill to within four inches of the top with water, preferably spring water. A single layer of burlap is secured over the top to keep the bugs out and to let the brew breathe and ferment. It's best to be kept at 70 degrees or warmer for best results.

After a few days the liquid is poured out and put into a copper still, and all the coils and other gear are set up to let it start coming out of the still. A low fire is kept under the still, and the potent stuff distills and drips into your jug. It's best to number the jugs in order as one, two, three, four and so on as they fill, for the first jug filled will be the most powerful. When all are full, you mix them together to get an average blend. The first jugful will blow your head off.

As I said in the beginning, this is just the overall process and not accurate in any way. As the warnings say, **"Do not try this at home."** Remember those cold winters down McAllister way.

"Yeah," Clyde spoke up. "The state may have supposed to have been dry, but you sure couldn't tell it by the amount of hard likker drank. And since it wasn't on the store shelves, then it had to be done as an at home project. Just proves that people are gonna have their drinking stuff regardless of the legality, huh?"

"You'd like to think that all that stuff went on in the olden days and doesn't happen today," Doc opined. "But we all know that isn't the case. As long as the fermentation process in nature goes on with fruit and grains, there's always going to be old boys who are going to try their hand at improving on nature."

"Good, bad or indifferent, that's just the way she is," said Joe Bob. "I'm making no judgment call on the activity. I also see that I'm sitting in the hot chair as the one for the next little lie ... whoops ... tale. Now, I know what a pun is and I just made one. I'm planning on spinning a tale on how my dear departed Ma used to make lye soap back on the ranch. I owe my soft-as-silk complexion to the fact that I washed my face with lye soap all the time I was growing up."

MAKING LYE SOAP

Ma used to say, before it gets too cold we'd better get our supply of lye soap made and put out to air dry. Could get mighty cold standing around that old wash pot, so let's get crackin' and get all the supplies gathered. If we don't, we're going to have a bunch of dirty clothes.

Used to be that if you really wanted to insult somebody big time, you'd tell them they were "as ugly as homemade soap." Now, folks, that was ugly.

There may have been recipes for making the soap, but I never saw my mother take a glance at one. She just did it as her mother had done and her mother before her. Later, as an adult I asked her for a recipe. She kinda grinned ... but eventually wrote me one. It's somewhere in all my junk, but I can't lay a hand on it, so I'll go the way I remember it.

With the coming of the cooler fall days the hog butchering had taken place, for it took a while to smoke the hams and bacons. In the cutting up process, lots of pigskin was left which was saved. Remember, we saved everything but the squeal. Now it was time to get some grease.

The skin was cut up in smaller pieces and placed in a deep-sided pan and shoved into the oven. The temperature was kept hot and the skins heated. In the process all the fat would cook out, and occasionally it would be drained off and collected in stone crocks.

When the pigskins were cooked all nice and crisp and the grease saved, one of the ingredients was ready. We didn't throw the pigskins away ... they were saved and "chawed" on by the family, for they were crunchy and tasty. They are packaged and sold today as "Piggy Pops."

The black wash pot had been placed onto the rocks that held it up, filled partway with water and a roaring fire built under it. Meanwhile, the grease had been strained to get the foreign objects out of it and brought to the wash pot, along with a can of lye crystals and a broom handle stirring stick.

With the water at a rolling boil, the grease was poured in and stirred constantly until the water was back at a boil. The tricky part now was adding the lye crystals. There would be clouds of steam boil up, and you had to avoid it for it was very caustic. Once again, you had to keep stirring the mixture briskly, stepping lively around the pot.

This was the finished mixture, and it was all simmered together until it started to thicken. Stirring had to be constant to keep it a creamy texture. Here again, it took the old master to determine when it was the right consistency and thickness. Mother would take some from the stick and feel it between her fingers, squeeze it and would know when to declare it done. This came only with lots of practice, but she had lots of that over the years.

She was just as proficient with her learned lore as Dad was in being the efficient and talented sorghum maker he was. Sadly, I don't believe any of the six children could ever have made either soap or sorghum, even on our best days. Lots of lore and learning was just not passed on down.

When it was pronounced ready, it was dipped out of the wash pot and poured into high-sided bread pans and set aside to cool. This generally was let set overnight, and the bars were ready to cut. Since it was of a smooth, creamy texture, it would cut into bars with a butcher knife real easy.

The bars were then stored in the washhouse to completely air dry out for several days as they were still wet and sticky. The soap had a fragrance about it that once you smelled it you would always remember the distinctive odor of home-made soap. Some women would add cheap cologne to improve on the smell, but we always used it in its natural state.

On washday the bars were taken and slivers would be sliced off and put in the wash water when the clothes were being boiled. Mother used the double tubs and washboard until about 1933 when we finally could afford a gasoline-powered Maytag machine.

"First off, Joe Bob," spoke up Jim, "you mentioned something about a soft-as-silk complexion. For the record I'd like to state that I've seen any number of these old horned toads whose skin looks like a little baby's when compared to that sun-tanned, wind-blown mug you put out front and brag about."

This last remark, at old Joe Bob's expense, brought down a loud, raucous burst of laughter and noise from the group, and once again Marvin came ambling over to see if his services were needed to bring peace.

Joe Bob enjoyed his few minutes of attention and grinned his best smile for the group. He mimed offering his soft cheek to anyone who might want to stroke it. This only brought forth more yowls and catcalls from the group, which was his objective.

In due time things quieted down, and Elmer took center stage with his offering. He felt it was appropriate to talk about advertising men right after the offering on soap.

ADVERTISEMENTS AND PITCHMEN

"I Root For Pigskin Davis" … does that phrase ring a bell with any of you guys who might remember hearing it or seeing it in the Tulsa papers back in the mid-'30s? You know how it is when you have an itch that needs scratching. Well, I have this strange name and phrase I can't put a handle on, and it really bugs me a whole bunch.

I well remember back in the '30s that there was an advertisement that ran quite often in the Tulsa paper. It was a picture of a huge old hog, and setting astride said hog was a big fat cowboy complete with a huge ten-gallon hat. The caption for the ad said, "I Root For Pigskin Davis." Now please help me. What manner of a store was he rooting for? What kind of store was it advertising? Car dealer?

I'd guess we've probably had advertising every since Noah had to put out the call for some of those hard-to-find pairs of animals he needed to take on board. Sure wish he'd not found any red bugs or skeeters ... but that's beside the point. As media sources have increased, we've gotten blasted with all manners and forms of advertising.

Sometime in the '30s a guy in Tulsa wanted to start a new radio station. He was getting a lot of flack on getting a license. Now it so happened that the call letters for his planned station were going to be KFMJ and his last name was Jones. Therefore, some of the wits around town said the call letters actually stood for "Keep Fighting, Mr. Jones." I wonder if it still exists.

The guy who sold tamales around Drumright had his name and product for sale emblazoned on the side of the wagon he pushed up one side of the street and down the other. We also had some guys who were sandwich board carriers. They'd put signs on wide boards with advertisements on the front and back of it and shashay up and down the streets on busy Saturdays.

I often wondered why it always seemed to be funeral homes that put advertisement on hand-held fans and gave them away. It was a soothing sight when you went to church on a hot summer day and get lulled to sleep with all the fans slowly waving back and forth.

Today we suffer the most from advertising when we tune in to TV. You'd have to be a recent visitor from Mars to not have seen/heard of good old Tom Park. Don't trust that dude as far as you can see him ... he's got the loyalties of a wayward tomcat. He'll hawk Fords in Tulsa, Dodges in Oklahoma City and Chevys in Wichita ... and extol each of them as being the best car ever invented ...

Right up there gracing the top of the list of all-time inventions should be placed the Remote Control device ... with a **zap** button to choke these guys off.

Remember the Crosley refrigerator? For many years they held exclusive rights to selling refrigerators with shelves in the door. It wasn't until the patent expired after many years that other brands could come out with door shelves and compete equally.

You old WWII survivors may remember the young bellhop named Johnny who, dressed in a red bellhop uniform, sang out, "Call for Phillip Morris" in a very "wimpy" voice. Along with Johnny was the ditty, "Lucky Strike Green Has Gone to War," when the company changed their package color from white to olive green. We could go on for days about advertising and commercials. They are a necessity if we're going to have our TV.

"You said it right," stated Doc Roy. "Without the advertising dollars, where would we be in publishing a paper, running a radio station or printing magazines. It's a cinch no one is going to go to the expense of putting one out just for the fun of it. There's gotta be a living made at doing it.

"I wouldn't mind the commercials so much if they would run more of the funny ones. Some of those that advertise sporting events are downright comical. However, it seems the more ridiculous they are, the louder they turn the volume."

"Well, Otto," continued Doc, "looks as if you're under the gun now. Appears as if you've been in deep thought, over there."

"I would like to help out Elmer on that story on Pigskin Davis a bit ago," said Otto. "I know what it was. It was a furniture store in Tulsa. I don't remember the name of it, but that's what it was. Maybe it was a Davis Furniture Company, I just don't remember."

Otto continued, "Other than that, though, wonder how many of you guys raised baby chickens in the living room of your house. My ma did it every spring, and I can still remember that smell."

RAISING BABY CHICKENS

All you who swear by the signs of the moon for doing stuff better check out the phases now. Looks to me like it should be about time to get the baby chickens ordered if they're gonna make fryer size by Memorial Day. What in the wide world the moon or its signs had to do with raising chickens is beyond me, but I won't argue with them or that weather-predicting Old Indian.

The calendar was actually the yardstick in our family for determining when to get the chicks ordered and on their way to some luscious eating. The worst of winter would have to be over and warm weather truly on the way. I have no idea where they were ordered from, but the RFD mailman, along with the regular mail, would deliver them.

One of us usually waited at the mailbox on a daily basis, and finally the

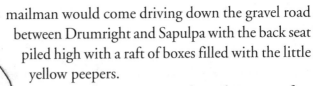

mailman would come driving down the gravel road between Drumright and Sapulpa with the back seat piled high with a raft of boxes filled with the little yellow peepers.

They came in a box about two feet square and four inches high and were separated into little compartments with a given number of chickens in each. Round holes about an inch in diameter were liberally spaced in the lid for ventilation. Some of you may remember the distinctive smell of them ... I sure do.

Now there's nothing cuter than a bunch of little yellow, newly hatched chicks, but since they were newly hatched, they had to be treated with lots of warmth and tender loving care. Since the weather could turn a tad coolish, it was necessary to keep them in a warm place. Some people had brooder houses and other facilities, but we backyard farmers had to keep them in the house until they were big enough and it was warm enough to move them to the chicken pen.

In the house meant behind the living room heating stove. An area was blocked off and a temporary pen built that was large enough to give them adequate living space and still had to be far enough from the stove so they wouldn't get too hot. We kept newspaper spread on the floor, which had to be changed daily. We used a kerosene heater at night to keep the chill off ... sure smelled awful.

While the little boogers were cute, they were also the dumbest animals in creation. There would always be an Alpha male chick that delighted in pecking on his brothers and sisters for no other reason than to show his status. He would be identified, and Mother would have to cut the tip end of his bill off to discourage this.

Occasionally the dumb things would all crowd up in a corner and some would be smothered to death. Each morning the flock might be reduced by one or more. Some would be sickly, and if you raised 90 out of an order of 100, you felt fortunate.

I remember the breed we ordered would be White Leghorn, but there were also Buff Orphingtons, Rhode Island Reds and Barred Rocks. Actually, I'm spoofing you a bit, for when push comes to shove I wouldn't know a White Leghorn from a Hampshire ... just wanted to show off my chicken knowledge.

When the weather was warm enough and the chickens were grown to teen-age size, they were moved out to the chicken pen to grow to fryer size when they would grace the table, making some mighty fine eating.

There was always the danger of losing some to various skunks, 'coons or other animals, but Old Shep was right there ... always on duty.

When we were fortunate enough to have a hen house, some of the new lady chickens would be let grow to maturity so they could become laying hens, but all others would go by the way of fried chicken, probably fried in lard ... we didn't worry about cholesterol back in those days.

Marvin had been listening in on the conversation and chimed in with this knowing comment, "There's nothing better than deep fried chicken fried in lard for a taste deluxe, in my book."

"Yeah," Phil replied. "And it didn't bother us all that much in the old days when we were working so physically hard. I guess our bodies just tended to burn up all the bad stuff that kills us off today."

"Otto," Phil continued, "you're gonna have to brush up on your breeds of chickens or you'll make me confused as to what I may be eating. Then again, they all taste like fried chicken regardless what breed they are. But now it's my turn on the wheel of fortune, so gimme a listen and I got a kind of funny one to tell you about."

WHAT'S IN A NAME?

Where in the world is Slapout, Oklahoma? Yep, that's what the T-shirt proclaims. And you can buy said T-shirt in the small crossroads store in sizes S-M-L and XL. Slapout is located way out there in Beaver County in the panhandle of Oklahoma, formerly known as "No Man's Land."

It's located on Highways 412, 3 and 270, which sounds like it would be a metropolis just booming with traffic coming in from every which direction. Actually, unless you're headed for Boise City, and the natives told me you don't sound the last letter in Boise, or maybe you're on your way to Colorado, chances are you'll never see Slapout, Oklahoma.

In fact, if you happen to blink as you pass the intersection, you'll stand another really good chance of never seeing Slapout, Oklahoma.

Now, my latest roadmap shows a population count of zero for Slapout, but that can't be right. Maybe everybody had gone to Woodward or Guymon the day the census guy came around.

According to my elderly uncle, who got the story from an elderly friend, the name came about from the old guy who ran the small store. Someone would come in to buy something and he'd say, "Why, you know, I'm slap out of that." It became such a commonplace happening that the unnamed little store was christened "Slapout." Now, the way folktales travel around there may be some who would doubt the story, but according to my uncle, "You can take this one to the bank."

As a kid we loved pouring over roadmaps and looking for strange named towns in Oklahoma. I'm sure many of you will remember this little ditty. We used to think we were being really naughty when we would use names and say, "Sallisaw Henryetta Wagoner Bowlegs" as a sentence. It usually was good for some chuckles and rolling of the eyes and droll looks. Dad used to say, "Eat'n more Hominy makes Pawhusky." Now there's a knee slapper for you.

Several years ago while visiting in North Carolina researching geneal-ogy, I found a book some local Tarheel had compiled. It was a listing of every city, town, village and hamlet in the state, giving the origin and history of the place name. It's a great bathroom book, and I've thought how this would be a great project for someone in Oklahoma to do for the places there.

Of course, a large number of the towns come from Native American heritage. In doing some research for the book, I'm thinking about writing I've found that Tulsa came from a Creek Indian word from the Coosa tribe for their town of Tallise. Maskoke or Muskoki became Muskogee. Won-derful … but on the other hand, what might be the origin of Whizbang or Lost City up there in Wagoner County.

Speaking of names, any time you hear of some old boy called with a bubba name like Bobby Joe, Jim Bob or Frankie Dean, you gotta know he's from either Oklahoma or Texas. I can rag on people with those old bubba names since I carry a name like Billy Gene. Growing up with that handle was almost as bad as "The Boy Named Sue" by Johnny Cash. My mother's excuse for the name was that she wanted a girl baby so badly, and that's the name the kid was going to get, regardless.

The old Cherokee medicine man, Dr. Orange W. Star, who delivered me, put the wrong name and date on the birth certificate for me and caused me no end of paperwork when I needed a birth certificate as an adult. My mother had to sign an affidavit that I really was who I said I was and was actually born.

Supposedly the Indians used to leave their children nameless until such a time as an event would happen or a physical characteristic developed that would suggest a name. Until that time a lot of kids must have come running when they said, "Hey, You."

We have Runs With Horses, Spotted Calf and Flying Eagle. Women became Blanket Woman or Bird Woman. What if we were to do the same thing with newborn boys and girls today?

The possibilities are endless and would be really descriptive. Boy Who Sleeps With Boom Box would be a natural. How about Women with Ring in Nose? Maybe She Who Burns the Biscuits or He with Purple Spiked Hair?

This is getting ridiculous and I'm gonna stop this blather.

"Oh, my sainted sister," said Harold, wiping tears from his eyes. "That's about as good a chuckle as I've had for some time, Phil. Have you been taking 'funny' lessons from Jimmy Boy, I didn't realize you'd become such a comedian in your old age. Looks like having that birthday today just mellowed you out somewhat."

It appeared that everyone had a small town name to tell about, and the hubbub of noise continued while each told his short story.

Phil chimed in again, "I kinda like this idea of taking turns, for the variety is great. However, I'd like to quit listening to you old guys for just a bit and see if we could entice our fair lady, Ivey, to join the group and entertain us with a story. What say ye, Ivey, lady?"

"Well, I don't mind if I do," she nodded assent. "I think I can entertain you with something just a bit unusual, and yet it has so much to do with our lives on a day-to day-basis. Today most everyone has a cell phone and would probably be lost without one.

"What we did long before the cell phones came along would seem to be as primitive as natives pounding on a drum to the younger generation. I'm referring to the party line telephone."

THE PARTY LINE

Ring-ring — ring — ring — ring. If you were one who owned a party line telephone you can quickly tell that you just heard two shorts followed by three longs. Well, at least that what it was supposed to sound like. Since you want a different story, I'll tell this one. It'll be a story about the party line, so hang up the receiver and take a chair.

Our family didn't personally have a telephone until about 1943, and it wasn't a party line. My experience with the party line, and the "hello girl" didn't come about until the 1950's.

For the younger set a little information about using the party line may help. There were certain rules of etiquette you were supposed to follow, but sad to say most of them were fractured on a daily basis. First off, everyone knew everyone's personal ring, and if your ring wasn't heard, then you weren't supposed to listen ... that was a laugh. Hey, we don't have TV or radio ... where else are we gonna get our news ... actually gossip ... so it was next to impossible to have a private conservation. Also someone might need help to fight a fire or something like that.

There was an all-call ring that everyone was expected to listen to. The operator at the switchboard in town would key that ring in and give everyone on the line important stuff like the war ending, the birth of a baby or somebody dying. The old lady in the tiny town we lived in would use her knowledge of the community to track someone down if it were an emergency. She'd just keep calling different exchanges and eventually someone would have seen him.

Most everyone knew their neighbors, and the telephone operator was a friend to all. You actually could chat with her on personal items. Remember when Fibber McGee and his telephone operator, Myrt, did their routine? In the skit he'd call and always say, "Oh, is that you, Myrt?" They would then go into some comical routine skit with each other.

Everyone knew you didn't go near the telephone during a storm with lots of lightning, for you could make your final call that way. It truly was and is dangerous even today with all our new and sophisticated equipment.

The crank-type party line telephone cases were a work of artistic skill and beauty. Most of them were made of oak and could be kept a high glossy sheen. When they were replaced by dial-type telephones, they became collector's items in antique stores. We bought one for $165 and felt we had a bargain.

Some people have taken the innards out of the old ones and converted them to regular telephones. We learned long ago that the value of an antique is lessened if you mess with them.

A real negative with the telephone was the noise you had to put up with on the lines. If a strong wind were blowing, it would whip the wires over each other, causing a whole bunch of static on the line.

We had a young daughter who thought we were saying the lions are cross when we were saying the lines are crossed.

Many times you had to carry on a conversation almost screaming, and when finished you weren't really sure if you understood what was said.

"Thanks, Ivey," replied Cece Damore. "I knew you had a good story there. We can always count on our lady to come through for us. And, yes, I'm addicted to my cell phone, but dog gone if they aren't handy. It saves me hundreds of steps every day, I know."

"Not me," countered Faye Bucklin. "That's just too much of trying to teach an old dog new tricks. I can handle a microwave oven and a few other electronic inventions, but I have to pass when it comes to using a cell phone. To be totally honest with you young sprouts, I lost out on all the new electronic inventions right after the flashlight was invented."

Faye gazed deadpanned around at the group while they hooted and catcalled his confession. Everyone knew just how sharp he was and didn't believe a word of his poor mouthing.

Faye went on to say, "Boys, here is something I knew a lot about, and I can tell you I surely do miss my lonesome old steam locomotive whistling late at night. I'll confess to have bummed around the country in my younger days riding the rail."

STEAM LOCOMOTIVES AND WHISTLES

Much of the romance of the railroad left us when the coal-fired steam engines, along with their steam whistles, were replaced with diesel oil and air horns. There are a few of us still kicking who remember the long, lonesome wail of the steam whistle in the dark of night as the engineer used his distinctive blasts as he pulled on the rope to send messages understood only by the railroading brotherhood.

It was the Atchinson, Topeka and Santa Fe Railroad that ran through Drumright, with a spur line over to Cushing. It followed a curving path as

it left town heading north, winding out the highway along Harley, through lease communities, past Fairview School and on toward Oilton.

We lived close to the track at one time, and the older guys used the coming and going of the train for fun times. Occasionally they would place pennies on the track and let the huge engine turn it into a mis-shapen, flattened blob, which would be carried around for luck.

At one time our family charged groceries at Hockett's Grocery Store. This store was located way north of town about where the by-pass presently crosses the old Oilton Road. A few stores would let the people with lesser means charge their groceries by the month, and we would use Sam Whitlock's until the grocery bill got too high, and then we would be forced to go to Hockett's until we could get them both paid off.

We were living on the hill at the east end of town, by the Quackenbush Gas Company. When we had to have some groceries, it was necessary for us to walk the entire distance to Hockett's Grocery, quite a far piece. We would walk west on Broadway to the railroad track. There we would follow the tracks north until we came to Hockett's where we would get our groceries and then walk the tracks back to town.

You remember how it is to walk the railroad tracks. The ties are too close together to step on each one and too far apart to skip one.

On this particular trip my brother and sister, old Shep and I were on the trek to get some necessities and were hoofing it down the track when we heard a train whistle from the rear, and we knew we were in for some excitement. It was always fun to have the rumbling cacophony of sights and sounds as a long freight passed.

Since the train was still within city yard limits, it was tooling along rather slowly and we were walking along the track bed not far from the moving cars. There must have been a couple of jokers as engineer and fireman in the cab of the train that day, or else they were mighty bored due to what happened next.

As the train came up even with us, one of the crew in the cab pulled on the valve that releases excess steam from the boiler. When they did this, we were right in the path, and the steam was vented out onto the three of us. Fortunately, we were far enough out that the steam wasn't scalding hot when it hit us, but it sure scared the puddin' out of three little urchins. We ran to the ditch and kept our distance. We didn't see Shep again until we got back home.

I'm sure the guys in the cab had a good laugh over the incident and surely knew they weren't going to scald us, but it made believers out of us and we never walked the tracks again when walking to Hocketts.

"Sure wasn't a nice thing that engineer did to you kids and also very dangerous," spoke up Cece. "Today doing something close to that would be cause for instant dismissal for that engineer. I don't suppose he meant any harm by it, but it sure could have burned you badly with that steam."

Pete rejoined with, "As kids we didn't feel we had much power in the society. We were just insignificant kids and accepted our roles as minor human beings and just bided our time and waited until we grew up. That still didn't make it right, but what were you going to do about it?"

Hank Blackwelder looked around the assembled group and saw that there were only two chairs left by ones who still hadn't spun a tale, and he occupied one of them. He cleared his throat and said, "I've enjoyed all these tales so much I kinda forgot to think of anything to talk about. My story won't begin to match what you guys have been telling, but here goes. It's a true happening, so you can't give me any static."

LONG WAY TO WATER

Good drinking water is always hard to come by and is a precious commodity wherever you live. We've talked before of the good old "sulfur water" many of us who lived in lease house communities grew up drinking, cooking and using for bath water.

When we were traveling the country in our motor home, we had many adventures with water. Just because it came out of the faucet was not a compelling reason to hook up to it when you pulled into an RV park. We usually drained out a bucket full and gave it a taste and smell test before putting our hose to it and running it into our pipes and storage tank. But I wander.

When I talk about water being a long way away, it doesn't mean a long walk to the water well. It has to do with the distance straight down that the well driller had to go before finding good potable drinking water to use.

This sharecropper farm we lived on was located way back in the boon-docks on some oil lease. We were living there and Dad had planted some cotton, corn and sugar cane. He raised some hogs and a few range-fed cattle. Mostly, though he and Ma raised kids … there were six of us with about that many miscarriages.

At some point a well driller had come in and set up rigging and put down a water well that must have been 150 foot deep or more. The water was delicious, but at what a price. There was a rope attached to a long cylindrical water bucket. The rope ran up over a large pulley, and then the bucket was let down until it hit water.

The water cylinder was equipped with a release flange that let about two gallons of water come into the cylinder and then closed. It was now up to the person at the top to haul that 16 pounds of water to the surface. As the rope was pulled up, it was coiled around a board sticking out for that purpose.

When the two-gallon bucket of water was brought up, the bottom end was put into whatever you wanted to hold the water There was a long wire with a ring at the top you pulled on which released the valve down at the bottom to let the water out.

This water might be for the water bucket to take to the house for cooking, or it could be the washtubs if it was washday. After a day of working the fields with the horses, it would be used to give a drink to Old Ben and Buck, the workhorses.

Dad had rigged up a system of troughs for the water to flow to the various places, and the older brother reports the horses were absolutely bottomless when it came to water. It took quite a while to let the water cylinder down into the well, let it fill and bring it back up. No mean feat for a pre-teen kid.

One of the absolute worst things that could ever happen would be for